Campaigning on the Oxus, and the fall of Khiva

J A. 1844-1878 MacGahan

CAMPAIGNING ON THE OXUS,

AND

THE FALL OF KHIVA.

BY

J. A. MAC GAHAN,

CORRESPONDENT OF THE 'NEW YORK HERALD.'

KIRGHIZ COURT OF JUSTICE.

WITH MAP AND NUMEROUS ILLUSTRATIONS.

NEW YORK:

HARPER & BROTHERS, PUBLISHERS,

FRANKLIN SQUARE.

1874.

PREFACE.

THE aim of this book is modest. It is rather a record of travel and adventure than a regular history of a military campaign. For the most part, I simply describe what I myself saw and heard. In doing this, I hope, however, to have at the same time succeeded in producing something like a picture of life and warfare in Central Asia. And I have done my best to give completeness to my narrative by describing not merely the military operations against Khiva, but also the physical features, the social life, and the political condition of the country itself.

It may be objected that I have dwelt too much —especially in my first chapters—on merely personal adventures. While pleading guilty in some degree to the charge, I venture to offer two pleas in extenuation. First, I travelled through a strange country under very strange circumstances. And, secondly, an account of my own adventures may serve to give the reader some idea of the manners, customs, and feelings of the almost unknown people among whom I moved.

The book is divided into three parts. In the first part, I give an account of my life in the desert of the Kyzil-Kum, while still in search of Gen. Kaufmann's army. The second describes the march on Khiva, and the capture of the city; and some chapters are devoted to a general account of the Khanate. In the third part is narrated the war with the Turcomans, which followed the fall of Khiva.

I am deeply indebted to Mr. Schuyler, Secretary of the American Legation at St. Petersburg, for the assistance he rendered me, on the way to Central Asia; but for his aid, I should probably never have been able to reach Khiva. To Mr. Robert Michell I also owe my thanks for many valuable suggestions.

I should add a sentence of explanation as to the method I have adopted in spelling the foreign words introduced into the narrative. The vowels are always to be pronounced as in Italian; the consonants as in English. In two cases, *dj* and *tch*, it may seem that a superfluous letter is used. This is done to prevent the possibility of error. The pronunciation of the letter *j* varies so much in foreign words, being sometimes *y* and sometimes *zh*, that I have thought it advisable to use *dj*; and *ch* even in English has two sounds. *G* is always to be pronounced hard, and *kh* has a deep guttural sound.

CONTENTS.

PART I.

LIFE IN THE KYZIL-KUM.

PART II.

❧ THE FALL OF KHIVA.

PART III.

THE TURCOMAN CAMPAIGN.

LIST OF ILLUSTRATIONS.

PART I.

LIFE IN THE KYZIL-KUM.

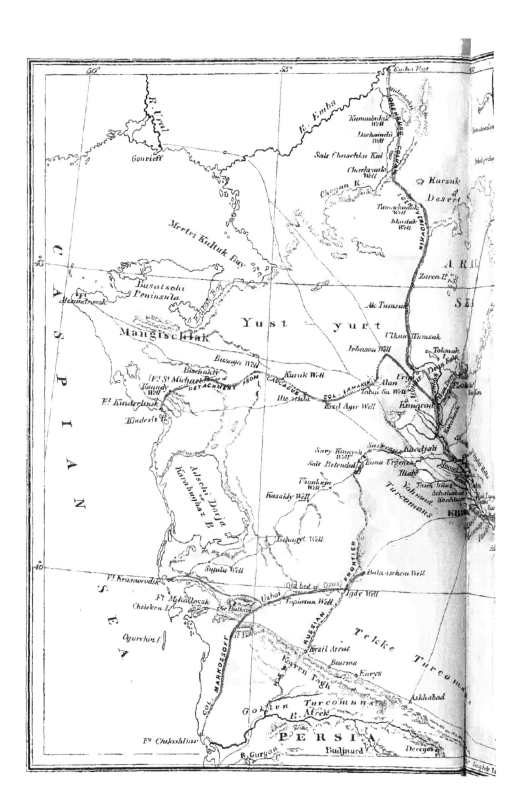

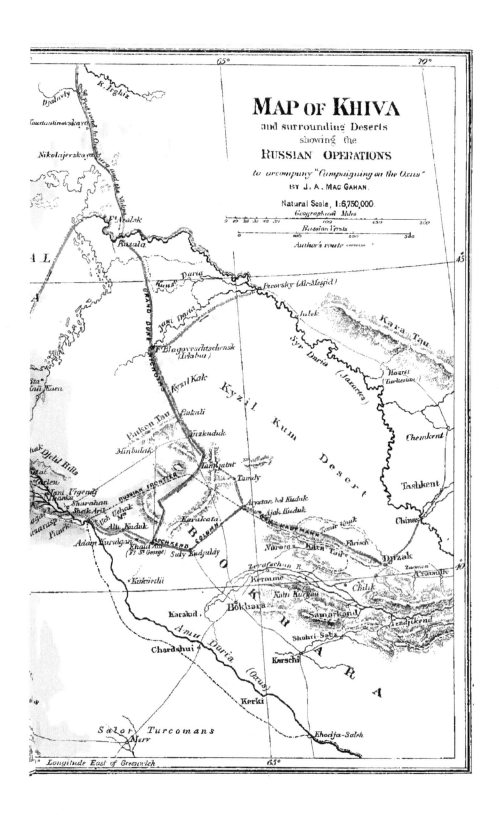

MAP OF KHIVA
and surrounding Deserts
showing the
RUSSIAN OPERATIONS
to accompany "Campaigning on the Oxus"
BY J. A. MAC GAHAN.

Natural Scale, 1:6,750,000.
Geographical Miles
Russian Versts
Author's route

CAMPAIGNING ON THE OXUS,

AND

THE FALL OF KHIVA.

———

CHAPTER I.

FROM THE VOLGA TO THE SYR.

A BRIGHT sunny afternoon. A wide level expanse of plain, cut up here and there by canals, and dotted with clumps of brushwood; on the south, extending to the horizon, a sedgy marsh, over which flocks of waterfowl are careering in swiftly changing clouds, that sometimes hide the sun; to the west, a caravan with its string of camels, creeping slowly along the horizon's edge, like a mammoth snail; to the east, the walls of a mud-built town, over which, leaning up against the sky like spears, rise the tall slender masts of ships.

The place is Central Asia, near the Syr-Darya River, or Yaxartes; fifty miles east of the northern shores of the Aral Sea; the time, the 19th of April, 1873.

In the foreground there is a *tarantass*—a long, low, black vehicle—in the midst of a swiftly-running stream; six or eight horses are splashing and plunging wildly about in the water, systematically refusing, with exasperating persistence, to pull together; four or five Kirghiz

postillions, some on the horses, some in the water up to
their waists, are pushing at the wheels, shouting with
savage energy, while the wheels sink deeper and deeper
at every movement of the maddened beasts. In the
tarantass two disconsolate-looking travellers, wrapped up
in rugs and sheepskins, who watch dejectedly but resignedly the downward tendency of the wheels, awaiting
despondently the moment when the water will be running
into the box, over feet, rugs, arms, and provisions.

The two travellers are Mr. Eugene Schuyler, *chargé
d'affaires* of the United States at St. Petersburg, on a tour
of observation in Central Asia, and the writer of this
book, on his way to Khiva.

Time was when we were neither dejected nor resigned,
when our hopes were high and our anticipations bright, in
the expectation of novelty and adventure. A time there
was when we offered advice to the Kirghiz postillions,
and swore at them for not taking it; when, growing
impatient and then enraged, we stormed and beat the
drivers as well as the horses, and spent an amount of
superfluous energy in trying to get forward, that astonished those easy-going Orientals, but, as far as could
be observed, produced no other appreciable effect.

That was, however, long since. To our benumbed
memories it seemed some few years ago. We now sat
resignedly in the *tarantass*, and let the horses plunge and
splash, and the drivers shriek and howl in their own way,
while the wheels steadily settled in the mud; never
offering to lift a hand or proffer a word of advice. Four
weeks of travel, day and night, across the level frozen
steppes of Russia, and the broad snowy plains of Asia,
with the thermometer ranging from 30° to 50° below
zero; of struggle with the exasperating perversity of

Russian *Yamstchiks*, the wearing, patience-trying sto-
lidity of Kirghiz *djigits*, the weakness of enfeebled,
half-starved horses, that were scarcely able to drag themselves along; the obstinacy of refractory camels, that
tortured us for hours at a time with their dismal half-
human howls, had reduced us to this dejected state of
apathetic resignation.

Travelling in Central Asia at this season is a never-
ceasing, never-ending struggle against difficulties. The
distance from Saratof or Samara on the Volga to Tashkent, the capital of Turkistan, is about 2000 miles,
a distance which in Europe and America would be
nothing, but which in Asia is a mighty undertaking, re
quiring weeks, and, under unfavourable circumstances,
even months, for its accomplishment. The Russians have
established a line of communication by means of post-
horses; and in the autumn, when the horses are still
fresh from the summer pastures, and the roads good, or
in the beginning of winter, after the first snow, the
journey may be made in three weeks—that is, if you
travel night and day. At this season, when the horses
are enfeebled by several months of starvation, you are
lucky if you reach your destination in three months.

Your first care upon starting is to buy a vehicle known
as a *tarantass*, the fore and after wheels of which are
united together by two long springy poles, the only
springs with which it is provided. On these is placed the
body of the carriage, a stout box, with a stout leather
hood and curtain, absolutely necessary to protect you from
the cutting blasts of the steppe. The wheels are taken
off, to be put on again when the snow disappears; and
the whole equipage is mounted upon a sledge. The
box is then filled with straw, a mattress is put in, and,

2

having procured a *podorozhnaia*, or government order for horses, you roll yourself up in sheepskins, and start. For days, even weeks, you eat, drink, sleep—literally live in this vehicle.

I interrupt the narrative for a moment to give an account of our progress from Saratof, on the Volga, to Kazala, near where the beginning of this chapter found us.

For the first day our course lay along the left bank of the Volga, through the German settlements established there by Catherine II. in 1769. Pleasant enough was our progress through the little old-fashioned villages, with their snug, comfortable wooden houses, half buried in the snow, and squat brick churches, and tall spires. The post-houses are clean and tidy; good coffee and bread and butter everywhere to be had; the people quick and obliging, the horses excellent, and we go dashing at a swinging gallop over the glittering snow. The sharp wintry air, resplendent with particles of flying frost that sparkle in the cold sunshine, the gusts of sleet and snow that beat in one's face like a shower of needles, only add zest to what is simply a prolonged sleigh ride. Out of one village into another, from station to station, we fly with almost the speed of a railway train. Arrived at one of these villages, we tumble out of our sheepskins, rush into the hot sitting-room of the post-house, and by the time we have warmed ourselves and swallowed a hasty cup of tea or coffee, the horses are ready, and we are off again, flying merrily over the snow to the sound of bells. Day and night we continue our flight; sleeping as best we can in our *tarantass*, and only stopping at distant intervals to bolt a hasty meal; until at last Nicolaievsk is reached. And here we bid farewell to the German colonists, and our own peace and comfort in travelling.

THE TARANTASS. *From a design by Vereschagin.*

From Nicolaievsk we struck across the country to Uralsk, and here we began to experience a change. We were on the free-post road, that is, a line of post communication not established by government, but by private enterprise. There were no regular post-houses, and we stopped at the end of each stage at the house of the peasant who happened to furnish the horses. These were usually poor, lean, half-starved, woolly-looking beasts, very unlike the sleek, well-fed animals that galloped us through the German colony; and were often scarcely able to drag us along. The stages, too, were longer, and in the houses neither milk nor butter could be obtained.

The Russian peasants do not seem to have learned anything from their thrifty German neighbours, in spite of their proximity. This is partly on account of the bigotry of the German and Russian priests alike, who vie with each other in their efforts to prevent any intercourse between the two people; and partly because the Russian peasant is not a very progressive being. At every stopping-place we had occasion to observe their way of life, and to contrast it very unfavourably indeed with that of the German colonists.

Arriving at one of these peasant stations, you enter first a kind of outer room, cold and dark, which is used as a store-room, and likewise serves to shelter the entrance of the main apartment from the penetrating wind. Groping through this room, you come to a large heavy door, lined with felt, which opens outward, and immediately behind it another of the same description, opening inward. You pull one and push the other, and step into a room so hot, that for a moment you feel that some extraordinary and untoward accident has precipitated you into a place popularly believed to be the hottest in the universe. The atmosphere strikes your face like a hot pillow, and you are almost suffocated; while your eyes, accustomed to the glare of the snow, can make nothing of the semi-obscurity. In a moment, however, you recover your breath and your eyesight, and you find yourself in a small room, ten feet by twelve, about one-fourth of which is taken up by a huge stove or mud furnace, from which comes the over-powering heat. There are one or two small windows with double sashes, the glass dim with ice; benches all around the walls, a rough table of undressed boards, two or three stools of the same material; in one corner of the ceiling an *obraz* of "Mikola," a gilded picture of St. Nicholas, or perhaps of the Virgin; in another an earthen pitcher half full of water, suspended by a string from the ceiling, from which you pour water over your hands when you wish to wash, and—that is all. Dresser there is none : no such accommodation being re-quired when the house has but a knife or two, a couple of plates, and three or four wooden spoons. There is no bed, for the whole family sleep on the top of the large furnace, among a heap of sheepskins and old clothes; there is no wardrobe, for they keep their clothes in a more convenient place—on their backs, never taking them off even to sleep. The *samovar*, the Russian tea-urn, which we always found at the stations, is seen rarely in a Russian peasant's house. That is an article of luxury much beyond the means of a single peasant; two or three doing duty for a whole village.

The first thing is to make a bargain for the horses. That done, we bring in our tea-things, the children gather around us in expectation of lumps of sugar; the samovar is instantly heated, we pour down incredible quantities of boiling tea, as a means of laying in a supply of heat for our battle with the fierce chilling winds, and again we are out on the wide, snowy, cheerless plains, plodding slowly forward.

One night, almost the coldest I think I ever passed, we were very much astonished at the end of a long stage, during which we had been assailed by a furious snow-storm, to see our giant driver—four feet across the shoulders, wrapped up to the point of his nose in sheepskins—climb down from his seat, and resolve himself into a heap of sheepskins, and a bright-eyed, rosy-cheeked little girl of twelve. We were, however, relieved to find that we had not been intrusted to her safe keeping only on the steppe, her father having driven the sledge before us containing our baggage.

From the land of the Russian peasants we come into a settlement of Bashkir Tartars, where we nearly stuck for the rest of the winter, owing to the contumacy of the Bashkirs in refusing to give us horses, except at rates that would have impoverished us long before reaching our destination. After infinite trouble, however, and an expenditure of diplomacy that would have astonished Gortchakoff himself, we succeeded in worrying through, and, crossing a southern spur of the Ural Mountains, found ourselves in the country of the Ural Cossacks.

From Uralsk, the capital of the Cossacks, along the banks of the Ural to Orenburg, our progress was something like what it was through the German colony. The horses were good, the station-houses clean, and but for the broken roads, which were worn into holes and gutters, our journey would have been a pleasant one, in spite of the bitter cold.

At Orenburg we stopped only long enough to get our outfit; and crossing the Ural on the ice, we leave Europe behind us, and are soon far out on the broad, level, almost boundless plains of Central Asia.

Here the post-horses are furnished by the Kirghiz, who have thousands running wild over the steppe. But at this season of the year, enfeebled by a long course of starvation, the poor animals are scarcely able to walk. Sometimes we have as many as fifteen or twenty starving brutes attached to our vehicle, yoked three and four abreast, who go shambling along before us like a flock of sheep, unable to raise the ghost of a trot. The camels, which were often furnished us instead, were just as bad, with the difference that some one or other of the lot usually set up a howl by way of protest against the whole proceeding, which he would keep up for hours without intermission. The stages were from twenty to thirty miles in length, so that we were often out in the cold for hours at a time. And then, arrived at the station-house, benumbed with cold, we find nothing but a hole in the ground covered with reeds and earth. But for the black and white post planted in the earth, you might easily pass one of these stations, never suspecting its presence, so completely is it hidden beneath the level floor of the plain. Admittance into this cheerful habitation is gained through a long underground passage. The horses are always far away at some distant *aul*, and have to be found and fetched after our arrival—a task sometimes requiring hours. At one place they flatly refuse to give us horses; averring there are none.

" When will there be any?" we ask the Kirghiz whose duty it is to supply the horses.

" He does not know."

" Does he think we are going to stay in the steppe all the winter?"

This is a question he declares beyond the sphere of his prophetic vision.

The last answer proves too much for Ak-Mamatoff, our Tartar servant, who, flying into a rage, draws an old iron sword, with which we had provided ourselves, and thrashes the Kirghiz soundly.

This stroke of diplomacy results in the production of a number of starving skeletons, which too plainly corroborated the assertions of the Kirghiz that there were no horses. There is nothing better to be obtained, however, and we take them at the risk of breaking down halfway to the next station.

And so we get slowly forward. The days pass—some in wild fierce storms of snow and sleet, that howl around us as though all the demons of the steppe were up in arms, some in bright sunshine, whose intolerable glare blinds us and blisters our faces. From time to time we drive down into darksome underground holes, hot and reeking, hover around the steaming samovar, pouring down oceans of boiling tea; then out on the silent steppe again to continue the weary struggle.

There are nights when we awaken from a half-frozen sleep, and remember we are in the heart of the mysterious regions of Asia, and see nothing but the wide snowy steppe, silent and ghostly in the spectral moonlight. For miles and miles there is no human habitation, but the burrow-like stations somewhere far ahead, buried under the snow, as though crushed into flatness by the grim uniformity above.

There is something strangely oppressive and awful in the changeless monotony of these wide, snowy plains, level as a floor, where for days and weeks you see nothing but snow and sky; where you are the moving centre of a horizon-bounded plain that seems to move with you, and hang upon you, and weigh you down like a monstrous millstone. There is the breadth and loneliness of the ocean without its movement, the cold and icy silence of the arctic regions, without the glory of arctic nights or the grandeur of the arctic mountains—the silent desolation of an unpeopled world.

Those broad, level, snowy plains, over which the icy winds from Northern Siberia come rushing down in furious blasts with an uninterrupted sweep of a thousand miles, and drive the snow about in whirlwinds that go scudding over the plain like giant spectres; the short days of sunshine, when the glare on the snow dazzles and burns; the long cold nights passed in a half-frozen, half-somnolent state, with the tired beasts trudging wearily forward;—I shiver now at the bare remembrance of it all.

Day after day, night after night, week after week, finds us on the road, gliding silently forward, changing horses at stations so much alike, that we seem to be arriving at the same place over and over again; the same endless plain, the same ever-receding horizon, until the steppe becomes to our benumbed imaginations a kind of monstrous treadmill on which, no matter how fast we travel, we always remain in exactly the same place.

As we approach the River Syr-Darya the weather begins to grow warmer. The snow gradually disappears, and then we have to struggle through long watery tracts of country where the mud is knee-deep, and we stick every few minutes, apparently without hope of rescue. Then the plain changes its snowy mantle for one of delicious green; the air grows soft and balmy with the breath of spring, and begins to be laden with the odour of wild flowers. We meet everywhere the Kirghiz with their tents and camels, out already from their winter quarters, on their annual migration northwards, and the plain is dotted with their flocks and herds. For us the winter is over, although in the steppe we have left behind us the snow is still many feet deep. Then we come into the desert of the Kara-Kum, through which we plod slowly; and at last, one bright, sunny afternoon, we ascend a sandy dune, at whose foot stands the next station, and hail with delight the dark-blue waters of the Aral Sea, lying in the midst of the waste of yellow sands, and glimmering in the sunlight like a turquoise set in gold.

Darkly calm and silent it lies in the midst of the sandy desolation that surrounds it. Here its banks are rolling hillocks covered with brushwood, but far away can be seen rising, abrupt and precipitous, the western shore, in a serrated, mountainous range, and standing out in the evening sunshine bare and bleak, like mountains of rugged brass. It is a picture of strange and weird loneliness, according well with the sinister desolation of the surrounding waste.

After a two hours' halt we resume our journey. One day more brings the town of Kazala, or Fort No. 1, on the Syr-Darya, within view; and here in sight of the unknown town, which has been the goal of all our hopes and the object of all our anticipations for so long, the beginning of this chapter finds us.

For hours we sit patiently in the *tarantass* in the middle of the stream. We know by experience how any suggestion on our part as to the advisability of sending on to the town for fresh horses would be a good and sufficient reason to our postillions for not doing so. We watch with some interest their futile attempts to extricate us, but feel that it is no affair of ours.

At length, after what seems to us an age of vain attempts to drag us through; after employing a number of expedients for raising the *tarantass*, which expedients seem to produce the contrary effect with a certainty and exactitude that are remarkable; after a series of angry altercations between the postilions, in the course of which they treat each other to a variety of disagreeable names as well as blows,—they at last decide to send on to the town for more horses.

After long waiting, the horses appear, we are finally extricated from our insular position in the middle of the stream, and in another half hour drive gaily into the wide unpaved streets of Kazala on the banks of the ancient Yaxartes.

CHAPTER II.

KAZALA.

KAZALA, or Fort No. 1, was the entering wedge of the
Russians into Central Asia. The fort was first constructed by General Perovsky, in 1847, forty miles lower
down, at the mouth of the Syr, and called Fort Aralsk.
In the course of time that position was found so unsuit-
able, on account of the surrounding marshes, that the fort
was moved up the river to its present position. Situated
on the banks of the Syr, the first strategic point occupied
east of Orsk, it was soon followed by the construction of
Fort No. 2. The capture in 1853 of Ak-Mesdjid, 250
miles farther up the river—now called Fort Perovsky—
assured the safety of the Russian position on the Syr.

The fort, a small earthwork about 200 yards square,
surrounded by a ditch, defended by a few light pieces
of cannon, and garrisoned by about 1000 men, is a fair
specimen of all the Russian forts in this part of the
world. A single battery of modern field artillery would
render it untenable in half an hour, but in Central Asia,
with such fortresses, the Russians hold an empire in subjection. Between it and the river is the navy yard, and
on the land side has sprung up the flourishing town of
Kazala, which numbers about 5000 inhabitants.

With the exception of the military, there are few Russians in the place. The greater part of the population are Sarts, or Tadjiks, Bokhariots, Kirghiz, and Kara Kalpaks, all speaking a dialect of Tartar, and all Tartar tribes, in whom the Mongolian type has been more or less modified by an infusion of Aryan blood.

The first view of Kazala is sufficient to show you, in spite of its broad streets, that you are in Central Asia. The low mud houses with flat roofs, without windows, and almost without doors; the bazaar with its rows of little shops or stalls, where long-bearded men, in gay bright-coloured robes, gravely sit, taking tea, among their wares; the strings of laden camels that come trooping in, the crowds of wild-visaged men, the heaps of strange-looking merchandise, all remind you that you are in the wild and legendary regions of the East.

It was with a feeling of lazy satisfaction, only known by those who have posted a journey of 2000 miles, that we at last drew up before the door of the only hotel of the place. The hotel accommodation, to be sure, was not of the most luxurious. A large room—with a table, a few chairs, a wooden sofa, and a bed to which are wanting sheets, coverlets, pillows, and mattresses—is not all that could be required in the way of luxury, if one were disposed to be exacting. But that we were not. Besides, we were provided ourselves with leather-covered pillows, mattresses, and sheepskins. So, after a Russian bath, which we obtained in a little mud out-house, fitted up for the purpose, we stretched ourselves out for one good quiet nap, the first for many days, and then awoke to a royal dinner of wild duck, brown and juicy, done to a turn by our Tartar servant, Ak-Mamatoff. Then we sally out to get a view of the famous Yaxartes of ancient history.

Leaving the town and fortress behind us, we are soon standing on the banks of the river. It is here about a quarter of a mile wide; its waters, brown and muddy, rush by with a sullen murmur between low sharp banks, sometimes covered with a rich sward, sometimes with forests of tangled brushwood, and tall reeds and jungle, the hiding-place of tigers; while beyond, away to the south, in the direction of the Oxus, are the yellow sands of the Kyzil-Kum melting into the hazy sky.

One of the first things that attracted our attention was the Aral flotilla. There were three good-sized side-wheel steamers, the 'Samarcand,' 'Perovsky,' and 'Tashkent'; two stern-wheelers, the 'Aral' and 'Syr-Darya'; a steam-launch, the 'Obruchef,' and many barges, of which three were schooner-rigged. We saw, besides, two new barges, one of which had just been launched, while the other was still on the stocks. Two or three of these vessels were built in Sweden, but the rest were all constructed in Liverpool or London. They are all of iron, and were brought here in pieces, and put together. When it is remembered that these boats had to be carried on the backs of camels, in pieces whose weight could not exceed 300 pounds, and through the steppe I have just described, the difficulties of the undertaking will be understood. The 'Samarcand,' which was built, I believe, in 1870, is by far the best of the fleet, and is an exceedingly pretty and comfortable craft. They are none of them well fitted for the shallows of the Syr-Darya, as they draw too much water to run on the river, except in the high water of spring and midsummer, when the snow melts in the mountain ranges. Here the Syr-Darya is deep enough; but near Fort No. 2 there are many shallows, which are constantly changing. A few weeks ago, in coming down the Yaman-Darya from

Fort Perovsky, the 'Samarcand' anchored for the night in deep water, but the next morning was on dry ground, and it required the labour of 500 men for a week to cut a channel and bring her off. The models for the Russian steamers on the Yaxartes should be sought, not on the Thames, but on those American rivers where vessels are constructed to draw no more than six inches of water.

Though it was Easter Sunday—the greatest holiday in the Russian calendar—the river bank presented a busy sight. The barges and steamers were being loaded as fast as possible with provisions, stores, and ammunition; for Lieutenant Sitnikoff, the commandant, expected to sail for the mouth of the Oxus in three or four days, to go up the river and meet the expedition of General Kaufmann as near as possible to Khiva.

We were now very anxious to hear something of the campaign against Khiva; we had learned nothing since leaving Orenburg, and, for all we knew to the contrary, the place might already have fallen.

When I left St. Petersburg, it was with the expectation of reaching this place before the departure of the column led by the Grand Duke, Nicolas Constantinovitch, which I knew was to start from here. I had long since given up that hope. I knew the column must have already taken up its march for Khiva. The only question now was, how far it had reached, and what were the chances for overtaking it. Intent upon obtaining information, we called, in the course of the day, upon the commandant of the fortress, Colonel Kozyreff. We found him a genial, hospitable old gentleman, and were only too rejoiced to accept his ready invitation to dinner.

From him we soon learned that the campaign against Khiva was already far advanced. There were in all five columns directed against the Khanate The Kazala column, under the command of Colonel Goloff, with the Grand Duke Nicholas leading the vanguard, had left here on the 21st of March, had reached a place called Irkibai on the Yani-Darya, on the 6th of April, and had there constructed the fort Blagovestchensk. When last heard from, some ten days previously, they were at the wells of Bukali, in the Bukan-Tau mountains, not more than a hundred miles from the Oxus, where they were to await the arrival of General Kaufmann, leading the Tashkent detachment in person. No news had been received from Kaufmann since the departure of his troops from Tashkent. Nothing was known of his exact whereabouts, but it was supposed that he must, by this time, have united his forces with those of the Kazala column, and he might even have already reached the Oxus.

It was not encouraging news for me to find that 300 miles of desert lay still between me and the column which, when leaving St. Petersburg, I expected to meet here in Kazala, especially as the greater part of the distance would have to be considered the enemy's country.

A courier, who had just arrived on his way from the Orenburg expedition, reported that the forces under the command of General Verevkin had already crossed the Emba, and were well on their way south. This column was due by the 13th of May on the southern shores of the Aral, where it was to be joined by the expedition, under Colonel Lamakin, from Kinderly Bay, on the north-east shore of the Caspian, an expedition, by the way, of which we had not heard before. Of the detachment under Colonel Markosoff, starting from the southern shores of the Caspian, nothing had been heard.

But perhaps the most important news we obtained

3

was that, three weeks before, an ambassador from the Khan of Khiva, the Bii Murtaza-Khodja-Abaskhodjin, had arrived with a letter from the Khan to General Kaufmann, and with the Russian captives. The ambassador had a suite of twenty-five persons, among whom were a Divan-Beg and an Ishan. The Khan, we were told, had ordered the embassy to comply in every respect with General Kaufmann's demands. At the time when the embassy was sent out, nothing was known at Khiva of the movement of the Russian troops; and, as it took the road close to the Aral, it did not meet the expeditionary forces. The embassy was a month on the road, and found snow enough to supply them with water. General Kaufmann had ordered the ambassador to be forwarded to his camp, and also those of the Russian captives who could stand the journey. The released Russians numbered but twenty-one, eleven of whom are Cossacks. They were all captured in 1869 and 1870 by the Kirghiz and delivered to the Khivans. It was said that these were all the Russians held as slaves in Khiva that could be found, with the exception of one old man taken in Perovsky's disastrous expedition, who, having become a Mussulman, married there, and preferred to remain.

The next day we called on Admiral Sitnikoff, who likewise received us with great cordiality, and entertained us handsomely, giving us every facility for a closer inspection of the fleet.

Having duly reflected on the matter, I determined to attempt crossing the Kyzil-Kum alone, on the trail of the Kazala detachment. I thought that, with swift horses and a good guide, I could reach the Oxus in seven or eight days, before Kaufmann would have passed it.

Once there, I would trust to my star, if the army had crossed, for getting over somehow, and evading the Khivan cavalry that would probably be hanging on its rear. This course was a dangerous one, and was regarded, as I soon learned, by the Russians as not only dangerous, but simply impossible. The Kirghiz of the Kyzil-Kum were hostile to the Russians, and had besides the reputation of being robbers and marauders, who would regard a small party, during these war times, as a lawful prize. Nevertheless, to cross the desert inhabited by them was the only plan that seemed to be left open to me. Remaining here, or going on to Tashkent, was equivalent to staying in St. Petersburg. I had already spent so much of the 'New York Herald's' money, that I felt morally obliged to push forward; and I was very certain that anything less than my entry into Khiva would not be a satisfactory conclusion of my undertaking. The position of a correspondent is often a very embarrassing one. He embarks, perhaps, on an enterprise without fully counting the cost, or foreseeing or appreciating half the difficulties to be encountered in its accomplishment, and then feels obliged to put on a brave face and carry it out at whatever risk, when in his inmost self he knows that if he were a free agent, he would be among the very last to undertake it. In this way he often gets a reputation for foolhardiness, or pluck, or perseverance, or "cheek," which he really does not merit.

I soon found that it was easier to resolve upon this course than to carry it out. I was casting about for horses, and a guide with which to perform the journey, when Captain Verestchagin, Colonel Goloff's successor, called upon us, and informed me that he could not take the responsibility of allowing me to start upon so dangerous a journey without the sanction of the Governor-General. He remained unmoved in this opinion in spite of all our arguments, and, as General Kaufmann was in the heart of the Kyzil-Kum, nobody knew where, and it might take weeks to communicate with him, this determination on his part was an insurmountable barrier to carrying out my plan. A moment's reflection served to convince me that a half-formed design I had conceived of escaping across the Syr in the night was impracticable. Besides the difficulty of crossing the river, there was the necessity of buying horses, finding a guide, and making other needful preparations, which could not be done in a small place like this under the watchful eyes of Captain Verest-chagin without his finding it out. I determined, how-ever, to make an attempt to carry out my original design from Fort No. 2, or from Fort Perovsky. Captain Verestchagin did not oppose our proceeding to Tash-kent, and I hoped to find an officer at one of these places who would not have such exaggerated fears for my personal safety. Captain Verestchagin was very polite, nevertheless, and readily agreed to despatch any letters we might wish to write to General Kaufmann by a special courier. Accordingly we wrote, asking permission to go to Khiva, and requesting an answer to be sent to Tashkent.

I may as well forestall my story here by saying that Kaufmann had no sooner received our letters, than he sent a courier with an invitation for us to come on, accom-panied by a map and instructions for the road. Had I waited for this answer, however, I should have only reached Khiva several days after its fall.

CHAPTER III.

FORT PEROVSKY.

As Mr. Schuyler, on his way to Tashkent, had no business in Kazala, and as I was only too anxious to get on to Fort Perovsky to try my fortune there, we hurried our departure, and after a halt of only three days, replaced our baggage in the waggon, took our seats in the tarantass, and were once again on the weary post-road.

Our course now lay along the banks of the erratic Syr, whose vagaries we had plenty of time to observe and study.

The Syr is the most eccentric of rivers, as changeable as the moon, without the regularity of that planet. It is a very vagabond of a river, and thinks no more of changing its course, of picking up its bed and walking off eight or ten miles with it, than does one of the Kirghiz, who inhabit its banks. The Russians have never been able to do anything with it, and I have serious doubts of its ever being turned to any account for purposes of navigation. If the country through which it flows were thickly populated, means, it is true, might be found to navigate it. But before that can come to pass the greater part of its waters will probably have been absorbed in irrigating the thirsty sands of the Kyzil-

Kum, the most useful purpose to which they can be applied.

We were four days reaching Fort Perovsky, which four days were to me days of intolerable anxiety and suspense. If Kaufmann had advanced as far as was supposed, it would require the utmost despatch to overtake him before the fall of Khiva, and here I was plodding along at a very snail's pace, without even the certainty of being allowed to go on at all.

At length we arrived at Perovsky in the middle of the night, to find the whole of the only hotel in the place occupied by a Russian officer. We were offered, however, a small room, five feet by eight, without a stick of furniture, dusty and dirty, into which we were fain to bring our mattresses and camp for the night.

Early the next morning I sent Ak-Mamatoff out to find a guide and horses. In spite of all remonstrances, I was fully determined to attempt crossing the Kyzil-Kum to the Oxus, whether the district superintendent should oppose me or not; and spent the day in filling cartridges, and making other needful preparations. Ak-Mamatoff returned in the evening, saying he had not been able to find a guide, and that no horses were to be obtained in Perovsky.

I was completely dumbfounded by this announcement. I should have been disposed to attempt the journey without a guide; but without horses, of course, this was impossible. I then asked him if any camels could be procured. He thought they could, and without any difficulty. But it was now already night, and nothing further could be done that day. The next morning he started out early in search of camels and of a guide, promising to return soon.

We spent the day in looking about the town. It was just such another place as Kazala. The same mud houses, the same little shops and bazaars, the same bright costumes and dark swarthy faces, the same array of strange outlandish wares, the same little fortress with its guns peering over the walls, and the same broad river rushing by. It was here that the Russians met with the first serious resistance offered them in Central Asia.

The place was defended by Yakub Bek, then in the service of the Khan of Kokand, with a skill, courage, and daring rarely equalled. After a siege of several days, it was at last taken by storm with a great loss of life on both sides. Yakub Bek escaped, and has since made himself Emir of Kashgar, the most flourishing and prosperous country of Central Asia. The place was then called Ak-Mesdjid, but the name has since been changed to Perovsky, from a mania the Russians have of changing names, often hundreds of years old, to flatter the vanity of some military chief.

Ak-Mamatoff did not return until evening, and then came with the same story; neither guide, camels, nor horses to be found. It appeared to me very strange that camels and horses should not be found in a place like this, where three-fourths of the property of the inhabitants consists in these animals. Ak-Mamatoff was evidently lying for some purpose of his own, and a moment's reflection served to show me what that purpose was When, just before arriving at Kazala, we disclosed to him my intention of going to Khiva, and asked him if he would come along with me, he entered into the plan with great zest and heartiness, and appeared anxious to undertake it. Since then, however, he had spoken of it with great despondency, having probably heard at Kazala something of the difficulty of the proposed undertaking, and had changed his mind. He had evidently adopted the ingenious device of telling me there were no horses or camels to be had here, in order to convince me of the impossibility of attempting the expedition. There may have been likewise behind this some intention of so increasing the obstacles to my starting, as to induce me to pay liberally in case he should find himself obliged to go in the end.

When I arrived at this conviction, and remembered that he had thus detained me two days, I felt a strong inward temptation to send him at once to his Muslim Paradise. By the application of some very forcible arguments, however, I succeeded in convincing him that any more lies on the subject of horses would result in very disagreeable consequences to himself, and he started out next morning faithfully promising to do his best.

I may as well state here that Mamatoff was a Tartar from Orenburg, who had been recommended to us by Bekchurin, a civilised Tartar in that place in service of the government. He was about fifty-five years old, spoke all the Central Asian languages as well as Russian, but proved to be the most worthless, lazy, thieving, contrary old idiot I could possibly have found. In spite of his being a Mohamedhan, he used to get drunk, and was continually finding pretexts for thwarting my wishes and disobeying my orders, as in the present case.

He returned in the course of the forenoon with a kind of renegade Jew, whom he proposed for a guide, and who said he had been in the Bukan-Tau mountains, where I expected to find Kaufmann, and knew the way there very well.

After having concluded a bargain with this individual, and agreed upon the number of horses that would be required, he suddenly disappeared, and we never saw him again—a flat, and somewhat unexpected ending to a long and satisfactory negotiation.

Another day was thus lost, and the result proved so exceedingly disagreeable to Ak-Mamatoff, that he started off next morning more than ever impressed with the expediency of fulfilling our commands. This time he brought us a Kara-Kalpak, named Mustruf, who had just returned from Irkibai, where he had gone as *djigit* or guide to a small detachment, which left this place to unite with the Kazala column. As this man talked as though he really meant business, and evidently knew the country, I engaged him at his own price, which proved to be an outrageously high one, a fact with which I duly credited Ak-Mamatoff. It only remained to obtain the permission of Colonel Rodionoff, the district governor, for the guide to accompany us, without which he would not go, however much I might have been disposed to start without complying with that formality. We called on Colonel Rodionoff, who so far from offering any objections to my departure, as had done Captain Verestchagin, gave the guide a passport, myself permission to depart, and rendered me every assistance in his power.

As soon as it became known that I wanted horses, at least a hundred were offered me. The street, in fact, around our door was soon full of them, thus giving the lie direct to Ak-Mamatoff. This he bore with great equanimity, however, not seeming in the least disconcerted at such overwhelming proof of his own duplicity. I bought six at prices varying from six to ten pounds, four for the saddle for myself, Ak-Mamatoff, Mustruf, the guide, and a young Kirghiz, whom I had employed at Mustruf's suggestion to help to take care of the horses, the other two for the baggage and a little forage, as well as the water, we would have to carry with us in many places.

Camels would have been far better as beasts of burden. With them I might have taken a tent, carpets, camp-stool, and table, and a supply of clothing as well as provisions, which would have rendered my sojourn in the desert comparatively pleasant. By taking horses only, I should, I knew, be deprived of even the comforts of the nomads; but with horses I hoped to make the distance in just half the time, and time was with me the great consideration. Had I known how long I was doomed to wander about in the desert, I would never have undertaken the journey with horses only.

CHAPTER IV.

AMONG THE ROBBERS.

It was three o'clock on the afternoon of the 30th of April, when I bade farewell to Mr. Schuyler, and stepped into the ferry-boat which was to carry me over the Syr-Darya. Three of my little Kirghiz horses had already scrambled in along with Mustruf, while Ak-Mamatoff was preparing to embark with the rest of the horses and baggage in a second boat.

The Syr here was about a mile wide, and the shore, with the fort, over which some pieces of twelve were peering, and the little mud-built town, with the natives who had assembled to see me off, fast receded and grew dim. I was soon obliged to take my field-glass to distinguish Mr. Schuyler from the crowd, where I easily made him out, giving old Ak-Mamatoff his last orders preparatory to sending him off with the rest of the baggage and horses.

On the other side of the river I found a small village of Kirghiz, consisting of five or six tents. The inhabitants gathered on the shore as we landed, and very good-naturedly helped us to unload our boat. Ak-Mamatoff soon arrived in the second boat, with the two horses. Of these, one was loaded with the barley we had provided as fodder, the other with about 100 pounds of biscuit, sugar, tea, a tea-pot, and tea-kettle, hogskins for carrying water, called *tursuks*, leather buckets with long ropes attached for drawing water from wells, and my own scanty wardrobe. A hundred rounds for each of my guns and revolver were equally divided, with many other little traps, among the four saddle-horses.

The baggage having been all packed on the two horses, and everything being ready, I slung my Winchester rifle across my shoulder, mounted my little Kirghiz saddle-horse, and waving an adieu to Mr. Schuyler, whom I made out far away on the other shore watching our proceedings through his glass, turned my horse's head to the south and plunged into the desert.

My little party consisted of the Tartar, old Ak-Mamatoff, employed as servant and interpreter; the guide, Mustruf, a Kara-Kalpak from Fort Perovsky, and a young Kirghiz, named Tangerberkhen, from the same place, whose duty it was to look after the baggage and the six horses. Being a man of peace, I went but lightly armed. A heavy double-barrelled English hunting rifle, a double-barrelled shot gun, both of which pieces were breech-loading, an eighteen-shooter Winchester rifle, three heavy revolvers, and one ordinary muzzle-loading shot gun throwing slugs, besides a few knives and sabres, formed a light and unpretentious equipment. Nothing was farther from my thoughts than fighting. I only encumbered myself with these things in order to be able to discuss with becoming dignity questions relating to the rights of way and of property with inhabitants of the desert, whose opinions on these subjects are sometimes peculiar.

My only thought now was to get away as fast as possible from Fort Perovsky, lest Colonel Rodionoff might change his mind and " send for" me. Once out of sight of the fort, with a few miles of desert behind me, I knew I should be safe from pursuit. Our departure, therefore, bore a strong resemblance to a hurried flight. My plan was to follow the course of the Yani-Darya, a small stream which flows out of the Syr in a south-westerly direction, to the springs of Irkibai, where, as has already been stated, the Grand Duke had constructed a fort. From that point I would follow his trail, and overtake the detachment.

Mustruf took the lead, myself, Ak-Mamatoff, and the young Kirghiz following, each of the two latter leading a horse. Our course lay to the south-west, and we left the river almost directly behind us. Its valley here was very sandy, and covered with tufts of coarse tall grass. Reeds and tangled masses of a fine wiry thornbush, that some-times attained a height of twenty feet, formed a dense impenetrable jungle, in which the tigers of the Yaxartes find a safe retreat. There were occasionally small patches of fine green grass, and little groves of a kind of thorny, scrubby tree, resembling the wild plum of America. None of these were out in leaf as yet, but the singing of birds, and the scent of early flowers betokened the approach of spring.

We occasionally met a Kirghiz horseman, with his old matchlock slung across his shoulders, who looked at me curiously as he rode by, but always saluted me with a respectful salaam. Of course my people had to stop and have a talk upon these occasions, and each man received a full account of me, where I was from, where going to, who I was, and what was my business, as far as old Ak Mamatoff knew it, probably with the addition of a good deal he did not know.

We continued our march till about sunset, when we

entered a dense thicket of the thornbush before mentioned. Through this a bridle path had been worn, which led us out into a delightful little glade, covered with a carpet of rich green grass. This glade was surrounded on three sides by the jungle through which we had just passed, while on the fourth it ran down to the edge of a broad river, which I was very much surprised to see was the Syr. I soon learned that the river made a broad sweep to the south, and at this point our path again approached its banks. In the middle of this little glade was a Kirghiz aul, consisting of four or five kibitkas or tents. An *aul*, it should be observed, is the Tartar word for village, but means here a nomadic or wandering village, because among the Kirghiz there are no other kind. Mustruf rode up to one of the tents, from which two or three women and several children had emerged, and asked something in Kirghiz. A larger tent farther on was indicated. Ak-Mamatoff then proposed stopping here for the night. Being now fairly started, and quite out of the reach of the Russian police, and as it was, besides, about sunset, I consented. So we rode up to the large tent, the owner of which had made his appearance at the door. He and Mustruf shook hands, stroking their beards and exchanging salutations, being, as it turned out, old friends. After a moment's conversation, of which I could see I was the subject, the Kirghiz motioned me to dismount; I complied, and he then shook hands with me, stroking his beard, and pronouncing a salaam. I was next led into the kibitka with the gravest politeness, and invited to seat myself on sundry bright-coloured rugs and carpets, which were spread across one half the tent for my reception.

I was now for the first time in the midst of the Kirghiz

of the Kyzil-Kum, and beyond the protection of the Russians. These people, as I have already said, have the reputation of being robbers and murderers; and I had sufficient property to make a rich prize for even the richest amongst them. When starting into the desert I knew I must adopt one of two systems in dealing with such a people Either fight them, or throw myself entirely upon their hospitality and generosity; I chose the latter system.

So, now, on entering the tent, I unslung my Winchester and handed it, along with my belt and revolver, to my host. Then throwing myself on the ground, I enjoyed, tired as I was, the soft rugs and bright fire, which burnt in the middle and sent up a column of blue smoke through a hole in the top. My host hung my arms up in the tent, and then went out to see what my people were doing with the horses, leaving me to the care of two very ragged, high-cheeked, small-eyed women, who, going about their household duties, cast on me from time to time a curious, but discreet glance.

The scene was a pretty one. Through the open side of the tent I could see the horses cropping the rich grass, the children playing about the green, the smoke curling over the kibitkas in a cozy way, and the river rushing by with a subdued murmur. The children of these nomads, so far from being shy of strangers, as is usually the case among savages, were not in the least afraid of me, and one half-naked, black-eyed little fellow came tumbling into my arms, when I held them out to him, with a childish trust that was captivating.

On Ak-Mamatoff's suggestion, I went out to a neighbouring pond, and soon brought down four or five ducks.

It was now nearly dark, and the Syr was rushing by

with a low threatening murmur, broken occasionally by a heavy startling splash, as its banks tumbled in. The other side lay buried in obscurity, out of which the tops of the trees defined themselves dimly against the sky. Judging by the time we had been on the march, I concluded that Perovsky was about fifteen miles distant. I returned along the bank to the aul, where I found that my ducks had created quite a sensation. The Kirghiz have such poor arms that they are rarely able to shoot anything; and to have brought down five was in their eyes a great feat.

The ducks were already roasted when I entered the kibitka, and inviting my host, as well as everybody else who happened to be present, to take part, we gathered around the cheerful fire in the middle of the kibitka, and made our supper on wild ducks, together with biscuits and some cold meat I had brought with me, the latter from Perovsky, the former from Orenburg. My host was delighted with the biscuit, it probably being the first time he had ever eaten white bread. Even black bread is a luxury among the Kirghiz, who live on milk and mutton. I now learned for the first time that in the hurry of my departure from Perovsky I had forgotten to take the knife, fork, tin plates, and teaspoon I had provided for the trip; I was obliged to eat with a jack-knife, like the Kirghiz, and stir my tea with a twig, hastily cut from a thornbush. The Kirghiz, as well as my own people, made their tea by the simple and primitive process of boiling it in a large iron pot, like soup, and drank it out of small porcelain bowls of Russian make, nibbling a lump of sugar the while. They do not indulge in the extravagance of putting sugar in the tea itself.

The fire having now burnt down low, a piece of felt was

drawn over the opening in the top by means of a rope, making everything snug and cozy for the night. We rolled ourselves up in sheep-skins, stretched ourselves out on a rug, and soon fell asleep. Thus pleasantly ended my first day in the dreaded desert of Kyzil-Kum.

4

CHAPTER V.

ON THE MARCH.

THE next morning we were in the saddle by sunrise, and after a kindly farewell to our host, we took up our line of march in the same order as the day before. Our course lay to the south-west across the country, where there was neither road nor bridle-path. We pushed straight forward, sometimes through tangled brushwood, sometimes through tall reeds in which we were completely lost; over low sandy dunes, and again across the bare plain, where there was only a little furze or coarse grass.

I soon remarked the cry of some bird, which seemed to be very plentiful in the reeds and bushes, as we heard it around us at every moment. It was a sharp discordant cry, resembling that of the peacock, and was always instantly followed by a rustling of wings as if the bird had flown. I was very much surprised to learn that this was the far-famed golden pheasant of Turkistan, and became anxious to have a shot at one. This, however, I found was no easy matter in the tall reeds. They seem to possess a remarkable facility for hiding, in spite of their brilliant plumage; and although I often heard their cries within fifty feet of me, I could never succeed in starting one, however much I beat the bushes. This was all the more provoking, as I had no sooner left the place than the cry would be repeated, apparently on the very spot where I had been standing. It was only after I got into more open ground that I succeeded in bagging one.

At last we fell into a beaten path, which led across the plain, and which made our progress through reeds and brushwood easier and more rapid. We passed many flocks and herds of cattle, sheep, and horses, that were quietly grazing in the open glades. They were always guarded by a Kirghiz on horseback, who usually came forward and accosted us; and then there was always a short halt and mutual exchange of questions. These shepherds were armed ordinarily with a curved sabre or a matchlock, sometimes with both, and would often accompany us a short distance on our way. The valley of the Syr is very thickly inhabited by these nomads, and many thousand sheep, cattle, and horses, are annually reared on its banks.

About ten o'clock we came upon an aul of four kibit-kas, and, as we had not yet eaten anything, we halted to make a light breakfast. The aul was situated in a little thicket of thornbushes, which shut it in on all sides, and we might easily have missed it had not Mustruf, knowing there was one here, been on the look-out. We found our way into it by a circuitous path cut through the brushwood. I was glad to take shelter in the shade of a tent from the sun, which was already growing hot This was a very poor aul. The felt of the kibitka was old, ragged, and full of holes, and there were no pretty rugs or carpets to be seen, as in the one where I had passed the night. The other kibitkas I perceived, upon visiting them, were no richer.

While preparations were going on for breakfast, I took my rifle and sallied forth in search of a pheasant, whose cry I had remarked just before arriving at the aul. The plain here was covered for the most part with a short kind of furze a few low shrubs, with here and there a dense thicket of thornbushes, like that in which was situated the aul, and I concluded I would have a better chance than among the tall reeds. I soon perceived a beautiful cock emerging from a thicket, with his golden wings, green neck, and long tail, almost equalling in beauty the rainbow tints of the peacock. He stepped proudly forth from the thicket and took his way leisurely towards another, occasionally stopping to pick up a worm or insect, apparently unaware or unmindful of my presence. Slowly raising my rifle so as not to frighten him, I took as accurate aim as I could with the sun in my eyes, and succeeded in breaking his wings. He ran into the thicket, but I got him out and brought him into camp, where he was soon stripped of his brilliant plumage and roasted for breakfast.

Observing that I had lost a button from my cap, I asked Ak-Mamatoff if he could not sew it on for me. He resented doing a woman's work with indignation, and went and brought me a young and rather pretty Kirghiz girl, and informed me, in an angry and aggressive manner, that she would do it, if I would find button, needle and thread. The necessary articles were soon produced, and she sat down on the ground beside me, amid the giggles of three or four friends who had come to see the stranger, and now stood around the door of the kibitka, looking in. She was a girl of about sixteen, very poorly dressed, for which, however, her long black hair, hanging over her shoulders in several braids, and her gleaming black eyes made ample amends. She handled the needle with a good deal of dexterity, without the aid of a thimble. Her comrades seemed to think it very funny, laughed, and made signs to me to kiss her, which hint of course I was not slow to act upon, she submitting with a very demure grace. I gave her some needles and thread, and a little present besides, and was somewhat surprised to learn that she was the sister of my young Kirghiz Tangerberkhen, who was an inhabitant of this aul.

After a nap of about an hour, and another cup of tea, which, by-the-way, tasted very strongly of mud, the water being far from good here, we were once again in the saddle. It was now about one o'clock, and the sun was fearfully hot. We were, however, on a very good bridle-path, and our horses went forward at a gentle, steady, but rapid pace. My horses were of the Kirghiz breed—a small, but hardy race. They all have, either by nature or training, the gait called the amble, which, as is well known, is a very easy one for both horse and rider, and this they will keep up from dawn until dark, getting over an amount of ground in a day that is astonishing. Their endurance is such that they will travel fifty miles a day for a month at a time, with nothing to eat but what they can pick up in the desert and an occasional handful of barley.

As has already been stated, I had six horses. Only four of these, however, were pure Kirghiz. the other two having a mixture of Cossack or mongrel blood. One of these, I have reason to believe, belonged to Mustruf, as he was very officious in urging me to buy him at a round price, assuring me that he was an excellent horse, and, what was of more importance to me, would perform the journey well. I took him against my own judgment, as, although a fine-looking beast, with heavy black mane and tail, he was rather lean to undertake a long journey. For

a distance that can be made in three or four days a lean
horse is best, but for a month's steady marching a fat one
is absolutely necessary; and I soon had reason to regret
not having had the courage of my own opinion, as this
animal became food for the jackals long before I reached
the Oxus.

The Kırghiz, unlike the Turcomans, take no care of their
horses. They never clean or groom them, nor stable
them, except in the very coldest weather, and they rarely
feed them with grain. In winter they give them a little
hay, if they have it, and if not, they clear the snow from
the ground, and let them take their chances along with the
sheep and cattle. In summer they live on what they can
pick up in the desert, just as do the camels; and although
on the Syr here the pasture is good, a little farther south
in the Kyzıl-Kum it is very different. The result is,
that they are probably the hardiest race of horses in the
world, can live anywhere a camel can, and they will
travel as far without water, but not for as many days.
They have neither the speed nor the size of the Turcoman horses, however.

In a half an hour from this aul we approached and
crossed for the first time the Yanı-Darya, along which
our course lay. It is very small and crooked, and was
almost dry. We did not follow its circuitous windings,
but continued our course straight to the south-west,
crossing and recrossing it several times before reaching
Irkıbai We now found ourselves in a country broken
up by canals for irrigation, which were for the most part
dry, owing to the fact that the Syr had not overflown this
year. The soil appeared rich enough, but was dry and
parched already, with great cracks running through
it, showing how hot it was here, although it was only

the first of May. There were no habitations, but many
little enclosures, some of brush simply stuck in the
ground, only sufficient to mark a boundary, and incapable
of preventing animals from passing, others simply formed
by the narrow banks of the canals. There was little
vegetation, as the extreme dryness of the ground seemed
to have soaked up the snow as fast as it melted, but the
ground was covered in many places with the dry stalks
of last year's weeds.

A few miles further on we left these signs of irrigation,
and came upon a rolling sandy country with here and
there a little lake or pond shut in by the small sand-
hills, and almost hid from view by the tall reeds. Two
or three of these were covered with duck, and I soon
succeeded in obtaining enough for dinner for the whole
party. The sun grew very hot in the afternoon, and
I could scarcely have believed that the difference in
the temperature could have been so great in a few
days. We even commenced to suffer from thirst, as we had
tasted no good water since morning.

We were now in the desert, or rather we commenced
crossing wide stretches of sand, varied by occasional
streaks of ground that had lately been under cultivation;
and it was curious to observe the difference between the
desert and these spots, the former having by far the
advantage. The land that had been irrigated only the
year before was parched and dry, seamed and cracked by
the sun, with not the slightest vestige of vegetation, while
the desert was almost green with the budding brushwood
and thin grass, which always shoots up immediately after the
snow melts, and flourishes until the summer heat scorches
it to death. There were plenty of wild tulips already in
bloom, as well as a good many other flowers, of which

I made a collection as I passed along. The tulips were
very pretty, the calyxes about the size of a small wineglass,
the petals a pale yellow, and the bottom a deep purple.
I observed that they seemed to have a very formidable
enemy in a small brown animal about the size of a rat,
called by the Russians *suzlik*, which digs down to the
bulbs and completely hollows them out, leaving only a
thin rind.

Towards evening we came upon a Kirghiz burying-
ground, consisting of several tombs and one tall hollow
tower of mud, with a winding stairway inside. Near
it was a well, the water of which was very warm, and
tasted besides so strong of something like straw, that
it was almost impossible to drink it. We slaked our
thirst as best we could, however, and, having watered our
horses and taken a short look at the graveyard, continued
our march.

The plain was almost level, so that we could see for
miles in every direction, but no sign of life greeted our
eyes. We had left the populous lands of the Syr behind
us. In another hour we came upon a well, the water
of which was deliciously cool and sweet; and before
proceeding farther we filled our leathern bottles, warned
by the day's experience not to trust too confidently to
the plain.

At sunset Mustruf began to look about for an
aul, which he thought must be somewhere in our
vicinity. We pushed on until dark, however, without
finding one, and were about casting around for a good
spot to camp, when a broad blaze of light lit up the
western sky two miles to the right of our path. We
immediately started in that direction, and in a few
minutes Mustruf and myself, who had put our steeds

KIRGHIZ KIBITKA. *From a design by Verestchagin.*

to the gallop, reached an aul of some dozen kibitkas, situated near a little pond whose banks were fringed with a rich greensward, affording delicious pasturage for our horses.

We had come to a fertile spot, a kind of oasis apparently, where there was plenty of grass and water, which I accounted for by supposing we had again approached the Yani-Darya.

This was my first day's ride, and as I had been in the saddle altogether about eleven hours, I was pretty tired; and no sooner had Mustruf led the way to the kibitka whose owner was to entertain us, than I alighted, and taking my saddle-blanket, stretched myself out on the ground. Our host first invited me into the tent—an invitation which I declined, preferring to enjoy the cool evening air before the door. Immediately he brought out a carpet, which he spread on the ground, and requested me to take a place on it, seating himself at the same time in order to engage me in a conversation.

As my knowledge of Tartar was, however, confined to a very few words, and as Mustruf knew no Russian, he was obliged to await the arrival of Ak-Mamatoff for more than an exchange of civilities. He greeted me gravely and politely, however, stroking his beard and bowing low. He was a large, finely-built man, and had a heavy beard —a thing very unusual among the Kirghiz. Indeed, I learned upon the arrival of Ak-Mamatoff that he was not a Kirghiz, but a brother of Mustruf's, and a Kara-Kalpak, which accounted for the beard. The Kara-Kalpaks, although nomadic in their habits like the Kirghiz, living side by side with them, and often intermarrying, seem to belong to an entirely different race of men. They are generally well-formed, much taller than the Kirghiz; and instead of the small eyes, high cheek-bones, flat noses, thick lips, and round beardless faces of the latter, they have large open eyes, long faces, high noses, and heavy black beards, and their skin, when not exposed to the sun, is almost as white as that of Europeans.

Who they are, how they came here, where they came from, is one of those historical, ethnological questions which will probably long remain unsolved. That they are not of the Mongolian race is very evident, but what they really are it would be difficult to say.

By this time supper and tea were ready; the ducks were roasted, and we all gathered around the cheerful blaze in the kibitka to partake of the meal.

After supper, I stepped outside the tent to take a look on the surrounding scene and enjoy the cool air of the evening. The new moon was just setting, lights were gleaming in every direction over the plain, showing that ours was not the only aul in the vicinity. The bleating of sheep and the lowing of cattle could be heard, mingled with the playful bark of dogs and the laughing voices of children, which came to us on the still evening air like music.

In places the weeds and grass of last year had been fired to clear the ground for the new growth, and broad sheets of fire crawled slowly forward over the plain, while huge volumes of dense smoke, that caught the light of the flames below, rolled along the sky in grotesque fantastic shapes like clouds of fire.

CHAPTER VI.

A KIRGHIZ CHIEF.

DURING the next day I began to observe a kind of plant that gave out a very fragrant aromatic odour when trampled under the horses' feet. This I soon discovered to be absinth. The plain was in some places covered with it, and I observed that the horses ate it with pleasure.

Here also were from time to time thickets of a kind of low scraggy, gnarly, bush, varying from a foot to six feet high. The wood is very hard and brittle, so that it is more easily broken than cut, and it is so hardy, that it flourishes even in the bleakest and most desolate places. It is called by the Kirghiz *sax-aul*, a name they give, however, to any kind of wood serving for fuel.

In the course of the morning we saw four or five "saigaks," a kind of desert antelope, resembling somewhat both the antelope and the goat. I tried to get a shot at them, but my people, who had not the most elementary notions of stalking, made so much noise that they soon took the alarm and were off like the wind. I gave chase, and followed them to a place where the stunted bushwood took the dimensions of small trees, ten or fifteen feet high, but it was all in vain. Nothing can overtake these animals but the fleet-footed greyhound of the Turcomans. While riding back to the path we were following, I remarked that the sax-aul here, although so large, owing probably to the greater richness and humidity of the soil or sand, still maintained its peculiar characteristics—hard, dry, knotty, scrubby, gnarly and twisted as a ram's horn. Half of it seemed to be dead or dying, and as the spring leaves had not yet come out, the whole presented a bleak forbidding aspect, like a goblin forest that had been scorched and withered by some terrible curse.

This morning's ride was delicious. The cool air, laden with the aromatic fragrance of the wild absinth that was crushed beneath our horses' feet, was a very delight to breathe.

At noon, however, the sun began to grow very hot, and observing a horseman a mile or two away to the north watching us, Mustruf galloped off to see him, suspecting the presence of water there. After a moment's conversation with the stranger we saw him making signs to us to advance, and leaving our path we struck across the plain, and soon rejoined him. We found not only one strange horseman, but four or five. They were Kara-Kalpaks, as their stalwart forms and heavy beards indicated, and they manifested their hospitality by taking charge of my horse immediately and offering me a cup of tea they had just made. I soon learned that they had chosen this spot for the noon halt of their aul, which was on its way, and which in fact soon arrived.

The work of breaking up camp, taking down the kibitkas, and packing them with the household goods on the backs of the camels, and driving forward the flocks and herds, devolves upon the women and boys; the men in the meantime mount their horses and ride forward to find a place for the next encampment. The men we now spoke to had chosen this spot on account of a pond, or puddle rather, of muddy water in the vicinity, and the grass, which was reasonably good for the desert.

The aul soon arrived; the camels with the women and children came trooping in in a long line, followed by the flocks of sheep and of cattle, which immediately scattered themselves over the plain in search of pasture; the camels were made to kneel by a jerk of the cord around the muzzle or through the nostrils, in guise of bridle; the women descended, and immediately commenced setting up the kibitkas and unpacking the household goods, in which task they were little helped by the men; fires were lit, kettles put on, and everything was bustle, life, and animation.

I was very much interested in watching the women set up the tents, and the speed with which they accomplished it.

The framework of the kibitka, or Central Asian tent, is composed of a number of thin strips of wood six feet long, loosely fastened together in the form of a vine-trellis, this frame opens out and folds up compactly, so that it may be placed on a camel. The sticks forming this frame are slightly curved in the middle, so that upon opening out it naturally takes the form of a segment of a circle Four of these frames complete the skeleton sides of the tent. On the top of this are placed some twenty-five or thirty rafters, curved to the proper shape, the upper ends of which are placed in a hoop, three or four feet in diameter, serving as a roof-tree.

As soon as the camel carrying the felt and framework of a kibitka arrived, he was made to kneel down, two women seized the framework, set it up on end, and stretched it out in form of a circle, one holding it while the other fastened the different parts together. Then the doorposts were set up, and a camel's-hair rope drawn around the whole, to bind it tightly together. One of them then took the wooden hoop, which serves as roof-tree, and elevated it inside the tent by means of a stick inserted in one of the many holes with which it is perforated, while the other immediately commenced inserting the rafters, some twenty or thirty in number, the bases of which are fastened to the lower framework by means of loops. The heavy rolls of felt are then drawn over this skeleton, and the kibitka is complete. It is about fifteen feet in diameter and eight feet high, and in shape not unlike an old-fashioned straw beehive. The whole operation only requires about ten minutes, and it is so solid that any wind short of a tornado will not budge it.

Upon returning from a short and unsuccessful search for game, I was surprised and pleased to learn that my comfort had not been forgotten in the general bustle and confusion. The chief of the aul had ordered a small kibitka to be set up for my own especial use, to which he now led me with grave politeness. I found it nicely carpeted and provided with several soft, bright-coloured coverlets and cushions, which were deliciously luxurious to my weary limbs.

I invited my kind host to share a pheasant I had killed in the morning and to take tea with me, which invitation he accepted. I was very much surprised to see him arrive shortly afterwards with a Russian *samovar* hot and steaming, all ready to make tea. And when he observed that I had no teaspoon, and that I was stirring my tea with a twig of sax-aul, he sent for one, and presented it to me. This, together with the offer of the nicely fur-

nished kibitka as a shelter against the scorching noonday
heat, was such a piece of real kindness and hospitality as
is rarely met with except in the desert.

For my own part, I made a display of all my wealth in
provisions. I had some of Liebig's extract of meat—
by-the-way, about the most villainous compound I have
ever tasted—which, with some dried vegetables, I had
made into a soup; also some pâté de foie gras, that
pleased my Kirghiz friend immensely, and a quantity
of dried fruit, known in Central Asia as *kishmish*.
Kishmish, which consists of raisins, dried apricots, and
peaches, is considered a great delicacy in the desert. I
had besides some chocolate, which so pleased my guest
that he sent off some to his wife and daughters. I then had
some fresh sweet milk boiled, into which I broke a quantity of biscuit. This was the great triumph of the meal,
and gave immense satisfaction. Then we drank our tea
from large bowls, which was the only thing I had in the
way of dishes. These bowls, enclosed in a lightly ornamented leather case, are attached to the saddle, and form a
part of the accoutrement of every horseman in the desert.

While taking tea, I offered him a cigar, which he at
first refused. When he saw me light one, he changed
his mind and followed my example with great zest, thus
showing that he first refused because he did not know
what the cigar was. He then showed me some paper
and tobacco for cigarettes, as well as a pipe, the use of
which he had learned from the Russians. He assured
me, however, that the cigar was better.

While smoking our cigars, I opened through Ak-Mamatoff
a general conversation with him, our few and desultory
remarks up to that moment having been confined to the
necessary questions and answers relating to the meal.

He informed me he was a chief, that his name was Dowlat, and that he governed under the Russians two thousand kibitkas. Each kibitka paid three roubles a year taxes to the Russians—that is, about nine shillings of English money. When I asked him if they were satisfied with the Russian rule, he said " Yes," but at the same time significantly shook his head. He added that they very often had to pay tribute to the Khan of Khiva, who likewise claimed as his subjects all the Kirghiz living between the Amu and the Syr.

I told him that when the Russians would have conquered the Khan and brought him to terms, this state of things would be put an end to ; but he shook his head sadly, as though the prospect were anything but pleasing. Probably he did not look with any great pleasure at the prospect of the last stronghold of his religion being subjected to a Christian power.

The mode of life of the Kirghiz is very peculiar. The three winter months are passed in mud habitations on the banks of some river or small stream. When the snow begins to melt, they start out on their yearly migrations. For nine months they never stop in one spot more than three days, and all the time live in tents. They continue their march often until they have travelled three or four hundred miles ; then they turn around and go back exactly the same route, reaching their winter quarters again when the snow begins to fall. It is hard to find what motive guides their selection of places beyond the respect for tradition. A spot which one aul deserts, another is glad to occupy : and often a body of Kirghiz leaves good grazing ground behind to travel hundreds of miles away to far inferior pasturage.

KIRGHIZ WINTER ENCAMPMENT. *From a design by Verestchagin.*

For instance, the Kirghiz, who winter on the Oxus, migrate in the spring to the Syr and even farther north; while some of those on the Syr go south to the Oxus, and others north to the Irghiz. Many · of those on the Irghiz migrate either still farther north or take a southerly direction to the Syr. To anybody unacquainted with their habits of life, there does not seem to be the slightest system in their movements. They have a system nevertheless. Every tribe and every aul follows year after year exactly the same itinerary, pursuing the same paths, stopping at the same wells as their ancestors did a thousand years ago; and thus many auls whose inhabitants winter together, are hundreds of miles apart in the summer. The regularity and exactitude of their movements is such that you can predict to a day where, in a circuit of several hundred miles, any aul will be at any season of the year. A map of the desert, showing all the routes of the different auls, if it could be made, would present a network of paths meeting, crossing, intersecting each other in every conceivable direction, forming apparently a most inextricable entanglement and confusion.

Yet no aul ever mistakes its own way, or allows another to trespass upon its itinerary. One aul may at any point cross the path of another, but it is not allowed to proceed for any distance upon it. Any deviation of an aul or tribe from the path which their ancestors have trodden is a cause for war, and, in fact, nearly all the internecine struggles among the Kirghiz have resulted from the encroachment of some tribe, not upon the pasture grounds, as might be supposed, but upon the itinerary of another.

The inhabitants of an aul are almost always relations. In many cases they seem to have been founded by two or three brothers, who, with their wives and children and grandchildren, make up a little community, occupying usually from five to ten kibitkas.

The Russians, when they first conquered the Kirghiz, found this system very embarrassing; and thinking it would be impossible to keep any account or control of the people while thus wandering from department to department, tried to make territorial divisions among them and to confine each tribe to a certain section of country. As might have been foreseen, the attempt was a failure. Besides the impossibility of enforcing the order, it was found that it resulted in continual warfare among the Kirghiz themselves, as they could not be made to understand what their rights really were.

Accordingly they soon returned to the old order of things; and the governors of the departments of Orenburg and Turkistan agreed to consider the winter quarters of the Kirghiz as their residence, regardless of their migrations, in order to determine which department should have jurisdiction over them.

I took occasion now to ask my friend why his people did not stay in the same spot, instead of continually wandering from place to place. The pasture, he said, was not sufficient in one place to sustain their flocks and herds.

" But why do those who live on the Syr in the winter not stay there in the summer, where the pasture is good, instead of wandering off into the desert, where it is thin and scarce ?" I ask.

" Because other auls come ; and if they all stayed, they would soon eat it all bare."

" But why do not the other auls stay at home on the Amu and the Irghiz, instead of coming ?"

" Because other auls come there too," he replied.

" But why do not they all stay at home ?"

" Well, our fathers never did so, and why should we not do as they have always done?" he replied. And I suppose this is about as near the true reason of their migration as any other.

To tell the truth, this nomadic mode of life is, probably, better adapted to the desert than any other.

I was further informed by my friend, that the Kirghiz live principally on milk, and sometimes a little flour, with an occasional piece of mutton. He himself, he said, had mutton or bread as well as tea and sugar every day. After an hour's talk my host left me, and, as the kibitka was delightfully cool, I stretched myself for a nap. When I awoke, I found the horses saddled and everything ready for starting. Swallowing a cup of tea, I mounted my horse and started, first giving a hearty shake of the hand and a half-dozen cigars to my kind entertainer.

Towards evening, we seemed to approach the Yani-Darya. Here there was a little forest of some kind of wood different from the sax-aul, and not unlike the American burr-oak; many of the trees being twenty-five or thirty feet high. In the middle of this wood was a low mound, partly surrounded by what appeared to have been a very deep ditch, and which looked like the remains of some ancient earthwork. I asked Mustruf about it, but he was unable at the time to give any satisfactory answer. I afterwards learned that it was the site of an ancient town, which had been abandoned on account of the drying up of the waters of the Yani-Darya.

Although there was plenty of grass and water here, Mustruf preferred pushing forward in search of an aul to camping. We accordingly continued our march until

long after dark. Leaving the Yani-Darya behind us,
we entered upon a dry, open, level plain, where there was
very little vegetation of any kind. Our horses trotted
silently along, their hoofs touching the soft, yielding,
dusty ground as lightly as though they had been muffled.
After hours of travelling, when I began to think we would
probably have to pass the night on the open plain, without
shelter, I was startled to hear the voice of a child. We
turned in that direction from which I had heard the voice,
and, after going half a mile, caught a gleam of light and
the glimmer of water in the spectral moonlight.

At the prospect of food and rest, our horses broke into
a joyful neigh, and after a few minutes' gallop brought us
within the precincts of a small aul.

INTERIOR OF KIBITKA.

CHAPTER VII.

A KIRGHIZ LOVE STORY.

A BRIGHT fire flashing up out of the darkness, and throwing a ruddy light over bright-coloured carpets, rugs, and cushions; around and above a light trellis-work of wood, covered by thick white felt, against which are hanging cooking utensils and various articles of household use, a sword and gun, saddles and bridles, a three-stringed Tartar guitar, thrown carelessly aside, was the scene that greeted me on stepping out of the desert into the tent.

The kibitka was the largest I had ever seen, being fully twenty feet in diameter; and the felt, with which it was covered, was clean and new, and of almost a snowy whiteness. It was easy to perceive that the young Kirghiz who had offered me his hospitality was one of the richer class. At a word from him, two young girls, evidently sisters, and probably twins, came forward with downcast eyes, and saluted me each in her turn by taking my hand between both hers, and then laying it on her heart with a pretty modest meekness that was perfectly bewitching. This is the manner, as I afterwards observed, in which the women always salute husbands, brothers, fathers, and lovers, and, judging by myself, guests also. It was done with such a simple pretty grace, accompanied by a timid glance of the dark eyes, that I thought I had never in my life seen prettier or more interesting faces. And, in truth, they were very pretty. Round, fresh faces, in which the Mongolian type had entirely disappeared; rich olive complexions that were perfectly transparent; their hair, black as night, hung down over their backs in two rich heavy braids, reaching almost to the feet, and their dark soft eyes were fringed with long heavy lashes, such as are rarely seen except among the Caucasians. They were dressed in khalats, or tunics of red silk, ornamented on the sleeves and around the edges with a kind of embroidery in various colours, and covered with a number of broad thin silver buttons. The khalats were fastened at the throat with a coral button, but hung loosely open in front, exposing a chemise of white silk, reaching to the knee, and worn carelessly open on the bosom in a very piquant manner. White trowsers of the same material, with red boots, completed a very simple, but, for the desert, very becoming costume.

The brother wore a short, tight-fitting jacket of some red stuff, half silk, half wool, likewise ornamented with silver buttons; wide leather trowsers of a bright yellow, and embroidered nearly all over in a variety of curious patterns; a sash of yellow silk, in which were stuck a knife and an old flint-lock pistol very prettily inlaid with silver, a light jaunty cap made of the fur of some animal, and loosely-fitted boots of unblacked leather.

Handing my rifle and revolver to him, I threw myself on the rugs before the fire with a delicious sense of repose, while Ak-Mamatoff drew off my heavy riding-boots and replaced them with a pair of slippers my host had instantly provided.

There is always a small space in the kibitka un-carpeted. When making your toilet you simply kneel down on the edge of this spot, while water is poured over your head and hands from a tea-kettle, or a leather pail or bottle, and sometimes from a copper ewer of a very elegant shape, often met with among the Kirghiz—from what-ever vessel, in short, comes first to hand. The dry sand drinks up the water instantly, and in a moment all trace of it has disappeared.

A large iron pot was set over the fire on a big iron ring. This ring had legs attached, and when afterwards set up on its edge, did duty as a crane to hang the tea-kettle on. My people soon came in, and, together with three or four neighbours, squatted down around the fire and set up a lively chattering. The Kirghiz do not sit down cross-legged like the Turks, but go down on their knee with their weight thrown down back on their feet, which are twisted and pressed down flat, with the heels outward. However natural and easy an attitude to the Kirghiz, a European, who ever hopes to walk again, should never attempt it. I was the subject of the conver-sation, as I could easily see from their occasional glances towards me, and I inferred, from certain bursts of as-tonishment and other signs of surprise, that Ak-Mamatoff was indulging his imagination by drawing the long bow to its utmost tension about myself. The Kirghiz, unlike the Turks and Arabs, are very loquacious and fond of gossip. The whole evening passed in a continual flow of conversation, in which there was much mirth and laughter.

In about half an hour the contents of the great pot were turned out into a large wooden dish; wooden spoons were provided, and I was invited to take my place with the others around it. Our meal consisted of a kind of

mutton broth, thickened with something like wheaten
grits, and very palatable.   We all ate from the same dish
in the most amicable manner, but there was unfortunately
not enough, and I had seen that afternoon neither duck
nor pheasant.   There was plenty of good fresh milk,
however, and ordering a quantity of it to be boiled, I
broke some of my biscuits into it.   My Kirghiz friends,
who had probably never tasted such a dish before, were
delighted beyond measure, and by the time we had concluded the meal with a little chocolate and *kishmish*,
we were all in the merriest possible humour, and had
forgotten the howling waste outside.   All this time the
two girls kept in the background, and it was only on my
repeatedly insisting, that they came forward and took
their share of the meal.

Our supper over, I asked my young friend for some music,
pointing at the same time to the guitar.   He complied
very readily, and sung three or four songs, accompanying
himself on the instrument.   One or two of the songs were
hailed with shouts of laughter and merriment.   He also
sung one or two war songs, in which he celebrated the
feats of some Kirghiz hero against the Turcomans, and
these also were greeted with applause.

The guitar was a small instrument, with a body in
shape something like a pear cut in two lengthwise, and
about a foot long, while the neck was three feet.   It was
made of some dark wood resembling walnut, and had one
brass and two catgut strings.   The frets were not arranged
so as to produce the chromatic scale.   The airs of the
songs would, I think, have been pretty, though very
peculiar, but for the shrill high key and disagreeable long
nasal whine in which they were sung.   This manner of
singing is universal in Central Asia; I remarked the

same thing at Khiva, and among the Bokhariots who accompanied the Russian expedition. This, however, did not prevent the singing from being very amusing, and, taken together with the surroundings, very interesting. The place, the wide desert without, the cheerful fire within, throwing a ruddy light over the wild faces and strange costumes, the arms, saddles, bridles, and accoutrements, and the two young girls with their wild beauty, made up a very pretty picture. I tried to get the girls to sing, but they modestly declined, and no inducement could prevail on them to do so. Then I laughingly got Ak-Mamatoff to make one of them a proposition of marriage for me, which they heard with many blushes and much laughing. Ak-Mamatoff told me, however, that I would have to make the proposition to the brother, who had the right to give them away if he wished; and that besides I should bestow on him a present, and on the girl a dower in advance. I accordingly offered the brother one of my rifles, and the girl a horse, a camel and a kibitka furnished, and twenty sheep. This proposition was received with grave faces by the girls, who began to look upon it as serious. But they told Ak-Mamatoff to inform me that I would have to marry them both, as they would not separate from each other. It was not for me to object to so agreeable an arrangement, and of course I readily consented. It would have been a pity to separate them. I may as well add here, that upon starting away next morning the brother told Ak-Mamatoff to tell me that he had talked the matter over with his sisters, and that when I came back that way they would give me an answer.

The Kirghiz may have more than one wife, as all Mohamedhan peoples, but they rarely avail themselves of the privilege. Marriage among them is looked upon as any other business transaction, and is not a religious ceremony at all. The man buys the girl from her father with a present or presents, in proportion to the wealth of the parties concerned. It is a fact worth stating, that this sum is not usually retained by the father, but returned to the young couple, and thus becomes the wife's dower. It is sometimes, however, held in trust by the father, as a protection to the wife in case her husband should send her back; for a husband has a right to put away his wife at any time, though the right is rarely exercised. If this has not been done, however, the wife, upon being sent back to her father, can take with her all the property originally given by the husband.

In other words, the husband, instead of seizing the wife's property upon marriage, as is the law in civilised countries, actually protects her against future want. This barbarous custom will no doubt be abolished with the advent of modern civilisation and enlightenment.

In case the husband dies, it is the custom, as in the old Jewish dispensation, for his brother, if he have one, to marry the widow—a custom which probably arose from a desire to keep the property in the family.

In eliciting this information, I drew out a story from the young Kirghiz, which shows that human nature is very much the same in all places, and that love rules supreme as well in the desert of the Kyzil-Kum as elsewhere. Polat, a young Kirghiz, was affianced to Muna Aim, the most beautiful maiden of the aul of Tugluk. The *Kalym* or wedding present had been given to Ish Djan, her father, and the day was fixed for the marriage. Before it arrived Polat died, and Muna Aim was freed from her promise. Then Suluk, the brother of Polat, came forward

and claimed her as his wife. He wanted to get back his
brother's property, which the girl had received as a dower,
and her father said she must marry him. But she considered
herself a widow now, and had enough to live on. So she
thought she had a right to do as she pleased, and refused
to marry. Her father drove her out of his kibitka. Then
she took her camel, her sheep and goats, her clothes and
carpets, and went out from her father's kibitka. She
bought a little kibitka, and lived all alone by herself, and
milked her own sheep and goats, and drove them to pasture, and drew water for them from the well. And when
the aul moved, she moved with the rest, and set up her
kibitka not far from the others. Then all the old women
got very angry with her. "What is the matter with
Muna Aim?" they said "She will not go to her husband,
but lives all alone like an outlaw. Let us go and reason
with her." And so they went, and scratched her face, and
pulled her hair; but Muna Aim only cried, and wrung her
hands, and would not go. And they used to gather
around her tent every day, and call her bad names, and
torment her until she nearly cried her eyes out. But
all the same; she would not yield. Then Suluk took
the matter in his own hands, and went with three or
four friends one night to her kibitka, and broke it open to
carry her off to his tent, and make her his wife by force.
But she fought like a wild cat, so that they all together
could not succeed. When they dragged her to the door,
she caught the door-posts with her hands, and held so fast
that they had to take their knives and cut her fingers to
make her let go. When they at last got her out of the
tent, she had not a rag of clothes left, and was covered
with blood from head to foot. But she still fought; and
Suluk got on his horse and caught her by the hair,

and dragged her until it came out by the roots, when he rode off, and left her on the ground, naked and half-dead.

"But why wouldn't she marry him?" I asked.

"Because she loved Azim."

"And where was he?"

"Away off in another aul, which wintered in the same place as this one, but went a different way in the summer. You see she never loved her intended husband, and only consented to marry him because her father told her to."

"But how did it all end?"

"Why, the Yarim Padshah heard the story, and sent some Cossacks for Suluk, and took him, and he was never seen afterwards."

"What became of him?"

"I don't know. They say he was sent so far away he will never come back again."

"And the girl, did she die?"

"No; she got well, and when she came back to the winter camp she met her old lover, and they were married."

"And did not the old women interfere?"

"No; they were afraid of the Yarim Padshah."

The "Yarim Padshah," the half-emperor, is the name by which General Kaufmann is known all over Central Asia.

I afterwards asked Kaufmann if the story were true. He corroborated it in every particular, adding the important detail that Suluk, the would-be lover, had been sent to Siberia.

About ten o'clock the girls retired to one side of the tent, drew a red curtain, which I had not observed before, across, and were soon fast asleep in each other's arms. After a look at the horses I threw myself on the ground before the fire, and watched its flickering, dying flame until I went to sleep.

CHAPTER VIII.

A GLOOMY NIGHT.

I WOULD here remark that my sojourn with the Kirghiz left a most favourable impression upon me. I have always found them kind, hospitable, and honest. I spent a whole month amongst them; travelling with them, eating with them, and sleeping in their tents. And I had along with me all this time horses, arms, and equipments, which would be to them a prize of considerable value. Yet never did I meet anything but kindness; I never lost a pin's worth; and often a Kirghiz has galloped four or five miles after me to restore some little thing I had left behind. Why talk of the necessity of civilising such people? What is the good of discussing, as Mr. Vámbéry does, the comparative merits of Russian and English civilisation for them? The Kirghiz possess to a remarkable degree the qualities of honesty, virtue and hospitality—virtues which our civilisation seems to have a remarkable power of extinguishing among primitive people. I should be sorry indeed ever to see these simple, happy people inoculated with our civilisation and its attendant vices.

Next morning, I bade my host and his pretty sister farewell, not without some feeling of sadness. To each I gave as a parting gift what I thought would be most acceptable: to the brother a pocket-knife; and to the sisters, earrings and other little articles of jewelry.

In the course of this day's journey we passed several Kirghiz tombs. These tombs are very large; consisting of a central dome, thirty or forty feet high, and enclosed by a high wall, forty or fifty feet square; and, in fact, could easily be turned into a formidable fortress for a small party.

Passing through a small forest of sax-aul, eight or ten feet high, we came out on a very poor aul, consisting of three kibitkas, which, covered with ragged felt and without rugs and carpets, presented a very miserable appearance. Here I tasted for the first time the well-known *airan* of the Kirghiz. This is made from the milk of camels, sheep, and goats, mixed together; which being set, while still warm from the animals, over a slow fire until it turns, takes a sharp acrid taste. It thus becomes a very agreeable and palatable drink in hot weather, and possesses the advantage of always tasting cold, even on the warmest day. In summer it forms almost the entire food of the Kirghiz. They have another kind of drink made of mares' milk fermented, which they call *kumiss*. It foams and sparkles, and has a taste slightly resembling champagne, very refreshing in hot weather.

As night approached, the wind rose until it became a regular hurricane. The air grew thick with dust, and the sun itself was hidden, so that night came on an hour earlier than usual. In such circumstances we thought it high time to look for an aul. On and on, however, we went until long after dark, scanning the horizon in every direction without success. At last we sent off Tanger-berkhen to scour the country, as Mustruf thought there

must be an aul somewhere in the vicinity. The wind, rising every moment, was making a deafening noise, and we could at times scarcely see ten yards before us, while the dust arose in tall whirlwinds, that went scudding along in the pale moonlight like desert spectres.

At last we heard Tangerberkhen calling to us, and his voice, borne, through the obscurity, on the gusty wind, had a strange unearthly sound. After some difficulty we made out the direction whence it came, and started towards him, hoping the longed-for aul had been found But no sounds of welcome greeted us here, nor bleating of flocks, nor lowing herds, nor merry voices of children, nor the thousand pleasant sounds of aul life. Only blasts of wind, and clouds of whirling dust, through which the moon's pale light struggled feebly, casting dim spectral shadows over the desert. We found Tanger-berkhen by the side of a puddle of muddy water, about ten feet in diameter, near a clump of sax-aul bushes. What was to be done? To go forward against this beating wind was impossible; to find an aul in this darkness hopeless. Plainly we saw that there was nothing for it but to camp in the open desert for the night, with the sand for a bed, and unsheltered by a friendly tent from the cold, the wind, and the dust.

We accordingly dismounted: Mustruf and Tanger-berkhen fed and watered the horses, while Ak-Mamatoff gathered fuel. In a few minutes a large bright fire was blazing, casting a ruddy glow over the desert. We bent together a few low bushes, and covering them with our saddle-cloths and horse-blankets, soon had a kind of half tent, affording us a little shelter from the wind.

Tea was soon made with the water we had fortunately brought with us, and our supper of a little cold mutton soon despatched. Then wrapping ourselves up in our sheepskin overcoats, we threw ourselves into the improvised tent. Our heads in our saddles, our faces to the moon, and our feet to the fire, with the wind still blowing a hurricane, we sink into a dreamless sleep.

After a hard day's ride in the desert, sleep comes easy, but the waking is bitter. At this season, the nights are as cold as the days are hot; and the hour before dawn is almost freezing. As you awake, you find your limbs stiff, sore, and benumbed; every movement is a painful effort, and your little hollow in the sand is a bed of thorns. A drowsy stupor hangs over your whole frame; and it is almost agony to think of the long, weary journey that must be commenced.

During the whole of the next day we continued our journey over rolling ridges of sand, entirely destitute of vegetation and of any track of the feet of men or animals. In the course of the afternoon I killed a saigak. Later on we came to a newly-dug well at the foot of a stunted tree in the dreariest little valley I ever saw. Nothing was to be seen but the yellow sandy dunes and the gravel-filled valley, upon which the sun poured down its hottest afternoon rays. A crow, that had built its nest in the topmost branch of the tree, which cawed hoarsely as it made vicious darts at us, was the only living thing visible. The ground was strewn with the shells of turtles which had been sacrificed to the appetite of the young crows.

Once during the day we lost our way. Upon consulting my compass, I found we were going towards Kazala, that is to say, in the very opposite direction to our destination; and for a while I suspected Mustruf of treachery. He explained the matter by saying that we would reach the road from Kazala to Irkibai by going a short distance in this direction.

The few hours that followed this discovery were the most painful I had yet passed in the desert. First, we wandered about without knowing the way, and apparently without any prospect of ever reaching it. And then, to add to our misfortunes, we had to undergo all the agonies of thirst. Owing to the negligence of Mustruf, we had brought no water with us. I had drunk nothing since the evening before but a little muddy tea; and the long, hot march of the day, together with the extreme heat, had utterly undone me. My exhaustion was not to be wondered at; for I was still fresh from the snows of Siberia. I had only been four days in the desert, and during each of these days I had ridden nearly fifty miles. My throat seemed to be on fire, and the fever commenced mounting to my head; my eyes grew inflamed and unsteady, in spite of all I could do. I began to fear seriously an attack of brain-fever. For miles around the desert presented the same bleak, parched appearance. And then, as we had lost our way, there was no knowing when we could quench our thirst; the thought of going another day or even passing that night without water was almost maddening. At length, after hours of intense suffering, just as the sun was setting, we struck the road from Kazala to Irkibai, over which the Grand Duke had passed. After some anxious searching we found near here a shallow pool of slimy water. It was thick with mud; and after drinking it my mouth, throat, and stomach were coated with slime, the taste of which remained for days. A hasty meal, and we threw ourselves in utter exhaustion on the sand.

When I awoke it was three o'clock in the morning,

and the stars were still shining. My people were saddling the horses preparatory to an early start; and long before the first streaks of day had begun to light up the eastern sky we were advancing on the trail of the Grand Duke's army towards Irkibai, which we hoped to reach before the heat became oppressive.

At nine o'clock we came to a spot where the country fell away in a kind of lower terrace, over which we could see for miles. It was thickly covered with a growth of sax-aul just coming out in leaf. This, though only four or five feet high, seen in the vast valley from our elevated position, had all the grandeur of an oak forest. In the middle of this plain was some kind of a fortress, which, in the distance, I at first took for the fort of Irkibai. We reached it after an hour's ride, and then found it to be an old ruin. To approach, we had to cross the dry bed of a very large canal and to ascend a little hill. We then discovered the crumbling founda-tions of an outer wall, and, mounting still higher, found ourselves among the ruins of an ancient city.

CHAPTER IX.

AN ANCIENT CITY.

THE ruin was all covered over with brushwood, but fragments of wall fast crumbling away appeared in every direction, and on the summit of the hill were two very large towers. Built of sun-burned bricks, they had crumbled away under the action of the atmosphere, and might easily have been mistaken for large mounds of earth, but for the fact that one side was pretty well preserved. The position of the gate was still distinguishable, and the rubbish filling it up might easily have been cleared away. Mounting to the top of one of the towers, which was about thirty feet high, I found it sunk in places, and giving forth a hollow sound to our feet, showing that beneath there was a very large cavity.

The city was about a mile in diameter, and completely surrounded on three sides by a wide, deep canal, now dry, while the Yani-Darya bounded the place on the north-west, and completed the circle. Inside the canal, at the distance of fifty feet, and extending entirely around the city, were the remains of a wall fifteen or twenty feet high in some places, with occasional watch-towers of greater height and in a better state of preservation than the rest. The whole place was built of the same sun-dried brick.

The side next the river was still good enough to make the use of a ladder necessary to get over the walls from the outside. The Yani seems to have been 100 yards wide here, judging from its ancient bed.

I was told by Mustruf that this city had been built by the Kara-Kalpaks, who, driven from the banks of the Syr, had settled here in 1760. They had not only built a town, but had brought the water all the way from the Syr, a distance of 200 miles, by excavating the bed of the Yani-Darya, thus actually making a new river. The name "Yani-Darya" signifies "new river," which gives some show of reason to Mustruf's story.

I have heard, however, from other sources that the bed of the Yani-Darya is of much more ancient date. Late investigations prove that it was once a great stream, and it is even supposed that it is no less than the ancient bed of the mighty Syr. It is a strange circumstance that there should be found indications tending to prove that the Syr, as well as the Oxus, formerly flowed in a different channel from its present one, and that the ancient courses ascribed to both rivers should be nearly parallel to each other, and should both run south to the Caspian Sea. Has some mighty convulsion, some volcanic upheaval of the country thus changed in a single movement the course of two great rivers, or have more simple means, working uniformly over the whole country, produced the strange coincidence?

However that may be, the banks of the Yani were evidently at no remote period teeming with life and covered with populous villages, instead of the few wandering tribes that now haunt them. This accounts for the works of irrigation, which so much excited my curiosity all the way from Perovsky. What causes have led to the sudden

abandonment of the formerly productive oasis is not clearly
known; but the drying up of the Yani-Darya is the direct
one. Mustruf told me that it had only been abandoned
since the arrival of the Russians, who had cut off the water
in order to make the Syr navigable for their steamboats.
This statement, however, I do not credit, as these ruins
evidently date further back than fifteen years ago, when
for the first time the Russians occupied this part of the
Syr. It is nevertheless true that the ruins are not very
ancient, as it does not take long for mud-walls to crumble
and disappear when deserted by man, and left to the
summer heat and winter snows to work their will upon.

The Yani formerly continued its course some fifty
miles farther, and then formed a kind of shallow marsh,
where it was lost. Now, marsh and river have alike
disappeared. The fact, however, of the river having been
made by the people is one of considerable importance,
as showing the capability of the Kyzil-Kum for irrigation and cultivation. The Syr affords probably a supply
of water sufficient to irrigate the desert between it and the
Oxus, and the fact of the desert sloping off to the latter river,
with a decline of 100 to 200 feet, makes it a comparatively
easy process. It is true that there would be no water left
in the Syr for the purposes of navigation unless, indeed, it
were turned into a large canal. But even were that
river made navigable, as it might be, it would be of little
use while it flows through a desert only inhabited by a
few wandering nomads. I believe that, with the progress
of the Russians in Central Asia, the whole country
between the Syr and the Amu will one day blossom as
the rose.

General Kaufmann has already undertaken extensive
works for irrigation near Samarcand, which, although

interrupted by the expedition against Khiva, will be resumed this year. He proposes assembling 50,000 Kirghiz on the line of the projected canal, providing them with implements and provisions, and hopes thus to finish the work in a single season. The Kirghiz understand thoroughly the importance of a work which will enable them to become proprietors of a rich piece of land, and enter into it with enthusiasm. Once the practicability of the plan is demonstrated, there is little doubt that, with an increasing population, many parts of Central Asia, now arid wastes, will become as rich in soil and productions as Khiva and Bokhara.

Resuming our march after a short halt here, and still proceeding along the valley of the river, we met in about half an hour two Russian soldiers coming along the well-beaten road. This told me that we were not far from the Russian fort. So we urged our horses forward, and emerging from a little forest of sax-aul, espied at a short distance an earthwork on the edge of a dry arid plain, before which stood a crowd of Russian soldiers and officers watching our approach.

CHAPTER X.

IRKIBAI.

"WHAT has kept you so long?" was the first question asked me upon riding up to the group of officers.

"I do not think I have been very long," I replied; "less than four and a half days."

"Four and a half days," exclaimed the officer who had addressed me; "why you left Kazala thirteen days ago."

I was considerably alarmed to find my interrogator so familiar with my movements, and began to fear that the same authority which had refused me permission to leave Kazala had sent forward orders to stop at this point my further advance. It was with a good deal of trepidation therefore that I replied:

"Yes, but I was detained four days at Perovsky."

"Perovsky!" said he, in astonishment.

"Why, yes," I replied, deprecatingly; "I left there only four days ago."

"Are you not with the Khivan ambassador, and is that caravan not yours?" he asked, pointing in the direction whence I had come. I looked back, and beheld immediately following Ak-Mamatoff, Tangerberkhen, and my pack-horses, a long line of camels, which moved forward with their slow, steady tread. This was the caravan of the Khivan ambassador.

It was now my turn to be astonished; for the embassy, leaving Kazala at the same time as myself, had been able to take a direct route, and had, unlike me, been subjected to no delays on the way. I had at one time even thought of accompanying the ambassador, had not my plans been frustrated by my friend, Captain Verestchagin, at Kazala.

"Who in the name of all the devils are you, then?" my interrogator next asked, finding I was not part of the Khivan party.

I explained that I was an American on my way to join General Kaufmann's army.

"Well this is the most extraordinary thing I ever heard of; I can hardly believe it. I suppose your papers are all right though, so get down from your horse and come in; you look tired."

In a few minutes the officer who had addressed me had a kibitka set up for my accommodation, into which he now kindly led me. His name was Captain Hiezing, and he proved to be the commandant of the post. During the short period of my acquaintance this officer treated me with a kindness and a hospitality I shall not readily forget. He invited me to dine with him, an invitation I was only too glad to accept, as I had not yet broken my fast; and afterwards showed me over the little fort. It was a simple earthwork, with two corner bastions, surrounded by a shallow dry ditch, and defended by two pieces of cannon. I did not wonder at the small size of the work when I learned that it had been constructed by the Grand Duke Nicholas on his passage, in twenty-four hours. The garrison consisted of two companies of infantry, with a few Cossacks. Soldiers as well as officers were supplied with kibitkas, and there was a large store of barley. The water was excellent and plentiful, but the position was exceedingly unpleasant. There was little sand here, and the hard dry soil was soon trampled into dust by the soldiers, and blown about by a strong wind in clouds that were at times almost suffocating; and this combined with the heat, which had become excessive, made my short stay here exceedingly disagreeable, in spite of the kindness of the Russian officers.

Upon inquiry I learned that nobody knew anything of Kaufmann, and that no news had been received of the Kazala column since its departure two weeks ago. From the fact of the Khivan ambassador having been sent on from Kazala, the commandant inferred that Kaufmann was awaiting his arrival somewhere or other in the desert. To this supposition I gave little weight. An army was by no means likely to remain in the desert, awaiting the snail-like pace of the Khivans. I had no doubt that Kaufmann was continuing his march to the Oxus with all despatch, and I resolved to start early next morning on the trail of the Grand Duke.

The commandant offered no objections to my departure, except upon the score of danger. He thought the way very unsafe, and advised me to go with the Khivan ambassador, who was provided with an escort of twenty-five Cossacks, besides his own followers. This proposal, however, I declined.

I paid a visit to the Khivan ambassador, who was not allowed to enter the fort, but camped outside at a short distance from it. He had some twenty-five or thirty camels to carry his provisions and baggage, and was what

7

would be considered in Central Asia a very great ambassador. Greatness here as elsewhere has its drawbacks. He was such a very great man that he could not compromise his dignity by any unseemly haste in his movements. Thus he had left Khiva with orders to meet Kaufmann at Kazala, but his motions had been so leisurely that he reached that place some days after Kaufmann had passed through.

After a halt sufficiently long to demonstrate to the Russian general how mistaken he was if he supposed the representative of Khiva in a hurry to treat, he started back with the intention of meeting General Kaufmann in the desert. But here again his greatness so retarded his movements that he only reached the Russian general several days after Khiva had fallen. By that time the importance of his mission had somewhat diminished.

The Khivan ambassador started early on the morning of the 7th of May, but I did not get off till the afternoon. Kind old Captain Hiezing had insisted on my breakfasting with him, and then made me stay and take coffee after my little caravan had already started. He had given me ten bushels of barley for my horses, for which he refused to take any pay, saying he would report the matter to General Kaufmann's quarter-master, who might charge if he thought fit. He likewise gave me several introductions to officers of his acquaintance, and altogether treated me like a long-lost prodigal son.

At last I mounted my horse, and shaking hands with all the officers for the last time, I galloped away from the little fort with Mustruf, who had been waiting impatiently for me more than two hours.

CHAPTER XI.

THE THIRSTY DESERT.

THE road we were following was broad and well beaten. It was a regular caravan route, and bore many marks of the passage of the Grand Duke Nicholas; amongst the rest were prominent the bodies of dead camels that had fallen by the wayside from exhaustion. An hour's gallop brought us up to my caravan, which was plodding lazily along. It had been augmented by the addition of two horses and a Kirghiz carrier, with the mail which Captain Hiezing had entrusted to my care.

Now we enter for the first time that part of the desert which offers the greatest danger to the traveller, and surrounds him with the greatest horrors. The friendly rivers and the frequent wells and pools of water have been left behind. Yet the face of the country is fair. Gentle elevations roll off in every direction, covered with masses of verdure of a dark rich green, that rival in exuberance the luxuriant carpet of an American prairie, and the sun, shining down from an unclouded sky, turns the spots of yellow sand, seen here and there, into patches of glorious golden light.

But all this beauty is deceptive. These gentle hills are only sand, and the verdure which clothe them hides horrors as great as those covered by the roses that twine themselves over sepulchres. Blossoms shoot up, ripen, die, and rot, in the course of a few days. The verdure consists of but a rank soft weed that breaks out into an eruptive kind of flower, which, dropping off at the slightest touch, emits a most offensive odour. Beneath the broad leaves lurk scorpions, tarantulas, immense lizards, often five or six feet long, turtles and serpents, and the putrifying bodies of dead camels. Once lost in this desert ocean, without guide or water, you may wander for days, until you and your horse sink exhausted to die of thirst, with the noxious weed for bed, winding-sheet, and grave.

Upon this world of desolate life, this plain of charnel-house vegetation, we enter with a sickening feeling of depression. Kyzil-Kak is the first well we can meet, and between this and us lie sixty miles of desert. For all this way we have but two hogskins of water—about eight gallons—which are to be divided among five men and eight horses. We urge our horses forward at a rapid pace. The angry sun sinks slowly down the western sky, as though loth to leave us, and then suddenly drops below the horizon. The shades of evening gather, the desert fades into the gloom of night, and then suddenly reappears again, weird and spectral in the shadowy light of the rising moon. The hours slip by; we pass the silent tents, and smouldering fires, and crouching camels of the Khivan ambassador, who has camped here hours before; and though the moon has now mounted to the meridian, we still continue our rapid course.

A hurried nap, and again we are on our way. The red sun flashes angrily upon the eastern horizon, and now there is scarcely any vegetation—not even the poisonous upas-like weed. Hotter the sun grows as we advance, and more fiery, until he reaches the zenith, and glares fiercely down on us from the pitiless sky. The sands gleam and burn under the scorching heat like glowing cinders; the atmosphere turns to a misty fiery glare, that dazzles the eye and burns the brain like the glow from a seven times heated furnace; low down on the horizon the mirage plays us fantastic tricks with its spectrum-like reflections of trees and water—shadows, perhaps, of the far-off gardens of Khiva and the distant Oxus; our horses plod wearily forward through the yielding sand with drooping head and ears, until at last I find myself, as evening approaches, lying exhausted on the sand by the well of Kyzil-Kak.

Three or four Kirghiz, with their camels and horses, had already watered their animals at the well, and were just going away. When they saw us arrive, tired and exhausted, they immediately stopped, and began to draw water for us and our horses in the kindest manner. The well was about sixty feet deep, and was walled up with the hard, gnarly, crooked trunks of the sax-aul. Near the mouth, which was very narrow, was a little basin eight or ten feet in diameter, formed in the earth with the aid of the same desert tree. Into this the water was emptied for the animals to drink. The labour of drawing water from deep wells for flocks and herds is no inconsiderable one, and the Kirghiz always employ the aid of a horse.

These wells are very curious. Nobody ever saw them dry, nobody knows by whom they were dug, and they are now in exactly the same state as when, centuries ago, the hosts of Tamerlane slaked their thirst at them. Centuries have gone by, and generations, and even races of men have passed away, the world has grown old, but the pure, sweet waters are as fresh and sparkling as ever.

After a short halt to feed our horses, and a light meal of biscuit, fresh milk, and *arran* obtained from the Kirghiz, we resumed our saddles a little before sunset. We were scarcely on the road before we met a caravan. Each camel, as he passes, turns his head and stares at you with his great intelligent eyes as though he would speak. The Caravan Bashi—or leader of the caravan —at last comes up; we halt, and there is an exchange of news.

After the usual salutation, we inquired if they had seen anything of the Russian army.

" Oh, yes !" was the reply, " at Tamdy."

" Where is Tamdy?" I ask, getting down from my horse and proceeding to look at my map.

" Ten days from here," was the reply.

" Ten days ?   Impossible !"

The map, however, showed that the place was about a hundred and sixty miles distant, in a straight line from Kyzil-Kak—probably two hundred miles by the road. And it would take, at the ordinary caravan's pace, the time mentioned by the Bashi.

It will be remembered that, when I started from Kazala, I was under the impression that Kaufmann, in going to Khiva from Tashkent, would first march in a north-westerly direction from Djizak to the Bukan-Tau mountains, there form his junction with the Kazala column, and then march south to the Oxus.   As I was now within a day's march of the Bukan-Tau mountains, I had reason to hope that I was on the heels of the army.

Imagine my state of mind on learning that I was almost as far from Kaufmann, after seven days' march through the desert, as I thought I was when I started from Perov-sky.   Perhaps, however, I began to think, he had not

yet reached the Bukan-Tau mountains, and had not yet
begun his march to the Oxus. And if he was marching
from the south towards the mountains, I, proceeding from
the north to the same point, would undoubtedly meet him
Must he not be there now, as the caravan had passed him
ten days ago?

"Which way was he going ?" I asked.

"South "

"South ? Why, Kaufmann is coming north-west towards the mountains here." I began to believe that they
had not seen the Russians at all.

"No. He had just marched for Aristan-Bel-Kuduk,
which was south." That was a name Commandant Hiezing
had spoken of, and this statement was therefore probably
true. Where was Aristan-Bel-Kuduk

"Two days' march south from Tamdy."

I began to grow uneasy. Aristan-Bel-Kuduk was
not on the map; but I had naturally supposed it to be
in the Bukan-Tau mountains. If it was therefore two
days' march south of Tamdy, and not west, Kaufmann
must have taken an entirely different route from the one
originally intended. He must have decided to march
due south to the Oxus more than ten days ago, instead
of to the Bukan-Tau mountains, and I was completely
astray. Instead of overtaking him in one or more days,
as I had fondly hoped, I might now be weeks. The
success of my undertaking seemed hopeless.

What was I to do? Go back? That was almost
as difficult as going forward. With many misgivings
I resolved to go on; and we resumed our march
We travelled nearly all night, and at half-past five
o'clock next morning, just after sunrise, we first came
in sight of the Bukan-Tau mountains, still about

twenty-five miles distant. The country here changed
its rolling character, and sloped off in an even slightly-
ascending plain, while the mountains themselves presented a dark grey united front, bare and barren, treeless
and lifeless.

While halting here to admire the scene, we were overtaken by an aul of fifteen or twenty camels and kibitkas
on its march towards the Bukan-Tau. The camels were
heavily laden, and it was curious enough to see a whole
family, with all its household goods, stowed away on the
back of one of these patient, gentle beasts. Often a
single camel bears not only a kibitka with all its furniture on its back, but also two women with three or four
children, the women as snugly seated as though in a
carriage; the children as soundly asleep as if in the
most fashionable baby-cart.

By nine o'clock we had reached the foot of the mountains. Here we found an aul or two, near a spring of
excellent water. We camped, and in a few minutes my
travelling friends had set me up a kibitka, into which I
threw myself, more utterly exhausted than ever before
in my life. Although it was still early in the day,
the sun shone down upon us with such terrible violence
that it was almost insupportable, and the shade furnished by the tent was a delicious haven of refuge
Besides, with the exception of a little tea, biscuit, and
airan, I had eaten nothing since leaving Irkibai, fifty
hours previously, and in that time I had travelled about
one hundred miles. After a cup of tea, that was speedily
prepared for me, and instructions to Ak-Mamatoff to buy,
if possible, a sheep, I threw myself on the rugs that had
been placed beneath the friendly shade of the kibitka, and
instantly fell into a deep and dreamless sleep.

CHAPTER XII.

THE BUKAN-TAU.

THE Bukan-Tau mountains are not more than a thousand feet high; are bare of vegetation; not even a shrub nor a blade of grass relieves their desolation. Their formation is of a very rotten kind of sandstone, which seems to be crumbling continually away. We were camped at the northern end of the range, and it was at Myn-Bulak, only some forty miles distant, that I expected to overtake Kaufmann when I left Fort Perovsky. Although so small, these heights presented all the characteristics of great mountains, in their miniature peaks, cone-like summits, deep valleys, and awful precipices.

We halted here the rest of the day; and next morning we took up our line of march around the northern slope of the Bukan-Tau. They fell off here into a gentle descent blending gradually with the plain. Once we had a slight scare, which served to awaken us to the reality of the danger to which we might at any moment be exposed. Mustruf and myself had left the rest of the party far behind, and ascended a low eminence to await their coming up. While here we beheld about a dozen horsemen approaching by the road before us. They had no camels with them, and therefore could not be an aul, and were all armed with guns slung to their backs. Mustruf looked frightened, for the Turcomans often make raids upon the Kirghiz as far north as the Bukan-Tau, and this might very easily be a party of marauders. As I afterwards learned, there actually was a party prowling about in the mountains at this very time.

We prepared our arms, and looked around anxiously for Ak-Mamatoff, whom we descried far away on the edge of the plain. Upon nearing us, however, we perceived they were Kirghiz, and Mustruf was soon among them shaking hands. We halted for a talk and an exchange of news. They gave information of the Grand Duke Nicholas, whose detachment they had accompanied from Kazala in the capacity of guides.

The Grand Duke, they said, had formed his junction with Kaufmann at Aristan-Bel-Kuduk ten days ago, and the two detachments had taken up their march for Karak-Aty. Here was more discouraging news. I looked upon the map, and found Karak-Aty about forty miles south of Tamdy, and if Kaufmann had marched from Aristan-Bel-Kuduk ten days ago, he must have already passed Karak-Aty on his way to the river. I observed that the latter point was no farther than Tamdy, from where we now were, and that a caravan route branching off to the south at a well a few miles ahead seemed to lead to it. This road, therefore, I determined to take.

At noon we descended suddenly into a little valley which came down out of the mountains. This was the valley of Yuz-Kuduk, or the hundred wells. It was completely bare of vegetation, except a very little thin grass, but there was a small stream of water trickling down through it which gladdened our eyes. It was very narrow, a mere gully coming down between two bare, gravelly, sandy mountains. Following it up about a quarter of a mile we came to the water. There were distributed along the valley about twenty-five or thirty wells or springs, in some of which the water came out at the surface, in others stood at a depth of from five to ten feet. In the latter it was deliciously sweet and cold, and quickly dismounting, we let down our tea-kettle by a rope. Ah! the sweet, cool water, how refreshing it was to our parched throats and swollen lips and sunburnt, grimy faces.

From here to the next well, a distance of twenty-five miles, the country, although still sandy, was high and broken up with occasional hollows and gullies, and I observed to the left a low range of mountains parallel to our route, extending north-east and south-west. This range is not down on any map yet published, but it seems to be the continuation of the Urta-Tau mountains, which are marked on the latest map of Khiva published by the Russian Staff. I found them here fully a hundred miles farther west than they are marked on that map They rose to the north-west in a succession of long slopes, each of which broke off suddenly and presented a bold declivity to the west. There were three of these between Yuz-Kuduk and Tandjarik, a distance, perhaps, of fifty miles

After travelling the greater part of the night, we reached about noon next day the well of Tandjarik. It was situated a mile from the road, and we only discovered it by perceiving some Kirghiz in the distance watering their sheep and horses. We found them, upon approaching, gathered around a low mud-wall, which served as the well-curb. They immediately gave places to us and helped us to water our horses. Afterwards one of them, better dressed than the ordinary Kirghiz, invited us to his aul, and offered me the hospitality of his kibitka. As the sun was at its hottest, and we were entirely without shelter, I accepted gladly, and after watering our horses, we mounted again, and followed our hospitable acquaintance. The aul was fully three miles distant, and after wandering through an interminable path, among the low sand-hills and sax-aul, we came unexpectedly upon it, snugly hid in a little hollow in the sand. It consisted of ten or twelve kibitkas placed without any regard to order or regularity.

We descended, and he led me in and presented me, as it seemed, to his wife and daughter-in-law, the first rather old and ugly, the latter young and pretty. They took my hand in both of theirs, and pressed it, and then laid it upon their hearts in sign of welcome. I threw myself down on the mats which the two women spread for me, and proceeded to get off a three days' accumulation of dust from my face, hands, and boots, and was just making myself comfortable for an afternoon nap, when an old woman came rushing in and stood before me, crying, wringing her hands, and pouring forth a torrent of words of which I could only distinguish the one word "Turkmen." I looked at my host for an explanation, but as we could not talk to each other without the help of Ak-Mamatoff, who was engaged somewhere about the horses, he only shrugged his shoulders; but I thought he looked as though it were an old story. The old woman, having finished her tale, sat down next the door, and watched me with eager eyes that made me uncomfortable.

When Ak-Mamatoff came in, she told the story over again, and he then gave it to me bit by bit. Some six weeks previously the aul had been in the Bukan-Tau mountains, near Yuz-Kuduk, pasturing their flocks. She was an old woman, and had an only son, she said, who took care of her, and was the staff of her old days. They had a tent and a camel, a horse and thirty sheep, and were happy. One day when her son, who was a fine young man, had wandered off among the mountains with his flock, a party of Turcomans, who had been prowling about, fell upon him, captured, and carried him off to Khiva, together with his horse and sheep. She had nothing left but her tent, and, worst of all, her son would be sold into slavery, and she would never see him again. Here she burst into tears again, weeping in a dreary, desolate sort of way, that was very affecting. I told Ak-Mamatoff to ask her what she expected of me. She replied, that I looked like a great man, and perhaps I would be kind enough to do something to help her to find her son, or get him set at liberty. I told Ak-Mamatoff to tell her that all the slaves would be liberated upon the arrival of the Russians at Khiva, and that I and my people would not only take particular pains to find her son, and have him set at liberty, but I would see that he had his horse, or a better one, back again, together with the same number of sheep, or their value. So she might expect to see him back, gaily mounted on a good horse, in two months at the most. When this was told her, she manifested her joy in a very vehement manner, and went off perfectly happy.

I then turned to my host, and asked him if the story were true. He said it was; that such things happened every year, and that there was the most deadly hatred between the Kirghiz and Turcomans in consequence. I asked him if the Turcomans were very terrible, and he said, no. They never attacked except in superior

numbers, as in the present case, when there was little or
no risk, and that the Kirghiz could always beat them in
an equal fight.

My host, I soon learned, was a subject of Bokhara,
and not of Russia; his name was Bu Tabuk, and he was
the chief of a tribe, which accounted for the superior
elegance of his dress and the wealth displayed in the
size and furniture of his kibitka. Naturally, my first
question was for news of General Kaufmann. Kaufmann,
he said, had indeed been at Karak-Aty, but was now at
Khala-Ata. He himself had just come from there, where
he had seen the whole army, and therefore he did not
speak from hearsay.

After a variety of questions concerning the distance to
Bokhara, I concluded that Khala-Ata must be about one
hundred miles south of Karak-Aty; one hundred miles
from the river, and the same distance from Bokhara;
and that instead of continuing on to Karak-Aty, the
nearest route would be right across the desert towards
the river, a little west of south. In this supposition I
was confirmed by Bii Tabuk, who said that would be
the shortest way, although there was no road, not even a
sheep path.

This way then I determined, if possible, to take, but I
foresaw that Mustruf would not be able to pilot me. I
asked Bu Tabuk if he could not find me a guide.
"Oh, yes, he would go himself; but he had to buy sheep
for the army, and he did not like to return without
them." "Very good; buy your sheep, have them driven
after, and we will go on together." "But they had given
him no money to buy the sheep, and he could not get any."
"Can you not trust the Russians so far as that?" "Oh
yes, but the Kirghiz won't let their sheep go without the

money." "How many sheep do you want to buy?" "About fifty." "Very good; I will buy, the sheep, if you will come with me as guide."

To this proposal he readily consented, and, after some

A KIRGHIZ.

more talk, it was arranged that he should go along with me and find somebody to drive the sheep to Khala-Ata.

Towards evening, when the sun was getting low, we mounted our horses and started forth in search of sheep.

We rode about over the desert, coming upon auls here and there in the most unexpected manner, hid away in little hollows in the sand. How we ever found them was a marvel to me, as you could never see one until you were right on it. We found plenty of sheep. They were all of the fat-tailed species, and generally in very good condition. We visited half a dozen auls, in all of which we were more or less civilly received. In one place, however, an old woman objected most decidedly to my presence; and although I did not descend from my horse, rated me soundly, if I could judge by her angry voice and energetic gesticulation. A bright pair of mischievous-looking eyes, which I saw peering through an opening in the kibitka before which the old hag was posted, disclosed to me at once the cause of her anger and her fears.

CHAPTER XIII.

KIRGHIZ HOME LIFE.

OBSERVING in the course of the evening that Ak-Mamatoff seemed to be very much interested in something Bıı Tabuk was telling him, I asked what it was about, when he told me the following story, which illustrates some of the workings of the Mohamedhan law relating to murder.

Among the Kırghiz, as among many other Mohamedhan people, murder is not punished with death, but the murderer is condemned to pay a fine to the relatives of the murdered man, proportionate to his wealth. And ın case he is not able to pay the sum fixed upon, he is obliged to serve them as a slave untıl the debt is paid. An old man, or woman, or a chıld—especıally a female child—is esteemed at less than a man or woman in the prıme of life.

Thıs was the story :—Two brothers who had quarrelled entertained a deadly hatred of each other. One determined to be revenged. He, therefore, one night murdered a little orphan niece—a deformed child left to his care by a dying sister—and placed the dead body at the door of his bro-ther's tent, where it was found. The circumstantial evidence was consıdered sufficient to convict the innocent brother of

8

the crime, and he was condemned to pay a heavy fine to the real murderer, as the only surviving relation. The injured man, however, cast around awhile, and at last found in another aul a great-aunt, about eighty years old, whom he murdered, and placed at the other's door. The first murderer was condemned in his turn to pay a fine to the second murderer; and as the old woman and crippled child were considered of about equal value, their accounts were squared.

The Kirghiz are generally allowed to arrange their quarrels in their own way, but among those who are Russian subjects General Kaufmann has established courts of appeal, composed of Russian officers. These courts do not, however, take cognisance of cases, except at the request of one of the parties to a suit, or for the punishment of certain very flagrant crimes, which would otherwise escape unpunished, and for the protection of women, as in the story I have related in a previous chapter.

The next morning I gave Bii Tabuk enough money to buy fifty sheep, and he and Ak-Mamatoff went off early, promising to have them all assembled, and ready to start by noon. While they were gone, I lay lazily in the tent and amused myself by watching the women going about their household work; I thus learned something of the daily routine of the interior of a Kirghiz family.

First, the sheep, goats, and camels were milked before being sent off to the desert to pasture. Then the carpets and felts were taken out and beaten, and re-arranged in their places, together with the other household implements. Two children, about as naked as robins, to whom belonging I could not quite make out, were fed with *airan*, and then sent out of doors to tumble about in the sand. A young camel that was tied just outside the

tent, and which kept up a dismal howling, was likewise
fed on the same nourishing food. Next, a sick ewe and a
sick colt were doctored, which operation was the cause of
much clamouring and chattering; and fuel was gathered
for the day. Suddenly there was a great commotion in
the aul. The women all rushed to a tent, chattering
in an excited manner. Something very extraordinary
seemed to have taken place, which I soon learned was the
birth of a child. In an hour the happy event was over,
and quiet was restored. The father came to me with
a broad smile on his face, and received my congratulations
and a present for the little stranger.

This episode over, the old woman, mounting a horse
which she bestrode like a man, took a tursook, or hogskin,
and went off to the well, some two miles distant, in search
of water, leaving me alone with the pretty young wife.
The latter soon came in, and sat quietly down without even
looking towards me; and taking out a bunch of wool and a
wooden spindle, on which a quantity of thread was already
wound, proceeded to spin, with a pretty, modest, house-
wifely air, that was charming. She had large black eyes,
fringed by long heavy lashes, a round face, to which the
Mongolian type, although very marked, only served to give
something of wild and interesting beauty. She wore the
high white turban of all the Kirghiz married women, and
a kind of short vest of red silk, embroidered with yellow—
worn provokingly open before—and upon the whole made
so pretty a picture, as she sat there twirling her spindle,
that I could not help envying with all my heart young
Bii Tabuk, and wondering whether he appreciated her
at her proper value. Was it not for such a woman as
this that a lover once served fourteen long years, " which
seemed unto him but a few days, for the love he had to

her ?" Was not this the life they led ? Was it not thus
they toiled, and lived, and loved ? I lie on my soft felts
in the deep shade of the kibitka and gaze dreamily
through the trellis-work, and, passing back over some
thousands of years, see the flocks and herds of Abraham,
and Isaac, and Jacob, and behold around me the living
forms of Sara, and Rebecca, and Rachel, and Hagar, and
Ruth.

The spindle with which she was working was made of
some kind of hard wood, worn very smooth, and I watched
the way in which she made that little bit of wood do duty
for our steam-engines, power-wheels, and spinning-jennies,
with a lively interest. Stretching out a little wool at the
point of the spindle, and slightly twisting it, she would
give the latter a twirl, and holding her hand high above
her head, allow it to whirl until it drew the wool out into
a fine long thread; then it was wound on to the back
part of the spindle, and the operation repeated. It was
very simple, and not by any means as slow as might at
first be supposed. The spindle was rapidly filled up, and,
curiously enough, took exactly the same form as that of
the thousands that may be seen in any great cotton
factory.

Bii Tabuk and Ak-Mamatoff, instead of returning at
noon, as had been promised, did not show themselves
until evening, and then they arrived without a single sheep.
Their story was that, although they might have brought
plenty of sheep, they could find nobody to help to drive
them to Khala-Ata. "But," said I, " I see plenty of young
men and horses, will none of them go for pay ?"

Ak-Mamatoff answered that they could not be induced
to do it, and Bii Tabuk returned me my money. I did
not believe this story, as there was really no reason,

judging by what I had seen, why men should not be found to help to drive the sheep, if I paid them well; and immediately attributed the difficulty to Ak-Mamatoff. I felt almost sure that he was thwarting me in this, as in everything else, for some inscrutable reason of his own; but as I could not communicate with Bii Tabuk without his aid, it was of course impossible to satisfy myself on the subject.

There was nothing more to be done; and as it was now too late to start that day, I unwillingly decided to stay here another night. I asked Bii Tabuk if he could not find me a guide. He said he thought he could, and, going off, soon returned with a young Kirghiz, who agreed to take me across the desert the nearest way to Khala-Ata for twenty-five roubles, or about three pounds. Although the price was exorbitant, I closed with him at once, as I was too much pressed for time to haggle. He promised to be ready early next morning, and with this understanding we separated. It was now sunset; the sheep and goats came trooping home, attended by their shepherds, enlivening the aul with their bleating and the movement and excitement they caused. The camels, too, came stalking in, some carrying water, others without any burden at all; with their beautiful, intelligent eyes they seemed to look around contentedly, as though recognising home. The ewes and goats were milked and watched until they lay down for the night; and the lambs and kids were all tied to a rope.

We passed a merry evening around the fire in the tent of Bii Tabuk, for although the day was excessively hot, the nights were cool enough to make a cheerful blaze a not unpleasant sight. This succession of hot days and cold nights is one of the most unhealthy characteristics of

the desert in this season of the year. I had made great
progress in the good graces of the two women, by several
little presents judiciously bestowed; and when I at last
withdrew to my side of the tent, I found a wide soft
carpet spread for me, with plenty of coverlets and rugs—
a very bed of roses after the sand I had been sleeping on
for several nights.

We were up next morning before sunrise, getting
ready for the march. I soon perceived that Bii Tabuk,
with the whole aul, was moving farther on, for the women
were taking down the kibitkas, loading them on the
camels, packing up their goods, and making rapid preparations for the march. For half an hour everything
was bustle and confusion. The camels commenced filing
slowly off in a long line, and soon the village had disappeared. I was astonished to see the woman whose
youngster was born the day before mount sturdily on her
camel with the brat in her arms, as though the birth of a
child were to her a matter of everyday occurrence.

I took an affectionate farewell of my hostesses, but
Bii Tabuk accompanied us a short distance on our way
before finally saying adieu. We shook hands upon separating, not without a feeling of sadness on my part. I
had been most kindly treated by him; and I had greatly
enjoyed my stay in his tent and the simple happy
life of the desert. Turning my horse's head to the south,
I was once more in chase of General Kaufmann. We
had not gone more than a mile when we stopped at a
well, where there were already three or four Kirghiz, to
water our horses. But when this task was accomplished,
we still lingered about; Mustruf, Ak-Mamatoff, and the
new guide, carrying on apparently an interesting and
pleasing conversation with our new acquaintances, with-

out any regard to the necessity of starting. I at last grew impatient, and ordered them to proceed, when Ak-Mamatoff coolly informed me that the guide refused to go unless I would, in addition to the twenty-five roubles, give him a horse, or the money to buy one. This demand I also attributed to the duplicity of Ak-Mamatoff, for the horse was evidently an afterthought.

I was determined not to be swindled in this way, however, as there was no telling when the demands of my new guide would stop, if encouraged. I told Ak-Mamatoff so in no very measured terms, giving him to understand that I held him responsible for the whole difficulty. I told him to ask the guide once more if he would go for the price agreed upon, and when he declined, I informed my own people that we would proceed without a guide Instead of cutting across country, as had been originally intended, we would go by way of Karak-Aty. This way was much longer, but we should have the advantage of a broad caravan route which could not be easily lost. At this they raised a clamour of opposition. They did not know the way; there was no water; we should be lost in the desert; it would be impossible to go without a guide. And this, although there had been no question of a guide as long as it had been our intention to go straight to Karak-Aty, now only distant a day's march. Arrived there, of course we should strike Kaufmann's trail, which could be easily followed. As the only objection to this route had been its length, this sudden opposition I considered a preconcerted thing. Determined to be trifled with no longer, I drew my revolver, and sternly ordered Ak-Mamatoff to mount and proceed. I had resolved first to reduce him to submission, and then to disarm Mustruf, take the horse he was riding, and proceed with Ak-Mamatoff and Tangerberkhen, who, I thought, showed a disposition to follow me at all hazards. I had no particular ill-will against Mustruf, for I knew very well that Ak-Mamatoff had been tampering with him in some way. But the arms and the horse were mine, and I was entitled to take them whenever he declined to go any farther. Ak-Mamatoff, who had probably not looked for any such energetic measures on my part, instantly submitted, and in a few minutes we were once more ready to start He then humbly proposed another plan for my approbation, namely, to go to an aul which, he said, was not far off, and try to get another guide. To this I consented, telling him, however, that we must be ready in any case —guide or no guide—to start in an hour; and that I would not give a kopek more than the amount originally agreed upon. He assured me there would be no difficulty in procuring another guide, and accordingly we proceeded to the aul.

This aul consisted of but three or four kibitkas, and the inhabitants seemed to be far less prosperous than those who followed Bii Tabuk. We soon found an old man, who readily agreed to conduct us at the stipulated price, a sufficient proof to my mind that the other guide had been trying—at the instigation of Ak-Mamatoff—to cheat me. He invited us all into his tent to eat with him, and instantly set about killing a sheep. In the course of the meal I heard, to my astonishment, that my host was the brother of Bii Tabuk. He had a horrible scar across his face, which, I learned, he had received forty years ago in a fight with a Turcoman, who was trying to carry off his wife. "This one?" I asked, pointing to a very ugly old woman, who seemed to be mistress of the kibitka.

" Yes."

She certainly did not look much like a prize that would be worth fighting for.   But then that was forty years ago.

Two girls came in from a neighbouring kibitka, and breakfasted apart with two or three other women.   They were not very pretty, but they seemed to be exceedingly merry and good-humoured, and kept up an amount of chattering among themselves that would have done honour to a bevy of the most civilised school-girls. I watched them narrowly, without seeming to do so. I observed in them a peculiarity, which I have remarked is common to all Tartar women : that is, the wonderful expressiveness of their faces, when animated.   In repose, when not interested, they have a hard, stolid, wooden look, like the carved face of some old heathen image ; but interested, pleased, or amused, they light up as with a ray of sunshine, their eyes sparkle, and the whole face seems to be aglow with some strange radiance from within.

Breakfast over, we set out for Khala-ata.   Instead of the broad caravan route, we were now following a very little sheep-path, which in places might have been hard to find, but for the sagacity of the guide.   No white man had ever been over this way before me.

The country presented the same general characteristics as heretofore, with the exception that the sand, instead of being disposed in little hillocks, covered with brushwood, lay in huge drifts as though heaped up and blown about by the wind ; and the earth in many places was bare and baked as hard almost as a rock.

Here, as in many other parts of the desert, were a great number of lizards, varying in size from two inches to a foot in length, which, together with an occasional little

land turtle, about six inches long, were the only specimens of animal life we saw. It is true there were said to
be plenty of scorpions and tarantulas, but although I had
come in the expectation of finding myself environed by
the deadly little monsters, and armed myself with all
kinds of antidotes to their stings, hardly hoping to
escape them, I never even saw one, nor did I do so much
as think of them while sleeping in the sand completely
exposed to their attacks. Several Russian officers were,
however, stung by them. The lizards were very inquisitive little animals. One day, while lying under the
thin shade of a brush, I observed one, whose curiosity I
had evidently excited. With his head up in the air, and
his tail curled up over his back like a dog's, in the most
comical way, he walked around me twice, and then, as
though satisfied of my peaceful disposition, crawled on
my foot, and perched himself there in triumph. They
sometimes attain an immense size, and I saw one that
had been captured at Khala-ata which measured nearly
five feet in length. They appear to be perfectly harm-
less, however, and the slightest blow kills them.

We passed another night in the sand without shelter,
and next morning changed our course from a little
west-south to south-west, and plunged into a desert
where there was not even a sheep-path to guide us—
the dreariest and wildest place I have ever seen. It
looked like a level plain, covered with a light spare growth
of brushwood, through which the sand was always visible;
but it was broken up into an infinite number of hollows
or cavities, from fifty to a hundred feet deep, and scarcely
more than that in diameter, resembling the crater of a
volcano. We were continually climbing out of these
little cavities, and descending into them again, while the

horses often sank into the sand up to their knees, making the march exceedingly slow and toilsome.

At noon we reached the well of Midyat-Kuz-ran, the water of which, in spite of its depth of eighty feet, was very warm—eighty degrees, I should say—and slightly brackish. It was impossible to drink it, but it made very good tea, which answered the purpose just as well. It is a fact not generally known, that hot tea slakes the thirst better than cold water. I could not believe this at first, and could scarcely bring myself to drink it, with throat and lips already parched with heat and thirst. Having been obliged to try it once, I found that it was much more effective than water. In a few minutes the sensation of thirst had entirely passed, and it did not return nearly so soon as after drinking water.

The road became very bad. The sand was heaped up across it in huge drifts, through which the horses struggled with difficulty. The little black horse, which Mustruf had particularly recommended to me for a saddle-horse, but which I had not ridden, had been showing signs of great fatigue during the past two days. We had removed his load, and distributed it among the other horses, leaving him only his light wooden pack-saddle to carry. It was all in vain. About nine o'clock at night he gave it up completely, and stumbling, fell his length in the sand with a groan. The poor beast was completely knocked up; I saw it was useless to urge him further, and taking off his saddle and bridle, we left him alone in the gloom of the desert.

Sadly we continued our march through the thickening gloom. Blacker grew the night, and more oppressive the darkness and silence. The loss of our horse cast a shadow over us. Here, in the heart of the wide dreary desert, there was something fearful in the necessity which compelled us to work a poor willing beast to death, and leave him alone to die.

How much longer was this to last? We had now been fifteen days in the desert, and were apparently as far from our journey's end as ever. Our horses had eaten nothing but what they could pick up in the desert for several days. How long before the others would fall like this one, from exhaustion, and leave us to continue our march on foot? It was evident that this phantom chase could not last much longer. Besides, although Bii Tabuk assured me I should find Kaufmann at Khala-ata, I did not expect it. Long ere this he must have reached the river. The savage Turcomans would be hanging on his flanks, harassing his march, and how should I with my tired horses escape their fleet-footed steeds, break through their lines, and reach the army? The death of our horse seemed but the harbinger of our own doom—the beginning of the end.

We persevere forward, stumbling through the low scrubby brushwood, sliding down into deep sandy hollows, almost slipping over our horses' heads; then again up steep ascents, where our horses pant and struggle, and wrestle with the heavy inexorable sand; over the hard earth where their hoofs clatter as over a stone pavement, until, late in the night, we throw ourselves in the sand to snatch a moment's repose.

We have scarcely shut our eyes, when we are called by the guide to renew the march. It is still night, but the desert is visible, dim and ghostly under the cold pale light of the rising moon. Vegetation has entirely disappeared, there is scarcely a twig even of the hardy sax-aul. Side by side with us move our own shadows, projected long and black over the moonlit sand, like fearful spectres pursuing us to our doom.

Then streaks of light begin to shoot up the eastern sky. The moon grows pale, the shadows fade out, and at last the sun, red and angry, rises once more above the horizon. After the sharp cold of the night its rays strike us agreeably, suffusing a pleasant sensation of warmth over our benumbed limbs. Then it grows uncomfortably warm, then hot, and soon we are again suffering the pangs of heat and thirst; our eyes are again blinded by the fiery glare, and our lungs scorched by the stifling noonday atmosphere.

At noon we have reached the summit of an eastern spur of a low range of mountains, which we have seen on our right nearly all the way from Tandjarik, and which here crosses our path. Although in reality nothing more than hills, they, like the Bukan-Tau, present, with their miniature peaks, deep gorges, and rugged crags and cliffs, all the characteristics of great mountains. Of a reddish, rotten sandstone formation, they lay barren, black, and bare under the burning sun, with no leaf, or blade of grass, or sign of life—unvisited by man or beast—the very picture of lonely desolation.

From the summit we stand gazing across a low level arid plain, beyond which, blue and misty on the horizon, rise the mountains of the Urta-Tau which had appeared on our left ever since Yuz-Kuduk. They sweep around to the west in a grand and noble curve, and are lost in the plain, far away in the golden light of the setting sun. Just beyond this range, the guide says, is Khala-ata, twenty-five miles distant.

Down the southern slope we plunge. It is very rugged and steep, and our horses' feet dislodge large masses of sand and gravel, which go rolling down before us in miniature avalanches. Half an hour brings us to the bottom, and we are again dragging over the weary desolate plain— a plain not of sand, but of dust.

Wherever there is sand, there is always at this time of the year a little wormwood, and here and there, perhaps, a spear of brown desert grass, as red as the sand itself. But nothing will grow in dust, and this plain was bare of vegetable life.

Long after dark we continue our march, in hopes of finding a spot where the horses can get something to nibble at. The guide gets down from time to time to feel the ground, in hopes of finding a little grass, but in vain. One might as well look for grass in a heap of newly-burned ashes. We camp at last, and make our tea with a bottle of water we have brought with us; carefully screening our fire from observation lest any parties of Turcomans that may be wandering about should see it; but our poor horses, after a march of fifty miles over a bad road, are obliged to go without food and water.

It is very evident that this cannot last much longer, and the night is one of intense anxiety.

At sunrise next morning we find a well of good water, and half an hour later we have reached the summit of the range behind which lies Khala-ata. The magnificent mountain chain, which looked so grand in the distance, has dwindled here into a low ridge.

The guide advances to the top, which is very sharp, and having peered cautiously over, motions me to advance. I do not know whether there is any necessity for this caution or not, but we are as silent and stealthy as if we expected to see, not the Russian, but the Turcoman camp in the distance. I advance my horse, and survey the scene with my field-glass.

A bleak arid plain, like the one we have just crossed, stretching away for miles to the south, and lost in the direction of Bokhara; in the middle, at the distance of eight miles, a dome-like mound, which I at first take for a monster kibitka, surrounded by small tents, that shine white in the morning sunlight; and finally, here and there, white masses of soldiers, and the glitter of bayonets.

Surely it is Kaufmann this time.

CHAPTER XIV.

KHALA-ATA.

IT was about six o'clock on the morning of the 16th of
May when I rode into the camp and fortress of Khala-ata,
dust-covered and weary after my seventeen days' ride
through the desert.   The camp was situated in the middle
of a level plain, bounded on the north by the low range of
mountains I had just crossed, and stretching away to the
south and east in the direction of Bokhara; without one
tree, without even the friendly sax-aul, which I had
seen everywhere, to relieve its dreary, soul-sickening
aspect—a wide expanse of sand that lost itself in the
distant horizon, and blended with the yellow, brazen
sky.   I was at first astonished that General Kaufmann
should have chosen such a spot to pitch his camp, but my
astonishment soon ceased when I beheld a spring of pure,
sweet water, gushing forth in a stream of six inches
thick, and affording a supply sufficient for an army of
many thousands.

   The camp itself was composed of tents and kibitkas, of
all sizes, shapes, and colours, scattered about irregularly
over a space of perhaps 200 yards square.   The large
dome-like structure which, in the distance, I had taken
for an enormous kibitka, proved to be an ancient mound

of earth, which, surmounted by a newly-constructed watch-tower of stone, now served as a corner bastion to the little fort which had just been constructed by General Kaufmann. Mud tombs, such as I had seen all the way through the desert, were scattered about here and there, some solid and well preserved, others broken and crumbling away; groups of soldiers gathered around the pools of water formed by the ever-gushing fountains, watering their horses; long lines of camels, starting out into the desert to hunt a scanty repast of sax-aul and wild absinth, a general appearance of dust, and heat, and discomfort—such was Khala-ata, the place where I first struck Kaufmann's trail, after a chase of seventeen days, and a ride of 500 miles.

It was with no little trepidation that I rode up to the young officer on duty, followed by my little caravan, and asked him where was General Kaufmann. The answer dashed my hopes to the ground. General Kaufmann had marched from Khala-ata five days ago, and was now certainly on the Amu-Darya. Five days! And by the time I could reach the river he would have crossed it, and taken Khiva. For a moment I was the prey to the most overwhelming disappointment, and mentally consigned old Ak-Mamatoff and Bii Tabuk to the lowest regions of the Inferno, for the three days they had detained me in the desert waiting for a guide and sheep.

I swallowed my chagrin as best I could, and informed the officer that I was an American on my way to see General Kaufmann, for whom, as well as for the Grand Duke Nicholas, I had letters of introduction. Would he kindly inform the officer in command of the detachment that I had arrived, and that I would like to call and pay my respects?

9

As soon as my informant learned that I was an American, he evinced the greatest cordiality, invited me into his tent, ordered tea to be made instantly, and told me Colonel Weimarn, the officer in command, was still asleep, but that he would soon be up, and would, he thought, be delighted to see me. He further informed me that Colonel Weimarn intended moving forward next

KHALA-ATA.

day with two companies of infantry, 100 Cossacks, and two field-pieces of nine, and that I could, of course, go with him. This suited me exactly, and I began to think that after all I might yet arrive in time. No news had been received from Kaufmann since his departure, except an order for the cavalry to advance, from which they inferred he had met the enemy; but further than this they knew nothing. They had already had one brush with the troops of the Khan, on the 9th of May, at the next well, the Adam-Kurulgan visited by Vambéry. General Kaufmann had, as usual, sent forward a small detachment to reconnoitre the ground, find wells, see if the water was good and in sufficient quantity, before advancing with the main body of the army. This detachment, under Colonel Ivanoff, a young and intelligent officer, approached Adam-Kurulgan a little after dark; but the Colonel himself, with four Cossacks and four Kirghiz guides, advanced rather imprudently a mile or two ahead of the column, and before he had even suspected the presence of the enemy in the neighbourhood, he suddenly fell on a body of Turkomens, 200 or 300 strong, camped near the well.

Both sides were about equally astonished, this being their first encounter. Before the Russians could retreat, they were surrounded and attacked on all sides. Quick as thought the Colonel dismounted his little force (it would have been folly to attempt running away from the swift-footed Turkoman horses), and made a most determined and resolute resistance. A desperate fight ensued, in which two of the little party were killed, and all the rest wounded, including the Colonel himself, who received a shot in the arm, and another in the leg. The fight lasted several minutes; and the Russians would have been certainly overpowered in a moment more, had not the troops in the rear, who rushed forward upon hearing the firing, arrived upon the scene in the nick of time. The Khivans, although still double the number of their opponents, immediately took to flight, and the gallant Colonel remained victor of a small but hard-fought battle.

I was very curious to learn the exact geographical position of Khala-ata, as it was not on my map, and how far we were still from the Amu-Darya. My informant, however, could give me no information on this subject, further than that Khala-ata was about 100 miles west of Bokhara, and the distance to the Amu was only a matter of conjecture even to General Kaufmann himself—it might be seventy-five or it might be 150 miles. He thought, however, that Colonel Weimarn might be able to give me the position as determined by the astronomers of the expedition. Its position, as I learned upon arriving at Khiva, is latitude 40 deg. 52 min. 52 sec. north, and longitude 33 deg. 10 min. east, from the Imperial Observatory of Pulkovo, near St. Petersburg, and 4 hours 13 min. 59 sec., Greenwich time.

I began to be reminded now, that although the forenoon was far advanced, Colonel Weimarn had not intimated to me that my presence was known to him—a circumstance which was far from reassuring.

The forenoon wears away. The soldiers crowd beneath their tents, or other improvised shade, to get a little shelter from the scorching heat; the camels come trooping home in long lines from their morning repast of sax-aul and wild absinth; the braying of donkeys, the neighing of horses, and the bleating of sheep become hushed in the overpowering heat, and the poor animals stand drooping in the sun, sweltering under its scorching rays; silence reigns throughout the camp; only the sentinel on the tower can be seen keeping his lonely watch. The sun rises to the meridian, and then slowly commences sinking towards the west, glowing in the brazen sky like a ball of fire, heating the atmosphere until it grows visible, and dances in misty waves over the sands of Khala-ata, like a phantom ocean. But I receive no intimation from Colonel Weimarn that he is ready to receive me. I grow impatient, and at last uneasy, at being treated in a way which I cannot help observing to myself is about as far removed from the polite as it well could be. I had brought the mail from Irkibai with no little trouble and difficulty; and Colonel Weimarn had not so much as thanked me yet. Thus far he had entirely ignored my existence. It was the first time I had ever been treated rudely by a Russian, although I had travelled about through the dominions of the Tsar for the last two years, and I concluded that this exceptional case boded no good.

At last I determined to put an end to my suspense, and see what kind of a man I had to deal with, by going direct to Colonel Weimarn himself, without invitation or announcement. After a while he was pointed out to me, walking leisurely about the camp, with nothing farther from his thoughts, apparently, than my request for an interview. I went straight to him, and having presented myself, the following colloquy occurred:—

"I owe you an apology, Colonel, for not calling on you sooner to present my respects; but the fact is they told me you were asleep."

"Well, what do you want?"

"As I before remarked, I wish to pay my respects."

"I am much obliged; but I do not suppose you have come all the way from New York to pay me your respects."

"Why, no, Colonel; my business here is with General Kaufmann."

"Oh, you have business with General Kaufmann, have you?" incredulously. "How are you going to get to him?"

" I'm going to ride."

" What is your business with General Kaufmann ?"

" That I can only tell to General Kaufmann himself."

" Have you the written permission of General Kaufmann ?"

" No," said I, proceeding to show him my papers, " but I have the permission of——"

" It makes no difference whose permission you have got ; without the written permission of the Governor-General you can't go. And as to your papers, I won't look at them."

" How can I obtain that permission ?" I asked.

" I do not know. You may send on your papers if you wish, but I am almost sure you will not be able to obtain it without a personal interview. He is too busy to answer letters."

" I beg your pardon, Colonel," I said. " His Excellency General Kaufmann seems to be a man very difficult of access indeed. I cannot see him without his permission, it would appear, and I cannot get his permission without seeing him. How do people who have business with him usually proceed ?"

" *Dass geht mir Nichts an*" ("That's your business, not mine"), he replied, turning on his heel and walking off, leaving me to my reflections, which, as may be readily supposed, were not of the most agreeable kind. Had I come all the way from St. Petersburg to Khala-ata, struggling forward sixty days against all sorts of difficulties, only to be stopped on the very banks of the Amu-Darya, the far-famed Oxus, and turned back in the middle of the desert by a military despot, without having caught one glimpse of its darkly-rolling waters ?

True I had the resource left of forwarding my letters to

General Kaufmann, and awaiting his answer (in case
Colonel Weimarn did not take it into his head to turn me
back in the meantime—a probability not to be over-
looked); but I could not expect any reply under ten
or twelve days, and in the meantime the Oxus would
be crossed, Khiva taken, and I would be too late.

As to breaking through the lines and escaping, the
attempt would have been folly, at least until I should see
what measures would be taken regarding me. If I was
to be held as a prisoner, either guarded or on parole, this
attempt would be simply impossible; and even if Colonel
Weimarn only proposed detaining me until he should
receive orders from Kaufmann, escape would present
difficulties of an almost insurmountable nature. It would
be dangerous as well as difficult, on account of the fleet-
footed Turcoman cavalry, that was probably hanging on
General Kaufmann's rear. Even if I succeeded in getting
away from the Russian camp, would I be able to elude the
vigilance of the restless and savage Turcomans?

As I had no desire for a personal explanation with
these latter regarding my business in their territory, I had
laid all my hopes on reaching Kaufmann before his
arrival in the enemy's country This hope had now
vanished for ever. I must reach Kaufmann, if I reached
him at all, by passing through the enemy's country, or
the country claimed by him, either alone or with a
detachment of Russian troops. The unaccountable
conduct of Colonel Weimarn made it very evident that
I could not count upon a Russian escort, and the more I
reflected the more it became apparent that I would have
to try it, not only without an escort, but probably with
twenty-five Cossacks giving me chase. This perspective
was so disagreeable that I at first refused to consider it

for a moment. A few minutes' reflection, however, sufficed to convince me that there was no other means of reaching Kaufmann.

Visions of a picture I had seen in Vambéry's book, with accompanying description, began to float in a shadowy way through my imagination; of a Turcoman emptying human heads out of a sack on the grand square before the Khan's police at Khiva, surrounded by the admiring and approving crowd; of an untold number of human heads piled up in regular heaps like cannon balls in the same place. I saw in my mind's eye the horrid pit of Bokhara, where prisoners were thrown to be devoured alive by millions of sheep-ticks, fed and kept alive by that disgusting monster, Nasrullah Khan; every unpleasant story, in short, illustrative of Central Asian life, recounted by Burnes, Wood, Vambéry, and others, recurred to my memory.

My position was not an agreeable one. I had reduced my baggage to the minimum; I was entirely without provisions for myself and people, and forage for my horses; and I had been living for the last two days on sour milk, the *airan* of the Kirghiz. Besides, I was without a tent or shelter of any kind—a privation not much felt when on the march, but which would become unendurable if I were to remain stationary under this scorching sun.

I wandered about the camp awhile; chewing the cud of sweet and bitter fancy, in which the bitter chiefly predominated; trying to think of some plan by which I might soften Colonel Weimarn, and occasionally calculating how many days it would take to starve to death; for I was ravenously hungry.

After a while I was accosted by two or three officers,

who, having heard of the arrival of an American, came to welcome me, and offer me their hospitality. I could see they were trying to make amends for the conduct of Colonel Weimarn, of which it was very evident they did not approve. Indeed, they expressed themselves to that effect at last, and in no very measured terms either.

The Russian officers combine a very severe discipline with a good deal of freedom of speech, and I was not a little astonished to hear the term "*canaille d'Allemand*" applied to Colonel Weimarn without the slightest compunction.

We were soon on the best of terms, and after having made a " square meal," for the first time for several days, I was conducted to the kibitka of Colonel Ivanoff, the officer who had been wounded in the affair of Adam-Kurulgan, already spoken of. When he learned that I had no tent, he immediately made room for me in his kibitka, and offered me his hospitality while I should remain in Khala-ata. I accepted, of course, and as the Colonel was on the sick list, and had the best of everything that was to be had, I could not have fallen into better hands. I was treated, not only by him but by the rest of the little party here, with a kindness I shall not easily forget, the more especially as I stood sadly in need of hospitality. I was an American, and, among them, as among all the Russians I had ever met, my passport was a sufficient letter of recommendation.

The next day I passed idly in the kibitka of Colonel Ivanoff, attempting to get a little repose after my long ride, in which endeavour I succeeded but indifferently, owing to the heat and dust. In the evening Colonel Weimarn sent me word that he would march at two o'clock next morning, and that if I wished to send in my letters to him I could do so. After some reflection, I decided to send one of my letters with him, but, nevertheless, to attempt escaping from the camp with the marching column. My plan was to leave the camp with the cavalry, trusting to the darkness to escape detection, make a wide circuit, reach the river, and pass the detachment. This, I thought, might be easily done, once out of the camp, as I could march at least twice as fast as the troops. I accordingly handed over one of my letters to Colonel Weimarn, to be delivered to General Kaufmann, and gave my people orders to be ready to march at two o'clock.

There were still the Turcomans to be dealt with; but I had to choose between that danger and the alternative of failing to accomplish the object of my mission, and I chose the former, trusting to the proverbial good luck of a war-correspondent for breaking through the enemy's lines with impunity. Had I carried out this plan at this time I would inevitably have fallen into the hands of the Turcomans, under Sadyk, a famous brigand in the service of the Khan, who, with 500 or 600 horsemen, were careering around Kaufmann's army, and who just about this time made a bold and dashing attack on Kaufmann's camels at Adam-Kurulgan.

At midnight, however, when we were ready to start, orders came from Kaufmann not to march. It appeared that he had not reached the Amu, as had been supposed, but whether he was at Adam-Kurulgan, or at some point further on, I could not make out, as everybody was extremely reticent on the subject. I gathered enough, however, from scraps of conversation I overheard, to make it pretty evident that something very nearly approaching a disaster had occurred.

This changed the aspect of affairs. If Kaufmann had not yet reached the river, I had still time to deliberate on the best means of overtaking him. As Colonel Weimarn would not march for three or four days, I concluded that I had better wait also, the more especially as it would have been very difficult to escape without the confusion attendant upon the night start of a detachment. I therefore remained at Khala-ata, the guest of the kind-hearted Colonel Ivanoff.

Life at Khala-ata I found was not a thing to be desired, even under the most favourable circumstances. Throughout the day the heat was of the most oppressive kind, gusts of wind filled and darkened the atmosphere, and even hid the sun itself with clouds of dust that was almost suffocating. Dust everywhere. Against this enemy a tent or kibitka was not the slightest protection. Once inside, it gently settled down over everything, filling eyes, mouth and nostrils, clinging to hair, eyelashes, and clothing, until you became the colour of the earth.

Besides, there was not the slightest scrap of anything to read, except a few newspapers which I had seen before leaving St. Petersburg. Nothing to do but lie on one's back all day long, and watch the heated atmosphere trembling in misty undulations beneath the glowing sun, and the storms of dust that from time to time came sweeping over the desert, or listen to the singing of the soldiers, which could be heard all day long, although the poor fellows had nearly nothing to eat, and no vodka to drink; and heap imprecations, not loud, but deep, on the head of Colonel Weimarn.

Poor fellow! Even if I had not outwitted him in the end, I could forgive him now. He was thrown from his horse in the gardens of Khiva, and so badly hurt, that he died in a few hours, without having caught one glimpse of the far-famed city.

Khala-ata is situated on Bokharan territory, and was occupied with the permission of the Emir, who consented, at the same time, to the construction of the little fort. The fort is about fifty yards square, and consists of a simple earthwork, two corner bastions, and a ditch that may be filled with water. It is defended by two brass field-pieces, and, although constructed in two days, is sufficiently strong to resist any attack that may be made upon it by a Central Asian force.

There is some reason to believe that Khala-ata is the site of an ancient city. When the Russians arrived, there were still remains of stone walls to be seen, which they quickly utilised in the construction of the fort, and I myself picked up a piece of carved stone that bore every appearance of having been the capital of a pillar. Not inappropriately this palace has been turned into a grave-yard by the Kirghiz. Mud-tombs and monuments replace lofty domes and minarets, and the dead city has become truly a city of the dead.

CHAPTER XV.

A FLIGHT IN THE DARKNESS.

DURING the next five days we heard nothing further from Kaufmann. I began to grow exceedingly uneasy at last, and to think that he had probably reached and crossed the Oxus, and would march to Khiva without waiting for the rest of the detachment to come up. Judging from the way in which I was treated by Colonel Weimarn, it was pretty sure that if he caught me in an attempt to escape, my position would be a very disagreeable one. Nevertheless, I determined to try it. I had watched the camp routine very closely, and decided that at break of day, just when the pickets were called in, while the officers of night duty were retiring to rest, and the other officers were not yet stirring, would be the moment the most favourable for flitting. I observed that the Kirghiz and Bokhariots came and went during the day at pleasure, with their horses and camels, and I concluded that my people could also slip quietly out of the camp without being noticed. I therefore decided to send them on ahead the evening before, and ride out of the camp next morning accompanied by Ak-Mamatoff only. As to the soldiers who would be up, they, having seen me about the camp for the last six days on friendly terms with the officers, could not be supposed to know anything of my real position, and would not think of stopping me.

In this way I hoped to get at least twenty miles start before my absence would be observed, and then—let Colonel Weimarn catch me if he could. In order to carry out this plan quietly and expeditiously, I had to take Ak-Mamatoff into my confidence; but he, as was usually the case when I desired to start anywhere, always found at least ten good and sufficient reasons that made starting perfectly impossible. He at last, to my utter chagrin and disappointment, flatly refused to move another step, except with the troops. Threats—my unfailing resource in the desert upon emergencies of the kind—were out of the question here, for the simple reason that any attempt to exert my authority would attract the attention of everybody in camp. Besides, I had to acknowledge to myself that the objections of my people were, to a certain extent, well founded. As they very well observed, I had not told them, when they engaged to go with me, that any such service would be required of them; and, even if we succeeded in escaping the Russian lines, we would probably fall into the hands of the Turcomans. They had families, they said; and had they known what was expected of them, they would never have come with me.

Besides the objections of my people, I found, upon looking at my horses, that the poor beasts were in a miserable plight. There was a large store of barley in the fort, but Colonel Weimarn refused to give me a grain, at any price; and had it not been for the kindness of Colonel Ivanoff and Colonel Dreschern, who procured me a little, the poor animals would have starved to death. As it was, two of them looked as though they would never reach the Oxus. If they failed me, there would only remain three—it will be remembered that I was obliged to leave one in the desert—to carry myself, my three men, and my baggage.

One week's standing in the hot sun, with nearly nothing to eat, had reduced them to their present pitiable plight; and when the brave little beasts, that had carried me so far and so patiently, came whinnying around me, asking in their equine language for something to eat, and biting ravenously at dry saxaul brushwood, in which there was not the slightest nourishment, I could, in a perfectly cheerful frame of mind, have seen Colonel Weimarn in a considerably hotter place than Khala-ata.

Upon the whole, my position was a good deal worse than when I arrived at Khala-ata. Then my horses, although tired, were still in a very fair condition, and would have reached the Amu without difficulty; now that was very doubtful indeed. To stop at Khala-ata, however, after having come so far, and remain there for an indefinite length of time, was too absurd an ending to my wanderings to be entertained, as long as the slightest hope of escape remained. I therefore determined to make the attempt, regardless of consequences. I went to my people and told them that if they refused to go with me, I would discharge them immediately, and they might get back to their homes as best they could, but if they would follow me, I would give them each a hundred rubles. This proposition staggered them, and after a good deal of murmuring they at last consented to start the same evening. In the meantime, however, Colonel Weimarn, as well as myself, had been growing uneasy at receiving no news from Kauffmann, and for exactly the same reason. He, too, feared Khiva would be taken without him—and he at last concluded to march, in hopes of meeting a courier with orders to move forward. Curiously enough, he took this resolution the very day I had planned to escape. This made escape comparatively easy, the more especially as Colonel Weimarn would know nothing of my flight for at least twenty-four hours, when pursuit would be out of the question.

At one o'clock, on the morning of the 24th of May, we were all in our saddles, and the column under march, already began to file out on the broad, sandy road, leading nearly due west, in the direction of Adam-Kurulgan and the Amu-Darya.

I had taken leave of nobody, and there was no one in camp who for a moment even dreamed of my undertaking such a project in the darkness. I dropped silently in the rear of the Cossacks, who led the column, followed by my people, and when we had gained the summit of the low sand-hill, a mile from the camp, over which the road led, I as silently dropped out again, turned my horses' heads to the north, and plunged into the darkness.

My intention was to get out of sight of the column before daylight, and, by making a slight detour, return to the road near Adam-Kurulgan, far enough in advance to water and rest my horses before the column should come up.

Guided by the north star, we proceeded slowly and cautiously forward through the darkness. For an hour we pressed on, crossing the sandy dunes, stumbling over broken and uneven ground, trampling through the sparse sax-aul and wild wormwood, or stopping to reconnoitre, as we thought we beheld some object moving in the darkness before us, and our excited imaginations made us catch glimpses of horsemen flitting through the obscurity around us. I began to feel that it was a wild and foolhardy adventure, and one which might end tragically. But the sense of freedom and exultation at finding myself once more in the saddle, after my monotonous and weary sojourn at Khala-ata, out in the open desert, with the stars above, and the fresh air of morning blowing in my face, was so great, that the danger appeared only a matter of secondary consideration.

With all its fatigues and dangers, there is, after all, something overpoweringly witching and attractive in the desert, that only those who have experienced it can understand. The long, hot marches over the yielding sand; the halts at the wells to draw the clear, cold water, the dreamy, weary noon repose, the fresh cool air of evening, when you throw yourself on the sand, and watch the stars come out, and the round, red moon slowly rise over the shadowy desert, the sublime, mysterious silence, and the sense of freedom, weave themselves into a kind of existence, full of an untold charm, that endures long after you have quitted the enchanted solitudes.

We continued to move forward as fast as the obscurity would permit, until the grey dawn began to appear in the east, when we increased our pace into a gentle gallop. As a red flare of light gradually mounted up the eastern sky, I looked around to see if I was well out of the clutches of Colonel Weimarn. Far away to the south-east I could make out a dark object moving forward, which I took to be the rear-guard, and which was soon lost on the horizon. Concluding we were far enough away, I turned my horses' heads to the west, and took up my line of march towards the Amu-Darya.

The country was rolling and uneven, with very little vegetation; the saxaul not more than a foot high, and

10

the wormwood very scarce. There was, however, a good deal of the fine, wiry, brownish grass that is to be found almost everywhere in the desert, and which forms the principal support of the flocks and herds of the Kirghiz.

At nine o'clock we stopped to take tea, having brought a little water for that purpose with us. Here it became very evident that one of my horses would not go much further, even with the very light load I had given him to carry. We had no sooner stopped, than the poor beast threw himself on the earth, already too tired to seek, as did the others, a scanty repast of the brown desert grass. I had still a little barley left, which I gave him, and he afterwards nibbled the grass within his reach, without attempting to rise. An hour's rest enabled him to continue the march better than I expected. I had foreseen that some of my horses would not reach the river, and had left nearly the last remnant of my baggage at Khala-ata, with a note to Colonel Dreschern, the commanding officer, left behind by Colonel Weimarn, apologizing for my unceremonious leave-taking, and requesting him to take care of it. Everything I retained could be carried by the four remaining horses. When it is remembered that there were four of us, and that each of my three followers had something in the way of luggage, without speaking of a tin kettle, forty pounds of dried black bread Ak-Mamatoff had bought from the soldiers, and which was destined to serve as sole nourishment for ourselves as well as horses, 100 rounds of cartridges for my guns and revolvers, and a little barley, it will be readily understood that my personal effects were of the slightest possible nature.

About two o'clock we ascended a dune covered with a growth of saxaul, five or six feet high, from which we beheld a low, level plain, two or three miles wide, covered with a whitish saline deposit. Beyond, more sand-hills among which was the famous Adam-Kurulgan, visited by Vambéry as a dervish.

What was my chagrin and disappointment, upon surveying the place with my field-glass, to perceive among the dunes the white uniforms of Russian troops! At this moment we perceived approaching two or three horsemen, who proved to be djigits, or Kirghiz guides, on their way to Khala-ata. They now informed us that the troops we saw were Cossacks, who had arrived that morning from Khala-ata. "The very same Cossacks," I mentally added to myself, "whom I had joined, and quitted so stealthily in the darkness!"

CHAPTER XVI.

CHECKMATED.

This was a circumstance which, in Dick Swiveller's choice phraseology, might be called a "stunner," and for the moment, indeed, I felt completely crushed. To add to my discomfiture, my people, who were only too glad, looked at me with a sly smile of triumph, which was exceedingly exasperating. They thought that now, being completely checkmated, I would be obliged to return to Khala-ata, or go and surrender myself to Colonel Weimarn. In either case they would be spared the trouble and danger of the present enterprise. The impossibility of pushing on to the Oxus without water was evident enough. With horses such as I had when I left Perovsky I might have done it, though with difficulty; with my present exhausted beasts it was not to be thought of for a moment. I did not even know the distance that still remained to be traversed, for Colonel Weimarn had not, of course, given me the slightest information regarding the position of Khala-ata, or of the supposed distance to the Amu. That it was not less than seventy-five miles, however, I thought very probable; and as I cast my eyes over the gleaming sands, in the direction of the historic river, how I longed for one good Turcoman horse—one of those noble beasts that make the distance from Astrabad to Khiva (500 miles) in four days, with only a little straw to eat. With one such horse I would have undertaken to reach Kaufmann alone, leaving my people behind to follow with the detachment. But there was no such horse near, unless, indeed, in the hands of his savage owner, who might now be prowling within a mile of me, and I must seek other means of reaching the end of my journey. I turned over every possible expedient in my mind for obtaining water, without seeing the slightest chance of success. At last, however, I remembered over-hearing a scrap of conversation, while at Khala-ata, in which mention was made of another well, somewhere between Adam-Kurulgan and the Amu, although no such well was known to Vambéry.

I had not the slightest idea of the position of this well, but I turned to Ak-Mamatoff, and told him to ask the djigits if there was not another well farther on. To my great joy, I soon learned that there was another, some twenty miles further on, called "Alty Kuduk," or the "Six Wells," that it was not on the road to the Amu, but some four miles to the north, and that Kaufmann had left some troops there. This was news, indeed, and I determined to push forward to Alty Kuduk without stopping at Adam-Kurulgan.

As to the Russians, I was pretty sure they were not under the command of Colonel Weimarn, and that the officer in command knew nothing of my detention at Khala-ata. In any case, it would be an unheard-of piece of ill-luck to fall into the hands of another such man as Colonel Weimarn, and I determined to take the risk. I therefore gave orders to mount, and push straight on. without stopping at Adam-Kurulgan.

As was to be expected, another contest with my people ensued. The horses, they said, had already made at least forty miles by the roundabout road we had taken, and they would never be able to go twenty miles more under this hot sun without rest and water It was impossible; we would all be left in the sands with no horses, and obliged to find our way forward on foot. But here I had no fear of attracting the attention of Colonel Weimarn, and I sternly ordered them to mount and proceed, without even stopping to discuss the question with them. They had got 300 rubles out of me among them the day before, because I was in their power; now it was my turn, and in five minutes we were moving forward.

I would here remark that although I was always in a state of chronic opposition to my followers, continually goading them forward against their wishes, they, nevertheless entertained for me anything but unfriendly feelings. I paid them well, and never refused them money for anything to eat that could be bought, shared everything I had in the way of delicacies with them, learned to drink boiled tea as they made it for themselves, in order to save them the trouble of heating water twice, and was every way good-natured, except on the one question of getting forward. On that I was inexorable; and although they possibly regarded me as one possessed of an itinerant demon, they only said, "Allah is great," and liked me none the less.

Leaving Adam-Kurulgan to the left, our way soon became difficult and toilsome. The sand grew deeper and deeper, and at last commenced taking the form of huge drifts, twenty and thirty feet high; which, piled up in all sorts of fantastic shapes, exactly like snow-drifts, were continually changing their form, and moving about

under the action of the wind. The wind kept sifting
the sand over us in little clouds, and the drifts were
so steep and so high, that working our way over
them was most difficult and toilsome. The horses sank
nearly to their bellies · and we were obliged to dismount.
Even then they only struggled through by a succession
of plunges, while we ourselves sank to the knees. This
continued for nearly two miles. One of those storms
that so often sweep over the desert would have sent
these huge drifts rolling over us, and in an instant
buried us twenty feet deep, leaving not a trace of
us behind.

The name of the place, Adam-Kurulgan, "fatal to
men," was well chosen.

I remarked that even here, impossible as it may seem,
there was more or less vegetation. Now and again we saw
a shrub of saxaul, in a more or less flourishing state.
Sometimes it was almost buried, showing only a few
leaves on the surface of the sand. Again, its short,
scrubby stem, and immense network of long, fibrous roots,
extending many yards, were completely bared to the sun,
without much affecting its condition apparently, so hardy
is the plant. Fortunately, this did not last long, or
the horses would have been completely exhausted. As it
was, we had only gone two or three miles farther, when
the feeblest of the horses suddenly stumbled, staggered
a moment, and then fell heavily on the sand with a
groan. We threw off his saddle and bridle, distributed
part of his load among the other horses, threw the rest
away, and resumed the march, leaving him to die.
Until long after dark we pushed forward, hoping to
reach Alty-Kuduk.

At length signs of fatigue in our horses warned me to halt and camp, if I did not wish to make the next day's march on foot. The poor beasts had to go without water that night, for it would have been impossible to carry enough with us, even had we foreseen the impossibility of getting water at Adam-Kurulgan. We offered them a feed of our hard, black, dried bread, which they were too thirsty to touch, hobbled them, and let them loose on the desert to pick up what they could find.

I could never cease admiring my own little saddle-horse. He had been now twenty-five days in the desert; he had carried me the whole distance from Fort Perovsky, sometimes as much as sixty miles a-day. More than half of the time he had nothing to eat, except what he could pick up in the desert, and yet he was by no means in bad condition. He would go the whole day, from sunrise to sunset, in the easy little trot of the Kirghiz horses, and in the evening would break into a gallop as lightly as though he were fresh from the pastures of the Syr-Darya. He was a pure-blooded Kirghiz; a light sorrel, nearly the colour of the sand; head, ears, eyes, and limbs exactly like an Arab, but the neck and body shorter and heavier. It was never necessary to tether him, as he never wandered away. He swam the Amu, and proved to be as much at home in the gardens of Khiva as in the desert, never hesitating, when necessary, to take a ditch or canal. In the end he was stolen from me by some of the liberated Persian slaves. Now the poor beast was crazy for water, as were the others, and refused to touch the black bread I offered him.

As to ourselves, we fared no better than our horses. We also were too thirsty to eat the black bread, even if our teeth had been capable of making an impression on it, without its first having been soaked in water. After the long day's ride my thirst was intolerable. The uncertainty of our situation, the ever present fear of Turcomans, who might be hovering around, the difficulty of finding the well we were in search of, the probability of missing it altogether, the condition of my horses—two more began to show signs of extreme fatigue, that told me plainly enough they would not go more than another day —the possibility of being obliged to drag on to the Oxus on foot, only to fall perhaps at last into the hands of the Turcomans; the darkness that settled down over us like a pall—making the stillness of the desert more fear-inspiring, and even the occasional chirp of an insect startling—all combined to make this the gloomiest night I ever passed.

After a two hours' ride next morning, our eyes caught, far away on the horizon, the glitter of bayonets in the early sunshine. Soon we made out the forms of two pickets, posted on a sand-hill, watching our approach ; and half an hour later we gained the little eminence from which they were keeping their dreary look-out, and beheld the camp of Alty-Kuduk. It was the sandiest, dreariest spot I have ever seen, not excepting Adam-Kurulgan itself.

A broad shallow basin, in which were three or four wells, and a quantity of forage and baggage; then a low ridge, with two brass six-pounders peering over it, and beyond another little hollow in which were pitched the tents of soldiers. Farther on, as far as the eye could reach, more sand heaped and piled up, rolling off in every direction in low mounds and ridges, with here and there in the distance, on a higher spot, a picket keeping his dreary watch in the hot sunshine.

Such was Alty-Kuduk—the place where Kaufmann passed the most critical period of the whole campaign—a week, during which he was well-nigh overtaken by the same terrible disaster that befel Markosoff.

CHAPTER XVII.

A FRIENDLY GREETING.

IT was still early in the morning when I rode into the camp; none of the officers were stirring. I sat down on a heap of baggage near, wondering what sort of reception was in store for me, and not without inward misgivings. I had not long to wait. I had only been seated a few minutes when a young officer, half-dressed, stuck his head out of a tent near by, and bawled out, "*Que diable faites-vous là? Entrez donc!*"

This was a promising invitation, and I entered accordingly, with a weight taken off my mind. The young officer in question was one I had met at Khala-ata, but whose face I had forgotten. He had left the day after my arrival, had joined Kaufmann here, and then had the misfortune to be left behind. He immediately ordered tea, and offered me a little dried beef and biscuit, of which I ate ravenously, for I had neither eaten nor drunk for twenty-four hours. It was all he had to offer me, and this was his last bit of beef; but he gave it with such hearty good will, that I had no hesitation in making away with the whole of it. He informed me that Kaufmann had been gone six days, and must be now on the

Amu, if he had not already crossed it. But they had heard nothing from him since his departure. They were in hopes of receiving orders to march every day, and that the camels which were to be sent back for their transport would soon commence arriving; that was all they knew. As to the road, it was very dangerous—probably infested by marauding parties of Turcomans, who would be harassing the rear-guard, and he would not advise me to attempt it alone. They would probably receive orders in a day or two to move forward, and I could go with them. I had already decided, however, that I would risk no more delays. It was just possible that I would be sent for by Weimarn, and there was more danger in waiting than in pushing forward.

I was glad, however, to stay a short time, in order to rest my horses after their long march of the day before. As I was very tired and sleepy, they prepared a bed for me, and I lay down for an hour's nap

When I awoke, I lay for a few moments with my eyes half closed, trying to make out where I was. The tent in which I found myself was large and roomy, lined inside with a stuff of brilliant colours, worked or cut in the most fantastic manner. I afterwards learned that this was one of several tents the Emir of Bokhara had presented to General Kaufmann, which accounted for its strangeness. While I was lying half awake, trying to make out my position, associating it in a dreamy way with some weird tale from the "Arabian Nights," I was aroused from my state of semi-somnolence by hearing the question, in very good English,

"Well, how do you feel after your nap?"

I looked around, and found myself surrounded by eight or ten officers. The one who had addressed me was Baron

Korff, and there were besides, Valuyeff, Feodoroff (several of whose sketches appear in this book), and many others. They were only waiting for me to awake to offer me a welcome, and the hospitality of Alty-Kuduk. We were friends in a moment. They invited me to breakfast, but they had to club together in order to find provisions wherewith to make the meal. One furnished a block of dried vegetables, another a pot of Liebig's extract of meat, another a piece of mutton, another some biscuit, another coffee, another preserved milk, and still another a bottle of *vodka*. This was about all the variety that could be found in the camp; but their welcome was so cordial, and their hospitality so generous, they appeared to be so glad to see me, and so anxious to do me a kindness, that I was not a little moved. I think now, as I thought then, that there were never better fellows in the world. They were terribly low-spirited on account of their being left behind, with every probability of their not reaching Khiva in time to take part in its capture. But they threw off dull care for the moment, and we were as merry over our solitary bottle of *vodka* as if it had been a dozen of *Cliquot*. Their only pastime seemed to be singing, to a most doleful air, a song they had adapted from the German, commencing, " In dem Alty-Kuduk, da ist mein Vaterland," into which they had introduced an astonishing number of variations.

Best of all, they gave me as much barley as I wanted for my horses; and, to tell the truth, matters had arrived at such a point, that success or failure, and perhaps my own life, depended upon a bushel of barley.

The water at Alty-Kuduk was tolerably good, and in sufficient quantities; but I had, nevertheless, to obtain a permit, in order to get any for my horses, the regulations adopted during the first days when water was scarce being still in force.

I was very much surprised and amused during the day to hear the crowing of a cock, which sounded strangely out of place here. He had made the whole distance from Tashkent, comfortably perched on the back of a camel. Originally destined for the table, he had shown such a pugnacious disposition, and offered so courageously to fight General Kaufmann's cook, who was proceeding to wring his neck, that the soldiers unanimously decided he should not die. This valiant disposition had been cultivated in him to such an extent, that he would give the road to neither man nor beast without a fight; and I actually saw him, more than once, attack and put to flight a dog in the most daring and resolute manner.

CHAPTER XVIII.

RUNNING THE GAUNTLET.

THE next day, towards noon, I was in the saddle again, on the road to the Oxus. My kind entertainers had used every endeavour to dissuade me from the enterprise, assuring me I could not escape the Turcomans who would be hovering round the army. But although I was not without apprehensions, and Mustruf knew as little of the way as myself, I felt too uneasy to remain longer. I had a presentiment there was as much danger behind as before. Colonel Weimarn would soon hear of my flight, and, everything considered, I preferred not meeting him again.

My presentiment of danger proved prophetic. Soon after arriving at Khiva, I learned that I had left Alty-Kuduk only a few hours, when an officer, at the head of twenty-five Cossacks, arrived, breathless, with an order to arrest, disarm, and take me back to Tashkent. He had come all the way from there, a distance of about 600 miles, hoping to intercept me in the desert. He had heard of me from passing caravans and wandering Kirghiz, who had seen me, had got on my trail, lost it, gone back, found it, and lost it, and found it again; he had killed several horses, and at last arrived at Alty-Kuduk a few hours too late.   They laughed at him there, and told him to follow me if he dared.   They assured him I was then either with Kaufmann or—the jackals; in either case, out of his jurisdiction.

The story is a curious one.   There is an order, which it is not now my province to discuss, prohibiting Europeans, not Russian subjects, from entering Turkistan. The reason given by the Russians for this measure is, that every foreigner who has ever gone to Central Asia, and got himself into trouble, has invariably accused the Russians of having a hand in it.   Two Italians who reached Bokhara were thrown into prison by the Emir, and, although only released upon the threats of the Russians to declare war, they went home and accused the Russians of having caused their imprisonment.   To save time, the Tsar, who has a very summary way of doing things, ordered that no more Europeans be allowed to go into Turkistan for the present.

I should have mentioned before that Mr. Schuyler and I had been confronted with this order at Kazala, and had evaded it by pointing out that we were not Europeans, and we then got permission to go to Tashkent, but not to Khiva.

But no sooner had a certain official in Tashkent, or Samarcand, I could never learn which, heard of my departure from Perovsky across the desert, than he determined to prove his zeal by catching me and bringing me back, probably as a spy.   Meantime the story got out that an American was in the Kyzil-Kum desert, making his way to Khiva, and that twenty-five Cossacks were in hot pursuit of him.   This created a good deal of excitement throughout the whole Russian population of Central Asia, everybody but the official in question taking the side of tho

American. He must be a "molodyetz" (a brave fellow), they were kind enough to say, and it was a shame to hunt him down in this way, as if he had not enough danger with the Turcomans. And the people of Tashkent were prepared to give me an ovation, if I had been caught and brought back. I was not caught, however, and the over-zealous official got laughed at for his pains. Another time, perhaps, he will remember the instructions of Talleyrand to his subordinates, "*Surtout, pas de zèle.*" What I regretted chiefly in the matter was, that he had authority to deprive Colonel Rodionoff, who had showed me some kindness at Perovsky, of his position, and actually did so. I hope, however, that Kaufmann has by this time given him another and better situation.[*]

Having thus given a rapid account of the danger that was hovering over my track, I will resume the thread of my narrative. I left Alty-Kuduk on the 27th of May, hoping to reach the river, and consequently Kaufmann's army, the same day. The exact distance to the river was unknown, but I thought it could not be more than fifty, nor less than thirty miles. As Kaufmann had only taken two of his six boats, I felt pretty sure he could not yet have crossed, and that I would find him camped on the banks. So I set forth on what I supposed was my last march with a light heart. Not that I believed all my difficulties to be at an end. On the contrary, the most dangerous part of my whole trip was before me. There would probably be parties of Turcomans hanging on the

---

[*] I have just learned that when General Kaufmann heard that Colonel Rodionoff had been deprived of his situation, he wrote, telling him that he did perfectly right in allowing me to pass, and that he would have been greatly displeased if he had not done so. He also gave the Colonel the position of district governor of Turkistan, which was not only reinstating, but promoting him.

rear of the army, and these I would have to avoid or fight. But I trusted to my star to come off successfully in either alternative.

Going due south four miles, we soon fell into the broad travelled road leading from Adam-Kurulgan to the river, the same road traversed by Vambéry as a dervish; and then turned our horses' heads to the west. The road was broad, well-worn, and easily followed; but even if it had been otherwise, there would have been no difficulty in finding the trail of the army, the dead camels that were scattered along every few yards serving as guide-posts. Even at night our noses would have guided us without the aid of the other senses. The sand was deep, and our horses sank to their knees at every step. I could see from time to time the tracks of the cannon, which must have almost buried themselves in this yielding sand, and was astonished to learn upon arriving at the river that eight horses to each piece brought them through with ease.

The characteristics of the desert here were the same as in the other parts of the Kyzil-Kum—rolling dunes covered sparsely with saxaul, and the brown desert grass.

After two or three hours' march, we began to come on the bodies of dead horses, which we easily made out to be those of the Turcomans, by their great beauty and symmetry; and I inferred that Kaufmann's sharpshooters had been at work with the breech-loading rifle. From here to the river we found the bodies of horses every few yards, showing that there had been a running fight the whole distance. I afterwards learned that, if I had attempted this passage two days sooner, when several hundred Turcomans were careering around the army, I should certainly have been caught. As will be seen, between the

Cossacks and the Khivans I had a narrow escape   Many of the dead horses were without tails. A tail serves a Turcoman as a certificate that his horse has been killed in the service of the Khan, who is obliged to pay for it. We advanced cautiously now, surveying the ground from the summit of every little hill before showing ourselves; and taking every precaution to avoid falling in with any wandering bands of Khivans who might be hovering about.

About five o'clock in the afternoon we reached a point where the desert suddenly changed its character, and instead of the rolling dunes through which we had been passing, we now beheld a level plain, which sank away into a lower kind of terrace.   Into this plain, but far away in the smoky distance, projected from the north a high ridge, which terminated in three or four low mountains These were the mountains of Uch-Uchak on the banks of the Oxus.

Forward we urge our jaded horses; to-day, we must reach the river, for we have neither water nor provisions. Lower sinks the sun down the western sky, until it hangs on the horizon round and red, and projects long shadows of ourselves over the desert: then drops out of sight. Suddenly flash up on the western sky broad flame-like streaks of red, purple, and golden light, beneath which, far away on the edge of the horizon, we at last catch the glimmer of water.

The Oxus at last!

When Kaufmann reached this spot and beheld the longed-for water, he took off his cap, and devoutly crossed himself, as did every officer on his staff; while the soldiers set up a shout, in spite of the Khivans who were howling around them, such as was never before heard in those regions.

We did not reach the river until long after dark. Stealthily we give drink to our horses, soak a little black bread in the water, and then silently withdraw among the dunes to camp, and wait for daylight.

What shall we see in the morning? The white coats of the Russians, or the tall black caps of the Khivans? We dare not light a fire, and we cautiously dismount in a little hollow, and throw ourselves in the sand, each man holding his horse's bridle-rein.

Daylight comes, we emerge from our bed of sand, ascend a dune, and look cautiously around. We find we are not on the river at all, but on the edge of a reedy marsh, just at the foot of the mountains of Uch-Uchak. Neither Russians nor Khivans are visible. The only sign of life is a white horse, halfway up the mountain-side, who, upon seeing us, gallops swiftly off, and disappears over the summit. Slowly we ascend the mountain. Cautiously we peer over its top, and scan the country lying beyond, in expectation of seeing friend or foe. We perceive neither; but, instead, we behold—the Oxus!

Broad and placid it lay, sweeping far away to the north and south, through the far stretching yellow sand, like a silver zone bordered with green, and sparkling in the morning sunlight like a river of diamonds. I forgot Kaufmann, the Turcomans, the object of my expedition, everything, in the one delight of looking on its swiftly rushing waters. It was almost with an effort that I could bring myself to believe that I was really looking on that river, which stretches its mighty course from the mountains of India to the Aral sea; and which has been the scene of so many historic events from almost the earliest ages of man It seemed still more strange when I thought how few of my race had seen this river , how few that had reached it had lived; and how if I had been standing here two days ago my life would not have been worth a pin's fee.

The hills or mountains of Uch-Uchak are scarcely more than 500 feet high. There are five or six little peaks of a rotten sandstone formation, inclosing between them a little crater-like valley a half a mile in diameter, which looks as though it had formerly been the bed of a lake. I thought I could distinguish around the almost perpendicular shores the old water line. Yet, as this valley is much higher than the surrounding plain, it does not seem possible there should have been a lake here.

But where was Kaufmann? I scanned the horizon in every direction with my field-glass. I could see up and down the river for twenty miles, and far beyond, where the sands were gleaming yellow and bare, but not a trace of the army, or of any human habitation, tent, or kibitka. And yet he had been here, for I had seen the tracks of the cannon at the foot of the mountain.

Where could he have gone? A prey to a vague terror, I dashed down the mountain, and in a few minutes was at the edge of the water. I saw the dead ashes of many camp-fires, and that was all.

CHAPTER XIX.

A NIGHT WITH THE OXUS.

I HAD now been seeking Kaufmann twenty-nine days. When starting from Fort Perovsky I expected to overtake him in five. I hoped to find him at the well of Myn-Bulak in the Bukan-Tau mountains, but before reaching that point, I learned that he was not there, and would not be there. Ever since then, with the exception of the short time passed at Khala-ata, I had been in quest of him, expecting every day to overtake him. I had learned to feel to its full extent how hope deferred maketh the heart sick.

Here again on the Oxus he had disappeared when I thought I was sure of him. Would I never find him? To my imagination, wrought up by so many repeated disappointments, and my wanderings in this strange land, Kaufmann began to appear like a phantom; I half expected to wake up in my hotel in Paris, and find the expedition against Khiva a myth, and my own strange adventures a troubled dream.

But no; here were the dead ashes of burned-out campfires, and the tracks of the cannon. He could not be far now   I could see no indication of his having crossed the river at this point, and there was nothing to do but to follow his trail.

I rode my horse into the river up to his belly, and, scooping up the water in my hands I tasted it. It was muddy, but sweet and good. The river was here, I judged, about 1200 yards wide. It was bordered on either side by a strip of green, varying in width from a few yards to a mile Beyond this, the sand commenced again as before. There was plenty of grass and brushwood, and we decided to stop and take tea, as we had tasted nothing but a little black bread and water for twenty-four hours.

Forward again in search of Kaufmann, with eager eyes and expectant faces. We ascend stealthily every little hillock and vantage ground, and peer cautiously over before advancing, determined at least to get the first view of the enemy, if enemy there be; and we survey continually with our field-glass the opposite shore.

The trail led along the right bank of the river in the direction of the Aral Sea. Sometimes it kept to the water's edge; sometimes it climbed the bluffs, here a hundred feet high, and skirted along their crest. All the day long we follow the trail, in momentary expectation of catching sight of the rear-guard, and all day long we are doomed to disappointment.

At one place, where the road lies along the water's edge beneath the overhanging bluffs, we are terribly frightened by a camel that, tumbling over the cliff, falls right among us with a broken neck. For a moment, we imagine that he has been thrown down upon us by the Turcomans, and that a shower of bullets will immediately follow. We seize our rifles, cock them, and for a few seconds await an attack with terrible anxiety. No shot is fired; no Turcoman appears; and at last, on going over

to the dead camel, we find that he is blind, and so conclude that he has fallen over of himself. This was but
one of hundreds of camels left by Kaufmann which we
saw wandering about alone. My people picked up three
or four, which they tried to utilise, in order to rest our
horses, but had never been able to get them to go for more
than a mile or two. When a camel thinks he has gone far
enough he will not move a step farther, and all attempts
to induce him to change his mind are thrown away.

Suddenly we meet five men on horseback coming around
a bend of the bluff, and once more we seize our arms.
They dash into the river, swim across, and scurry off on
the other side in the direction of Khiva, until they are
lost in the sand. Judging from their rapid flight that
they have no reinforcements near, I try two or three
shots at them with my Winchester, but without effect
Later the guide with my glass catches sight of a group
of fifteen or twenty men, probably Khivans, camped near
the river. As they outnumber us, we think it prudent
to give them a wide berth. They are in the valley
below, and we on the bluffs, and thus we have the advantage of seeing them before they can see us. Striking into the sands, we ride a short circuit, and cautiously
approach the river a few miles farther on.

In the afternoon we come upon fields of excellent
wheat and clover, which our horses eat with avidity—the
first clover they have tasted for a month—and we soon
begin to make out habitations, or something resembling
them, on the opposite bank. But the sand still approaches the river very closely on either side.

Towards nightfall we perceive, on the other side, a
group of horsemen, who appeared to be watching us,
but they, as well as the opposite shore, are lost in the

darkness, which soon envelopes everything but the pale and ghostly river

And still there are no signs of Kaufmann, except here and there the ashes of burnt-out camp fires. Through the darkness we continue our march, gliding over the sand as silently as ghosts. Our nerves are strung to the utmost pitch of expectation; for in truth the situation is becoming critical in the extreme. We have already been seen twice from the other side; the smallness of our force must have been remarked, and the enemy have but to cross the river to find us. We are expecting every moment to see Kaufmann's camp fires flaring up in the darkness, or to hear the "*kto idiote*," the "who goes there," of the Russian sentinel.

The road now leads us high up on the bluffs overlooking the river. A dark storm cloud has gathered in the west, in the direction of Khiva, and seems to hang over the fated city. From time to time it throws out flashes of lightning, that are reflected in the pale river below, making the succeeding darkness ten times more sinister.

Once, while the guides are on foot leading their horses, I think I see a flash of light far in advance. We stop and wait anxiously. It appears no more, and I conclude it is only a phantom of my over-wrought imagination. It is now eleven o'clock. Our tired horses have made forty-five miles since daylight, and we decide to camp. We turn off to the river, give the horses water, and prepare to wait till daylight.

I tried to get one of my people to stand guard, but, although they were fully aware of the danger, they showed such a disinclination to undertake the task, that I saw it was useless to order them. They would only sleep on their post, and I resolved to keep watch myself. In five minutes they are all sound asleep, each with his bridle-rein tied to his wrist, and I am left alone with the murmur of the river for company. For hours I pace up and down, for I am so sleepy and tired, that I cannot trust myself to sit even for a moment.

The sky is overcast; the darkness is impenetrable; I can scarcely see a yard before me. All night long I keep my gloomy watch and listen to the voices of the river, that sound almost human in their murmur. From time to time there is a flash of lightning, and the lowering clouds, the broad river, the tall bluffs, and the white faces of my people, with the tired horses standing over them silent and motionless, start into being for an instant; and then again—darkness.

Daylight comes on once more, and once more we are in the saddle. A mile farther, and we pass a still smouldering fire. I was not deceived then when, the night before, I thought I saw a flash of light. A Khivan fire, or a Russian fire? If a Russian fire, it could only have been an outpost; and in that case the army would still be in sight. It was then a Khivan fire; and so we had camped the night before just in time to keep from falling into a Khivan camp.

Until a half hour after sunrise we push on, when suddenly our ears are struck by a report that goes through us like an electric shock. The report is succeeded by another, and another, at short but regular intervals, and they come rolling up the valley of the Oxus, awakening the long silent echoes, like distant thunder.

It is the roar of cannon!

CHAPTER XX.

A MAUVAIS QUART D'HEURE.

It was Kaufmann this time, sure enough. But, as I had all along feared, the Turcomans were with him, and now was the most critical moment of the whole journey. The roar of the cannon still continued; a battle was evidently in progress. How to find out the position of the contending parties, and avoid the Khivans—this is my difficulty The Turcomans might be between us and the Russians, in which case our position was bad enough.

The river here made a sudden curve to the left, whereas the cannonade was directly before us. I decided to ride straight to the cannon, and leave the river. I had some difficulty in inducing my people to do this. They were terribly frightened, and, for some unaccountable reason, wished to keep to the water. I even found it hard to get one of them to go with me to the summit of a little hill, to try and make out the position of the contending forces The cannonade still continued, and appeared to be about five miles distant.

We ascend the summit of the first slope, and cautiously peer over, but can see nothing. A mile farther on is another little hill, that cuts off the view. So far at least the coast is clear. We are about pushing on, when five horsemen suddenly come dashing over the hill, and, seeing us, wheel off towards the river, and disappear. It begins to grow exciting. We urge our horses to their utmost, but the sand is so deep, and they are so tired, that it is impossible to force them out of a walk. The cannonade suddenly ceases. We approach the summit of the hill, which is covered with a short growth of sax-aul, and again peer over. This time we see something that may well give us pause.

At the distance of about two miles there is a number of horses right across our path, probably 100 in all, scattered along a line of a mile in length. I cannot see any men, but Mustruf assures me he can make out some, and that by their costume they are either Kirghiz or Turcomans, he cannot say which; certainly not Russians. This looks bad. If Kirghiz, they are friends; but if Turcomans, then, indeed, our position is almost as bad as it well could be. In that case we have three courses before us, all of which seem equally impracticable. Go back to Khala-ata; make a circuit of ten to twenty miles through the sand, and thus slip around them; or try to hide until night, and then steal through their lines. Our horses are too feeble to attempt either of the first two plans; and as to hiding, there is no cover but a few hillocks. In all probability we would be discovered before night.

As the cannonade had ceased, I could not tell how far the Russians were, nor their exact direction. So we halt in the sand to await events. Two horsemen suddenly detach themselves from the line, and start towards us, as though they had seen something in our direction, and were coming to investigate. Matters are now coming to a crisis. Retreat is impossible; and there is no cover within two or three miles that would tempt a rabbit. I order my men to dismount and hide, as well as they can, and get their arms ready. They are all well armed, having among them two revolvers, two double-barrelled breech-loading guns, and four single-shot guns loaded with slugs. The misfortune is, none of them can be counted on to hit anything farther than ten feet; probably they will even run away. My intention is to allow the two Turcomans to approach within ten yards, kill them, and if possible seize their horses; for with one good horse I would risk my chance of reaching the Russians. The attempt is certainly desperate, for the rest of the enemy will be down on us as soon as they hear the report of fire-arms, and then—but I have no time to think of my further movements.

The two Turcomans are within fifty yards, coming forward cautiously, as if they suspected the presence of an enemy. I look around on my followers, to see which of them I can count on. Old Ak-Mamatoff seems perfectly stolid, as though it were a matter of the utmost indifference to him. I had made life a burthen to him by dragging him here, where he had never engaged to go, and the sooner he got rid of his existence the better. Mustruf looks shaky. The only one of the three who seems to be ready for the fray is the young Kirghiz, Tangerberkhen. The cannonade suddenly recommences. I am lying down among the bushes with rifle cocked, and ask Mustruf every moment if he still thinks they are Turcomans. He still whispers "Yes," until they are within twenty-five yards, and I am about to pull the trigger, when he springs up, gives a shout, and throws up his cap, wild with joy. He has recognised a Kirghiz and an acquaintance. I feel very light-hearted myself, and we shake hands with one another all around. The two Kirghiz proved to be djigits in the Russian service, who were returning to Khala-ata. They informed us that the Russians were only three miles farther on, that they were bombarding a fort across the river, and that the Khivans had all been driven to the other side We sprang into our saddles, and pushed on. In half an hour we reached a dune near the river bank, where we had an extensive view of the river and valley.

The Oxus here was about three-quarters of a mile wide. When I arrived on the scene, the opposite shore was covered with horsemen, who were galloping about, while two pieces of cannon, placed down near the water's edge, in front of a little fort, were booming away with might and main. Looking down the river on my own side, I beheld the Russians, at the distance of about half a mile, scattered about, quietly looking on, while the two six-pounders were throwing shells. We drew rein, and watched the battle. The opposite bank was apparently about fifty feet high, while that on our side was low and flat. The enemy seemed to have thrown up earthworks on the other side. What appeared earthworks, however, afterwards turned out to be the high banks of the canal of Sheik-Arik, which here entered the oasis. On the top of these the Khivans had built their fort to dispute the passage. Beyond, glimpses could be caught of gardens and trees. Here the gardens of Khiva really commence With the exception of a few wheat and clover fields, that we had passed on the way, the river banks were uncultivated and uninhabited. But now on our side of the river, below where the Russians were, I could see rich green grass and fields of waving grain.

The Khivan artillery was worked nearly as fast as the

Russian, and I was astonished to see that their cannon-balls, so far from falling in the water, as I should have expected at that distance, seemed to plough up the ground right among the Russians. Although I could not at that distance see their effect, some of them, as I afterwards learned, carried a quarter of a mile over. The effect of the Russian shells was very easily observed, as they tore up earth in every direction. The Khivans stood their ground pretty well, considering the disadvantage under which they were labouring, in having only solid shot instead of shells.

This cannonade had been going on for about an hour. The Russian shells had been tearing up the ground all around them during this time, and still the two pieces down at the water's edge held their ground.

It was a curious scene; and I suppose the old Oxus, since the time it first broke from the ice-bound springs of Pamir, had never heard such music as this. Five times before had the Russians attempted to reach this very spot, and five times had they failed. Five times had they been driven back, beaten and demoralised either by the difficulties of the way, the inclemency of the season, or the treachery of the Khivans. The one detachment which had succeeded in capturing Khiva had afterwards been slaughtered to the last man; and now the Russians stood at last, this bright May morning, on the bank of that historic river, with their old enemy once more before them.

For my own part, I sat on my horse watching the progress of events with an interest all-absorbing. There was a sense of difficulties overcome and dangers passed, after my thirty days' chase, which, with the exciting scene before me, was well calculated to put a war correspondent into good humour. I could not help thinking how curiously fortune had favoured me. If I had the selection of the moment when I should arrive at the army, I could not possibly have chosen a more favourable one than the present.

Suddenly a shell, which exploded among the cavalry up on the opposite bank, seemed to produce great panic and confusion. There was a scampering off in every direction, a moment afterwards horses were brought down, the two pieces at the water's edge were quickly hauled off, and a few minutes later there was not a soul to be seen on the other shore. And thus ended the battle of Sheik-Arik.

CHAPTER XXI.

AT LAST.

I NOW started down the river towards the Russians, and, after crossing innumerable canals and ditches which cut up the valley in every direction, I succeeded in reaching them.

As soon as I was within earshot, an officer, who had advanced towards me, cried out in Russian

"*Vui kto?*" "who are you?" with a very strong emphasis on the you.

"*Americanetz,*" I reply.

When I got within talking distance,

"You are the man who crossed the Kyzil-Kum alone, are you?"

To which I answered in the affirmative.

"All right, come along, and I will present you to the General. We heard you were on the way to join us a few days ago."

I dismounted, and he led me to General Golovatchoff, whom I found sitting on a cannon, smoking a *papyross.* Near him was another piece, dismounted; and not far off the bodies of two horses that had just been killed; I soon learned this was the only loss the Russians had sustained.

12

Although the ground was ploughed up in every direction by the enemy's cannon-balls, not a single man had been touched. If the solid shot of the Khivans had been shells, the Russian loss must certainly have been heavy.

General Golovatchoff—a large, broad-shouldered man, with a long beard and a frank, open expression of countenance that was very pleasing—shook hands with me cordially, told me I had done a very daring thing, and then invited me to breakfast, which he assured me would be ready in a few minutes.

I suppose I looked as though I needed a breakfast, and something more. Hollow-eyed, hollow-cheeked, dirty, dust-covered, uncombed, unkempt, and ragged—my rifle, which I carried for a month, slung over my shoulder in a *bandoulière*, had worn my coat into holes—I presented but a sorry spectacle among the Russians, who were all spruce in their white coats and caps, and gold and silver buttons, as clean and starchy as though they were on parade in Isaac's Square, St. Petersburg.

The breakfast consisted of cold boiled beef, cold chicken, with a box of sardines, and a little *vodka*, and the cloth was spread out on the grass, which was here rich and luxuriant.

They were all very friendly, and manifested a good deal of curiosity about my experience in the Kyzil-Kum, as well as surprise that I should have undertaken such a foolhardy journey alone. They said there were a hundred chances to one against me, and gave me such a lively account of the dangers I had escaped, that I really began to be frightened. I experienced something of the feeling of the man who, having killed, as he supposed, a fine large wolf, was aghast upon being told he had slain the largest and most magnificent lioness that had ever been seen in the country.

They were very jubilant over the affair of the morning, and I found that I could not have arrived at a more favourable time. Everybody was in good humour. The great difficulties of the campaign were over, and the interesting part of it had just commenced.

While at breakfast, Golovatchoff was informed that some of the enemy had returned, and were setting fire to a large boat or kayuk that was lying under the fort. The sharp-shooters were already at work, trying to drive them away. When they had at last succeeded in doing this, the General despatched one of Kaufmann's small iron boats immediately to the other side, with twenty soldiers and an officer of the topographical corps, to capture the burning boat and make a hasty map of the river and surrounding country. In a couple of hours the officer returned with the kayuk, which was but slightly damaged.

I now learned that this was not the main body of the army, but only a detachment sent forward to reduce the fort. Kaufmann, with the rest of the army, was en-camped some five miles farther down the river.

Instead of occupying the abandoned fort, General Golovatchoff gave orders to march back to camp. It was not Kaufmann's intention to cross the river at this point, but at Shura-Khana, three or four miles farther down. The affair of the morning had been brought about in order to allow some boats, captured at Uch-Uchak, to pass. The fight had really commenced the evening before, when General Kaufmann was riding up the river-bank, very uneasy because these boats had not arrived.

As he was passing this place, the enemy opened on him in a very unexpected manner, for he had not until then suspected the existence of a fort here. The firing was very correct, the cannon-balls falling right among the staff, and in fact the correctness of their aim was, as the Grand Duke Nicholas laughingly expressed it, " remarkable—even disagreeable." The boats were already arriving, and as the enemy were no longer there to offer any resistance, we returned to camp to commence the passage next morning at a point lower down. Upon reaching the camp, I accepted the hospitality of the officer who had first accosted me. His name was Chertkoff, and he proved to be an old friend of Mr. Schuyler's.

My first duty was to call and pay my respects to General Kaufmann. I found him sitting in an open tent, wrapped up in a Bokharan khalat, or gown, taking tea, and smoking a cigarette. A man between forty-five and fifty, bald, and rather small of stature for a Russian, blue eyes, moustache, no beard, and a pleasant, kindly expression of countenance. He shook hands with me, asked me to sit down, and then remarked that I appeared to be something of a *molodyetz* (a brave fellow), and asked me, with a smile, if I knew what that meant. After a few questions about my own adventures, he gave me an account of the campaign up to that time, which I have reserved for the next chapter. He showed no hesitation in allowing me to accompany the army the rest of the way to Khiva.

I next called on the Grand Duke Nicholas, whom I found living in a Khivan mud house, the first house in which he had lived for three months. By him I was likewise received in a very friendly manner.

GENERAL KAUFMANN. *From the 'Illustrated London News.'*

Then I returned to Chertkoff's tent, and, for the first time in two months, slept tranquilly.

From this time forward until the end of the campaign against Khiva, and afterwards, during the war against the Turcomans, I was with the Russian army. I would here take occasion to speak of the kindness with which I was treated on all hands. I arrived among them almost destitute. I had neither sugar nor tea, the very necessities of life in that country, nor anything else to eat; but I never went hungry. It is true that for the first three days after my arrival I came nearer starving to death than ever in my life before. This was partly because I was enfeebled by a long course of semi-starvation, but principally because there was nothing to eat for anybody. Supplies were exhausted, and none had as yet been received from the other side of the river. For some time nobody had anything, and we would have been glad of the black dried bread which I had previously thought such hard fare. Some horses were killed, but they did not last long, as many could not be spared. It was the first time I ever tasted horse-flesh; I found it exceedingly good, and would have been glad to get more of it.

But, from the time they had anything to offer me, I never passed a tent where they were eating or drinking that I was not invited to join. From the Grand Duke down to the smallest officer in the detachment, they were all the same. I was invited on all hands, twenty times a day, to eat or take tea. Indeed, until I reached Khiva, I made no arrangements for having my servants prepare meals for me, but simply lived on the community at large. And now, as I write, I cannot think of the hospitality I received without a throb of grateful remembrance. I take

this occasion to thank them ; to thank not only those
with whom I became intimate, but the many whose names
I do not even know, but whose kindness and generosity I
have experienced, and whose friendly faces I shall not
easily forget.

PART II.

—

THE FALL OF KHIVA.

CHAPTER I.

KAUFMANN'S MARCH FROM TASHKENT.

IT is now time to give the history of General Kaufmann's march from Tashkent.

His force was composed of eleven companies of infantry, 1650 men, one company of sappers and miners, half a battery, or four pieces of horse artillery, six pieces of foot-artillery, breech-loading, all of the newest models; half a battery of mountain-pieces, a battery and a half of rockets, and 600 Cossacks; in all about 2500 men. This detachment left Tashkent on the 15th of March.

The train was composed of between 3000 and 4000 camels, hired from the Kirghiz at the rate of twelve rubles per month, with the proviso that each camel dying on the way should be paid for at the rate of fifty rubles apiece. The whole force was united at Djizzak by the 25th of March, which place the head of the column left on the same day.

As far as the well of Aristan-Byl-Kuduk the march of General Kaufmann presented nothing remarkable. The cold at first was very severe, and was rendered more unendurable by the absence, in many places, of anything that would serve as fuel. The sufferings of the troops during this time were extreme, but they were soon ameliorated by the rapid approach of warm weather.

By the 13th of April they had reached the well of Aristan-Byl-Kuduk.

It was near here that Kaufmann decided to change his route, and march to Khala-ata, instead of continuing on to the Bukan-Tau mountains, as he had originally intended. He accordingly sent orders for the detachment from Kazala to meet him at this place, instead of waiting for him at Myn-Bulak.

The Kazala column, of which it is now necessary to speak, was composed of eight companies of infantry, half a battery of mountain-pieces, half a battery of rockets, two mitrailleurs, and 150 Cossacks, in all about 1400 men. They set out from Kazala, or Fort No. 1, on the 11th of March, and were to meet the column from Tashkent at Bukali, in the Bukan-Tau mountains, 120 miles from the Oxus. They had already reached this point, when they received the order to join the other detachment at Khala-ata.

This change of route appears to me to have been a great mistake. Although, for the Tashkent detachment, the way by Khala-ata was the shortest and best, it was quite otherwise for the Kazala column. At Bukali they were within 120 miles of the river. It was then only the middle of April; the weather was still cool, and there being several wells they would besides have been obliged to carry water only half that distance. The river might thus have been reached in ten days, just one month sooner than they actually did reach it. Instead of this, however, they had, in carrying out Kaufmann's order, to make a retrograde movement, which required two weeks, and at the end of that time they were no nearer the river than before. The same time was consumed by Kaufmann in waiting for them. And the time thus lost was the most favourable for marching, as the weather was still cool, and the fierce heat which afterwards assailed them had not yet come on.

When it was decided to change the route, it would have even been better to push on to the river as fast as possible, and let the Kazala detachment follow the original route marked out for it.

General Kaufmann was deterred from this course by prudential reasons. He thought the Kazala detachment too weak to encounter the enemy alone; and although the result proved that this opinion was wrong, there was sufficient reason to dissuade a prudent general from taking the risk.

Kaufman reached Khala-ata on the 6th of May, and the junction of the columns took place on the same day.

Here they halted several days, in order to explore the road before them, ascertain the position of wells, and the supply of water to be obtained, before advancing farther.

It was while advancing from here to Adam-Kurulgan with a small party, to search for water, that Colonel Ivanoff was attacked in the manner already related in another chapter.

Having driven the enemy away from Adam-Kurulgan, and obtained, by digging wells, a sufficient supply of water for the army, they advanced to that point on the 12th of May, leaving a small garrison at Khala-ata.

This was the last point at which water could be obtained before reaching the Oxus. Every preparation, therefore, was made for a rapid march to the river. The distance was unknown, but it was thought it could be reached in two days, or three at the outside. Accordingly a supply of water was taken for three days, and on the morning of the 17th of May they marched from Adam-Kurulgan.

Their hopes of a speedy arrival at the river were doomed to disappointment.

The weather had now become excessively hot. The camels, enfeebled by their long march from Tashkent, and scarcity of food, were fast becoming worthless Instead of carrying 600 pounds, the ordinary burden of a camel, many of them only carried half that, and some even less.

The advance-guard halted as usual about eight o'clock in the morning, having made about fifteen miles. According to the order of march usually followed, the rear-guard should arrive at ten in the morning; then the whole army would halt until three in the afternoon, when the heat had somewhat abated, before making the afternoon march. Instead of this, however, the rear-guard, owing to the extreme weakness of the camels, only arrived at ten o'clock at night. Many of the camels had been left on the way, and their loads had been transferred to the others, which were thus overburdened. Instead of thirty miles, as had been intended, the troops had only made fifteen, and upon examination it was found that nearly the entire supply of water had been exhausted.

The utter impossibility of proceeding without more water through an unknown desert—a distance that might indeed be only thirty miles, but which might also be 100 —was only too evident. A single retrograde movement might be the signal for a rising of the whole Central Asian population; and the possibility of staying where they were, and sending back for more water, was not to be discussed for a moment. They could not advance, and they dare not retreat. From a position of secure confidence they had passed to one of utter desperation in a single day.

General Kaufmann passed through one of those moments of despair which every general who has ever commanded an army has probably experienced at least once in his life. The situation was hopeless. The men were without water, the camels almost exhausted, the artillery horses already suffering. The thermometer marked 100° of Fahrenheit. He was on the very verge of a similar disaster to that which, unknown to him, had overtaken Colonel Markosoff only a few days before, in the Turcoman desert, on the other side of the Amu-Darya; but failure to him entailed consequences a hundred times more tremendous. The Russians only maintain their authority in Central Asia by convincing the people that they are invincible and infallible. One mistake, one defeat, and this illusion would be destroyed; for the people finding the Russians could be beaten would rise. Kaufmann was about to give the order to retreat, when he was saved by one of those trivial circumstances which often intervene in the most unlooked-for manner in the affairs of men.

Among the fifty or sixty guides in General Kaufmann's employ, there was one who had been picked up by Colonel Dreschern in the Kyzil-Kum. He was in rags and tatters, and had presented himself, offering to serve without pay, in order to revenge himself on the Khivans, or, what was the same thing to him, Turcomans, who had captured and murdered a part of his family, and carried off the rest to be sold into slavery. He was employed to serve with the other guides, and no other attention was paid to him. This man now came forward, and, although the other guides declared there was no water nearer than the Amu, said he would find some in the immediate neighbourhood.

General Kaufmann took out his pocket flask, and said, "Bring me that full of water, and I will give you 100 rubles." The guide was then provided with a good horse, and he was off like the wind. This was at daylight of the morning of the 15th, and by a little after sunrise he had returned with the flask full of water, foul and nauseous, but water, nevertheless, that would support life. He declared he had found three wells, four miles north of the caravan route leading to the Amu, unknown to caravans, and never visited by them, and that the water, such as it was, could be found in sufficient quantities to supply the army.

Kaufmann immediately gave the order to march, and two hours afterwards the advance-guard had arrived and encamped on the spot, which has since been called Alty-Kuduk, or "Six Wells." They found water, as described by the guide, in three wells, at a depth varying from fifty to one hundred feet, but very bad, and in insufficient quantities. In one was the body of a dog, which had probably been thrown there by the Khivans. But, bad as the water was, it had to be portioned out to the men at the rate of a pint a day, in order to prevent the whole supply from being instantly exhausted. Although Kaufmann gave orders to have three more wells dug, each of which supplied more or less water, it was still so scarce that two or three of the native guides died of thirst.

The sufferings of the troops for two or three days, exposed to the broiling heat of a desert sun, on a pint of water a day, can be easily imagined. It was something terrible.

In the meantime, as there was no water for the camels,
Kaufmann sent the whole train back to Adam-Kurulgan,
to let them drink, and to get a fresh supply of water before making another attempt to proceed. The camels
were sent with an escort of four companies, or 600 men
It was against this escort that the troops of the Khan
made their first serious attack.

Sadyk, then probably camped on the Amu, having been
informed by his spies that Kaufmann had sent all his
camels back under a small escort, determined to fall on
them, and cut them off. He understood very well that if
he could capture the camels, the army was beaten, and
would have to retreat. He took 500 Turcomans, each
provided with two horses, and, passing Kaufmann at Alty-
Kuduk, reached Adam-Kurulgan early on the morning of
the 18th of May.

It was about four o'clock in the morning when the
Russian pickets were driven in, and the alarm was given
By the time the troops had seized their arms, the Turcomans were very near the camp. The attack was conducted
with considerable spirit and vigour. The Khivan standard
was borne by Sadyk himself, who rode a splendid white
horse, and he advanced so near, that if any of the sharpshooters had known it was Sadyk they would certainly
have picked him off. But what can men, undisciplined,
and armed only with sabres, however brave individually,
do against breechloaders? Soon perceiving the impossibility of advancing in face of the superior arms of the
Russians, the Khivans finally retreated, completely dis-
comfited. Sadyk, as appeared from the reports of the
prisoners taken, had been confident of a complete victory,
having been misinformed as to the real number of troops
he would have to deal with, and supposing he would only

13

find a mere handful of men. This was the first serious encounter the Khivans had with the Russians. They were very much discouraged by it, although still not without hopes that Kaufmann would be unable to reach the river.

Sadyk, it may be stated, is a soldier of fortune, who was then in the service of the Khan, and who used to exact a good deal of tribute from rich caravans on his own account. Immediately after the fall of Khiva, he made a pilgrimage to the tomb of the prophet, but has since returned, I believe, to Merv.

Kaufmann, in the meantime, suffered the greatest anxiety, and his soldiers the greatest hardships at Alty-Kuduk. Only those who have experienced it can form an idea of the horror of being among a mass of men who are suffering the pangs of thirst. Although the remarkable discipline of the Russian troops prevented anything like the least disorder, the consciousness on the part of the officers that the time might come when no discipline would be possible, and that then they would fall an easy prey to the enemy, who were relying upon such an eventuality, was not the least among their woes. Gradually, however, the water grew better and more plentiful, the daily wants of the army were supplied, and immediate pressing need was not felt. But their forebodings for the future were of the darkest. A week had been consumed by the return to Adam-Kurulgan; the camels were growing weaker every day, and less capable of carrying their burdens; many of them would certainly have to be left on the way.

The camel is a very strong beast, and capable of carrying immense burdens, and of enduring great fatigues when in good condition. But once enfeebled by a succession of long, hard marches, as were those of Kaufmann, he soon becomes worthless, and months of repose are required to restore him. Instead of a load of 600 pounds, the burden allotted to each camel at the commencement of the expedition, they were now only capable of carrying 200, and even 100 pounds each. Every day the number of animals which became too feeble to carry anything, and that had to be abandoned, increased. The camel, it should not be forgotten, plays the same *rôle* in a war like this as railroads in European wars. For the army to be deprived of transport here in the desert, was to perish.

The position then of Kaufmann, it may easily be imagined, was a most difficult one; not only the success of the expedition, but the life of every one of his men, was dependent on him—a disaster here would be certain death to every soul in the detachment—and the distance to the Amu was still a matter of conjecture. At last, after a week had been consumed, a fresh supply of water was taken, the camels returned to Alty-Kuduk, and the troops started once more for the Oxus, with the only alternative left them of reaching it, or of leaving their bones in the desert. It had been found, however, that the camels that were still in a condition to travel would not be able to carry the whole of the baggage. So, very reluctantly, orders were given to leave nearly the whole of it behind, together with four of the six iron boats Kaufmann had specially made for the passage of the Oxus, two pieces of artillery, and nearly all their remaining supply of forage. They took with them only what was of the most absolute necessity.

Two companies were left behind to protect the baggage, and this is why I found troops at Alty-Kuduk.

From Alty-Kuduk their march had been very difficult

and trying.   The last day before reaching the river they
had been surrounded all the time by the Turcoman light-
horse, who kept galloping around them the whole distance,
harassing the march.   The army had pushed forward for
several miles with a continual fire on the skirmish lines,
while the heat was almost overpowering.   It was here I
had seen so many dead horses.

The discipline of the troops was excellent.   Although
many of them were mad with thirst, upon arriving at the
little lake of which I have already spoken, not a man
broke ranks to get at the water, along the edge of which
they were marching, until they had received permission.
Kaufmann spoke of the conduct of his soldiers almost
with tears in his eyes.   He said there were no other
soldiers in the world capable of doing what they had done.
And I am fully of his opinion.

Once arrived at the water, and the safety of the army
assured, the General soon changed his plan of action from
the defensive to the offensive, he threw a few shells among
the Turcomans who had gathered in a mass near the foot
of the mountain Uch-Uchak; charged with the cavalry,
pursued the enemy eight or ten miles along the river
bank, and captured eleven " kayuks," or boats.   Without
these boats he would never have been able to cross the
river.   From Uch-Uchak to Sheik-Arik, they had seen
little of the Khivans, until the fort unmasked its battery
the day before.

CHAPTER II.

CROSSING THE OXUS.

THE next morning at daylight we took up our line of march, but instead of going to Shurak-Khana down the river, as originally intended, we went back to our position of the day before. Upon consideration, Kaufmann had decided to cross at Sheik-Arik, the scene of the previous day's engagement.

We were soon on the spot, the boats had arrived, and within an hour the first boat-load of fifty men had started across the river. This was the 30th of May The morning was bright and warm, and we threw ourselves on the fresh green grass before our tents, which we had pitched at the water's edge, and lazily watched the scene before us. It was extremely beautiful and animated. The sunlight danced over the surface of the broad Oxus. The other shore, dim and misty, was lined with dense groves of fruit-trees and elms, through which could be seen, here and there, the grey walls of an " Uzbeg " farm-house, or the slender façade of a graveyard mosque. It lay silent and lonely, without any moving figure to give it life, this strange, unknown land of Khiva; and seen, away over the water, bathed in a sleepy, glorious splendour, looked as beautiful and dreamy as the fabled land of the lotus-eaters. Idly I watched it, thinking of all the stories I had ever heard of it; of its cruel and despotic Khans; its wild fanatical Mohamedhan population, its beautiful women; its strange mysterious character; and its isolation, which had rendered it inaccessible to Europeans as the enchanted caves of the mountain. I was unable to realise the situation, and half expected to wake up and find myself some thousands of miles away in another hemisphere.

In strange contrast to the quiet of the other side was the life, animation, and movement of ours. The shore was covered with horses and camels, Cossacks and soldiers—some just arriving, some splashing about in the water, climbing into the boats, dragging in the artillery, forcing in the unwilling horses, tumbling in the baggage, and shouting and crying to each other madly the while.

The soldiers seemed perfectly at home in the water; and, although there were many of them who never saw so much water in their lives before, they appeared to take to it as naturally as young ducks. Twenty or thirty brawny, muscular fellows, stripped naked, would plunge into the river, seize a rope, and drag a boat up stream to give it a fair start for crossing; while General Kaufmann, sitting on a camp-stool at the edge of the river, encouraged them from time to time with the word "molodtsi," "brave fellows." All was bustle and animation.

It took a boat only about twenty minutes to cross, and the same time to return; but it was borne down the river so far each passage, that dragging it back to the starting-point against the current required fully an hour. There were three large boats, capable of carrying each fifty or seventy-five men, and eight small ones that would hold

FERRY ON THE OXUS. *From a design by Vereschagin.*

only about ten. These boats, called "Kayuks," are constructed of the trunks of small trees, rough-hewn to an even thickness of about six inches. They are nearly flat-bottomed, with a very heavy piece of timber forming the stem and stern, which project three or four feet above the hull—on the whole, a very heavy and unwieldy craft.

All day the passage of the river was continued without any opposition on the part of the enemy. Their utter incapacity for defending themselves was shown by the fact that they thus quietly allowed Kaufmann to cross the river here without the slightest molestation. They might have hid behind the banks, out of reach of the artillery, and overpowered each boat-load of soldiers in turn. It would have been impossible for the Russian artillery to protect the troops under such circumstances.

In a few hours, two companies and four small four-pounders had safely crossed and taken up a defensive position in and about the fortress. This put them out of danger of being overpowered by any sudden assault, and thus the passage of the Oxus was assured.

Meanwhile we knew nothing of what was passing at Khiva, and our imaginations were excited by the mysterious silence that reigned on the other side.

Would the Khan think of making any serious resistance, after thus giving undisputed passage of the Amu, his strongest line of defence? Or would he simply run away, and betake himself to the desert? We had no means of deciding this question, and could only conjecture as to what his future line of action would be. We had not then learned that Verevkin, at the head of the Orenburg detachment, was rapidly advancing on the other side, and that the poor Khan had his hands already full. That night, about twelve o'clock, when everybody had gone to sleep, we were suddenly awakened by the reveille. Springing to our feet, in the half belief that the enemy were making a night attack, we found that it was not the Khivans, but the water, that was advancing upon us. The old Oxus, angry, perhaps, at being crossed, had suddenly commenced rising since dark, as though hoping to catch us napping. It had risen about six feet in the course of three hours, and threatened to drown us out. The order was given to decamp, and move to higher ground—an order carried out in considerable confusion. My comrade and I got separated from our servants and baggage in the darkness, and were unable to find them—a misfortune which was not lightened by our being obliged to swim our horses over a canal, along with camels and Cossacks, so that we got wet to the skin. As it was impossible to find anybody, we had nothing to do but throw ourselves on the damp grass, with our saddle-blankets for a cover, and wait until daylight.

The next morning the entire aspect of affairs had changed. The Oxus was so wide, and the current so rapid, that Kaufmann was obliged to change his base of operations, and move up the river about a mile. This effected, the passage continued without interruption, but much more slowly than the day before. It now required fully three hours for a boat to make the round trip. The horses swam over for the most part, and nearly all the camels were sent back for the detachments of Alti-Kuduk and Khala-ata. I crossed with General Kaufmann and his staff on the 1st of June.

CHAPTER III.

AMONG THE KHIVANS.

UPON setting foot on shore, my comrade and I made a rush for the bazaar, which had been opened that day for the first time by the Khivans, in response to a friendly proclamation of General Kaufmann. For twenty-four hours we had eaten nothing but a handful of djugera, or millet. Now, fasting for twenty-four hours under ordinary circumstances, when you are in good condition physically, is a matter of no consequence at all. But when you have been on short rations for a month, during which time you have consumed your superfluous store of fat, it becomes a serious matter indeed.

The Khivans had responded to Kaufmann's proclamation with cartloads of flour, fruit, chickens, sheep, fresh wheaten cakes, "hot and hot," apricots, rice, sugar, tea, great quantities of white mulberries, together with clover and djugera for the horses. They had drawn up their great lumbering wooden carts just outside the camp, and were now surrounded by the Russian soldiers, with whom they seemed on excellent terms. A few of the soldiers spoke Tartar, or Kirghiz, but those who could not managed to get on somehow by signs, and the most lively exchange was going on between them and the natives when we arrived upon the scene. The Russians were paying, as I observed, triple and quadruple prices without hesitation. Where they got the money, I do not know, and cannot guess to this day, but the fact is they all seemed to have money to spend.

My friend and I bought hurriedly several pounds of flour, a sheep, a calf, a quantity of warm bread, some Bokharan honey, apricots and mulberries—enough provisions, in short, to last a month, never doubting for a moment but we should eat them all the same day. We were so hungry, that we were not even then quite satisfied that we had enough to supply our present wants. The Khivans who brought us these things were the "Uzbegs" of the environs; and, having satisfied my craving of hunger by two or three wheaten cakes and a little honey, I commenced examining the strange people around me with great curiosity.

They were generally medium-sized, lean, muscular fellows, with long black beards, and something of a sinister cast of countenance. Their costume consisted of a white —or what was once white—cotton shirt, and loose trousers of the same material, over which was worn a " khalat," a kind of long tunic, cut straight, and reaching to the heels. The khalat of the Khivans is very ugly, of a dirty brown and yellow, disposed in narrow stripes—entirely unlike the beautiful khalat of the Bokhariots, with its brilliant colours. Most of them were barefooted, and they wore a tall, heavy, black sheepskin cap, weighing fully six or seven pounds. Altogether, the costume of the Khivans is, I think, the ugliest and most inconvenient I have ever seen. The heavy sheepskin cap alone is enough to destroy the working of the most active brain, and upon seeing their monstrous hats, I no longer wondered at the backward state of their civilisation. The khalat, besides being hideously ugly, is most inconvenient; and although generally wadded with cotton, and very warm, is never taken off apparently, not even during the hottest days, when the wearers are performing manual labour.

They appeared very friendly; and, so far from being afraid of their conquerors, did not hesitate, as I before remarked, to ask triple and quadruple prices for everything they sold. They had at first thought the Russians would simply take what they wanted without pay, not even excepting their wives—a very natural proceeding, according to their ideas, and one which they themselves would certainly have adopted. But when they found this was not the case, they, with true Asiatic acuteness, commenced driving the best possible bargain.

To tell the truth, I was considerably surprised at the orderly proceedings of the Russians. I had expected that upon entering Khiva they would sack and burn the place, and slaughter the inhabitants. This was one of the principal reasons given for refusing correspondents of newspapers permission to accompany the expedition. The Russian authorities, it was said, did not want these atrocities reported. This reason, of course, was given to hide the real one, which was to prevent any Englishmen from going to Khiva.

General Kaufmann adopted a very different system in dealing with the Khivans. As soon as he reached the river, he issued a proclamation, assuring them that if they would stay quietly in their homes they would not be molested; that their property and their women would be respected; and that the Russians would pay with ready money for supplies, provisions, and forage brought into camp. But he warned them, that if the Russians had to go into the country to forage for supplies, they would take what they needed without paying for it, and would, besides, pillage and burn every abandoned house they should find. The supplies brought in that day were in answer to this proclamation.

Nor did the soldiers show any disposition to give the lie to Kaufmann's promises. There were no attempts to take anything by force. They paid the prices asked without grumbling, as though long accustomed to this mode of dealing with conquered enemies. To tell the truth, I think the world in general has a very imperfect and exaggerated notion of the Russians, and especially of the Russian soldiery. I remember what my idea of a Russian soldier was, not many years ago. A tall, giant-like fellow, with enormous bristling beard and moustache, fierce eyes, and a terrible aspect, with all the ferocious instincts of a savage, and nothing in common with civilised troops except his discipline;—such was my idea of the Russian soldier, and I suppose there are few of my readers who have not had very similar notions. This is a great mistake.

The Russian soldier is very far indeed from being a savage. He is neither cruel nor bloodthirsty, as far as I have seen, but, on the contrary, rather kind and gentle, when not enraged; and I saw many soldiers do little acts of kindness to the Turcoman children, during the campaign against the Yomuds, which greatly struck me. The lower classes of the Russian people, although ignorant and superstitious to the last degree, are not by nature either cruel or brutal.

The Khivans at first refused the Russian paper money, as they had never seen it before, and did not understand it. They accepted with eagerness, however, the small silver money in pieces of ten, fifteen, and twenty kopecks, of which the Russians had a large supply. A piece of twenty kopecks, about sevenpence of English money, passed readily for one " tenga," a silver coin of the Khivans.

The most curious things they brought us were the white mulberries, a kind which I had never before seen. The wheaten cakes, too, were peculiar. They were made of unbolted flour, mixed simply with water, rolled out thin about the size of a large dinner-plate, and baked a nice brown on the inner sides of a mud oven. This is the only bread known in Khiva, and when eaten warm, is really excellent. The gardens and cultivated land do not extend quite to the river at Sheik-Arik, but stop short within about half a mile of the fort. As there were neither trees nor grass here, we found we were much worse off than on the other side, where there was plenty of grass at least. The dust was terrible—worse even than at Khala-ata. The banks of the canal, formed of dry, soft earth, had first been trampled into powder by the Khivans, and then by the Russians, until it was a foot deep; and the wind blew it about in whirlwinds, that at times were suffocating. I never suffered so much from dust in my life; and the fresh green gardens, and the cool, dark shade of elms, which were within a quarter of a mile of us, and which we were not allowed to approach, only made the contrast more painful.

We found the fort of Sheik-Arik a very small affair indeed. It was not more than thirty feet in diameter, a mere toy-house, and utterly insignificant as a place of defence. The situation, however, was capable of a very formidable defence, if the troops of the Khan had known how to use it. Sheik-Arik, as its name indicates, is a

canal, now dry. It formerly received and conducted water
from the river into the interior of the Khanate, and may
do so yet, when the water is high.   Its banks, which are
from twenty to thirty feet in height, run for a short
distance almost parallel to the river, and form an earthwork of formidable dimensions.   The six-pound shells of
the Russians might have exploded here a long time before
making any impression on the solid banks of earth.   The
utter ignorance of the Khivans of military matters was
most strikingly shown in the construction of the little
toy-house of a fort, whose walls were so thin, that shells
went through them like cardboard.

CHAPTER IV.

THE GARDENS.

WE had been three days at Sheik-Arik, when suddenly the Khivans ceased bringing in provisions. As this was the only dependence the army had for food, it became necessary to take active measures for procuring supplies, and Kaufmann prepared to put his threat of foraging into execution. It appeared that the troops of the Khan, having recovered from their fright, had returned to the neighbourhood, and threatened with death anybody who should bring in supplies to the Russians.

Kaufmann sent out a reconnoitring and foraging party, under the command of Colonel Cherkovsky, consisting of 300 infantry, two little four-pounders, and 250 Cossacks. The latter were to forage, but not to take anything by force which could be had for money. They had permission to pillage any abandoned houses they might find, and the officer in command was to inform the inhabitants that if they did not immediately bring in supplies for money, he would send and take them for nothing. The infantry were to advance into the country, reconnoitre the ground, and endeavour to find and feel the enemy.

We marched out of camp about noon, on the 3rd of

14

June. Up to this point we had seen little of Khiva and the Khivans; for the right bank of the river was uninhabited here, and the gardens on the left bank did not quite extend to the river. We had seen nothing, therefore, but the still and silent trees that seemed to hide the secrets of the place so mysteriously. Now we were about to enter the renowned gardens. After crossing the short space of country between them and us, which was cut up in every direction by canals, we passed over a bridge that spanned a deep and narrow ditch; and, advancing along a broad, well-kept, but dusty road, soon found ourselves among the trees in the mysterious confines of Khiva.

The change from the red-hot glare of the sand to the cool shade and fresh, green verdure which greeted our weary eyes, was as sudden as it was agreeable. There were little fields of waving grain; fruit-trees of all kinds, bending under their loads of ripe and green fruits; tall noble old elms, spreading their long arms, thick green foliage, and dark shadows over little pools of water; grey, battlemented walls of houses and farmyards peeping out from among the trees. The newness, the strangeness of the place, the mystery hanging over it, its isolation and impenetrability, made us survey the scene, that was thus opened for the first time to the gaze of Europeans, with a delight and admiration only equalled by that of Columbus, when first setting foot in a new world. Over the road hung mulberry-trees, with their rich, luscious berries; apple-trees, with their mass of dark green foliage, apricot-trees, aglow with the rosy bloom of their delicate, delicious fruit; cherries, gleaming rich and red among the leaves Tall young poplars lifted their slender forms against the sky, and streams of water, shaded with bushes, ran about in every direction. To us, accustomed to the red-hot glare of the desert, it seemed a very garden of Eden.

This part of the country is inhabited by the Uzbegs. Their houses and farmyards are inclosed by heavy walls, from fifteen to twenty feet high, strengthened with buttresses and strong corner towers. The entrance is through an arched and covered gateway, closing with a very heavy wooden gate. Built on the same rectangular plan, from twenty-five to seventy-five yards square, each farmhouse is a little fortress in itself, far more formidable than the one at Sheik-Arik, and is actually intended to serve that purpose. The walls are composed of mud, but of a kind that gets comparatively hard. It is not worked up into small bricks, like the adobes of the Mexicans, but into huge blocks like granite, three or four feet square, and as many thick. Within the inclosure are contained the stables for horses, cattle, sheep, and all the live stock, as well as the dwelling of the inhabitants. Near the dwelling is always a little pool of clean water, thirty or forty feet square, shaded by three or four large elms.

The elms of Khiva are very beautiful. I saw many of a size and beauty that would make the heart of the "Autocrat of the Breakfast Table" leap for joy, and which were probably many hundred years old. Under these trees, during the summer, the family spend most of their time. Here they prepare and eat their meals; here they while away their hours of idleness, of which there are a good many in the life of an Uzbeg, and here the women weave and spin the golden threads of the silkworm. The interior of their houses is dark and gloomy, for they are only lighted by small holes in the walls, window-glass being unknown. But they are very often fitted up with a quantity of carpets, bright-coloured mats, rugs, and cushions, that render them very comfortable.

We rode into the first farmhouse we came to—the gate was standing wide open—and found three or four men sitting quietly under the elms beside the little pool They were a little startled at first, and came forward with their hats off, bowing very humbly. The Colonel told them we were in search of provisions, and required to know why they had ceased bringing in supplies. To this they replied, that the Khan had threatened to cut off their heads if they sold anything to the Russians. The Colonel told them to take whatever they had to sell to the camp, and he would see that they were protected. They promised to obey, and we advanced to the next house, where the same scene was repeated.

We found a few houses deserted, but we did not pillage them; indeed there was nothing to pillage, even if we had wished to do so, as there rarely remained anything but the bare walls. The Cossacks meanwhile spread themselves about through the country on each side of the road for the purpose of foraging, while the infantry marched forward to reconnoitre.

The country was most admirably adapted for defence; and if the Khivans had known how to avail themselves of its advantages, they might have made a formidable resistance. Every few yards there was a bridge, which ought to have been destroyed. Everywhere there were walls, hedges and ditches, clumps of trees, and houses in great numbers, in which masses of men might have found cover and protection. Our cavalry, would have been practically useless; our artillery as well as breech-loaders reduced to equality with those of the enemy, while their heavy brass pieces, charged to the muzzle with slugs and iron, would have been quite as effective at short range as the Russian shells. Every house was a fortress, whose walls would have to be battered down and stormed, with loss to the Russians, and little or none to the defenders. The Russians would, of course, have borne down all opposition in the end, but with loss; and they were, after all, comparatively few, while the Khivans were numerous. And then, too, a war of this kind, carried on for a few days, would have so reduced the invaders, that they would have been unable to take advantage of their victory.

But the Khivans showed neither inclination nor capacity for self-defence, and the Russian march was almost unopposed. Our little column moved forward through green fields of beautiful wheat, djugera, rice, and barley; the road, crooked and tortuous, was lined with mulberry-trees, from which the soldiers plucked the ripe fruit in passing. Sometimes it was shut in by huge mud walls, over which the branches of the apricot-trees hung in rich profusion; or bounded on each side by deep canals, full of running water, whose high banks were covered with verdure; and again it led beneath giant elms, whose thick shade fell over us with refreshing coolness. As it rarely rains here, the road was very dry, and we raised clouds of dust which, rising high above the trees, marked our approach for a long distance, ominous to the Khivans of approaching doom.

At length, after we had advanced about six miles, we began to see signs of the enemy. First we came upon abandoned houses in great number, whose owners had been forced to fly by the Khan's troops. Then a horseman would start out from behind a wall, and scurry off along the road, comet-like, leaving a train of dust after him.

At last cavalry began to appear in numbers, and we caught glimpses of them through the trees, galloping among the gardens on either side of us.

Our skirmish line was thrown out, and almost immediately the sharp ringing report of the rifle broke on the still afternoon air. The silence which had reigned until then was instantly disturbed. Shouts and cries were heard all around us, coming apparently from thousands of throats, and the firing on the skirmish line grew lively. The skirmishers dodged forward, sheltering themselves behind trees, walls, or whatever else they found in their way, and firing their pieces at every opportunity. We could catch glimpses of the Turcoman cavalry scurrying through the trees, with their tall hats and beautiful horses, in groups of fifteen or twenty, while the whole country for miles around seemed to re-echo their wild cries. To judge from the noise, one would have thought we were surrounded by thousands of the enemy. I expected we should be fired upon from behind the walls and embankments; but if they had ever had any such designs, they were forced to relinquish them by the skirmishers, and the column steadily continued its march. This went on for about three miles.

At last we came upon an open space of ground, about half a mile wide, across which the road led on a very narrow causeway. Beyond were more trees, gardens, and houses, and there, massed to the number of several thousand, were the enemy, apparently waiting to give us battle. They were firing their falconnettes, as the Russians call them—a kind of heavy matchlock. Some of these falconnettes were mounted on wheels, like a cannon, four and five together, and when fired at once reminded one somewhat of a mitrailleuse. They were

capable of doing considerable execution, too, at short range; but were too far off now, however, to do us any harm.

Our two little pieces of artillery were brought forward, and commenced throwing shells. Two or three exploded among the Khivans, who scattered in every direction. Then they took shelter behind the walls, and seemed disposed to stand their ground, without, however, showing any disposition to attack. We were now very near the town and fortress of Hazar-Asp, but our force was too small to attempt an assault. The Colonel had already sent back word that he had engaged the enemy, and that he wanted reinforcements; and he concluded to await orders before taking any further steps.

The two armies, therefore, stood confronting each other for nearly an hour, keeping up a lively fire the while on the skirmish lines. I was astonished that the enemy did not open upon us with their artillery, as at that distance, not only small shot, but slugs and stones fired from their pieces might have proved very effective; but either because they were afraid of our capturing their pieces, or because they had no confidence in them, they did not bring them forward. As it was now growing late in the afternoon, and we were some six miles from camp, Colonel Cherkovsky thought it prudent to retire. The Khivans were immediately after us, and followed so closely, that the rear-guard was kept continually engaged. Several of them were seen to fall, but were immediately picked up and carried off by their comrades. We were fired upon once from a house on the side of the road, and an officer was so severely wounded that he afterwards died—the only loss we sustained during the day.

We had got about halfway back to camp, when we

met the Grand Duke Nicholas, hurrying forward with a
detachment to reinforce us. He expressed a good deal of
chagrin at finding us on the homeward march, and was
for-returning and attacking Hazar-Asp at once. He was
dissuaded from this, however, by Colonel Cherkovsky,
who convinced him that it was now too near night to make
an attempt on a fortified place.

We nevertheless galloped back again, as the Grand
Duke wished to see the ground, and observe whether the
enemy were still disposed to hold out. We soon came to
the corpse of a dead Turcoman, lying beside the road.
He had approached too near the retiring rear-guard, and
had been shot fairly through the head He had fallen
apparently unnoticed by his comrades, who would otherwise have carried off the body, as it is considered dis-
honourable among them to allow either killed or wounded
to fall into the hands of their enemy. The corpse, dust-
covered, grimy, and horrible, was lying in the mud beside
the road.

As it was now growing very late, we turned back once
more, and started for camp.

"I think," said the Grand Duke, turning to me,
laughing, as we rode along, "I would like to forage a
little. The orders are to bring in everything in the way
of sheep and cattle for which there are no owners. Will
you come along?"

So we leaped over a canal which bordered the road, and
commenced galloping about among the gardens, taking low
walls and ditches at a bound, and penetrating into farm-
yards and inclosures in search of prey. We were not very
successful, however. There were plenty of cows, sheep,
and even horses, but the moment we had seized any, an
ill-advised owner put in an appearance. We, thereupon,

delivered up our captured prey, giving the owners instructions through Ak-Mamatoff to bring whatever they had to sell into camp, under pain of not escaping so easily next time. These orders were given with such a good-natured smile, however, by the Grand Duke, that the natives, I am afraid, were not very much impressed by the necessity of obedience. We generally found them sitting under the trees near the house, with their women and children — a little frightened and timid, but soon restored to confidence and composure upon seeing that we were not at all evilly-disposed. They offered us milk, a little fruit, or sometimes fresh wheaten cakes as a peace-offering, and seemed immensely relieved when we accepted. Once the Grand Duke seized the most hideously ugly donkey I ever saw, over which he went into ecstasies. "*Quelles oreilles, mon Dieu! regardez donc!* My arms are nothing to them. And his eyes! What an expression! It's enough to put us all out of countenance—the very impersonation of obstinacy and *entêtement.* He must be at least 500 years old. *Charmant, charmant!* If he only let us hear his voice!" and the Grand Duke was about handing it over to one of his followers, when, alas! the inevitable owner appeared and claimed him. "*C'est dommage,*" said he, delivering him up with regret; "*il était si laid !*"

I had just reached the road again, and was turning into it in the direction of the camp, when I was hailed in English in the following terms :—

"I say, American, don't you want a drink of sherry ?

I looked around, and beheld a young officer holding up a pocket flask to my delighted gaze.

"Certainly," I replied.

"It is capital sherry," he added, handing it to me. "I just got it from General Kaufmann."

I tasted it, and found it to be, as he said, capital; and we then rode along together towards the camp, conversing about the excursion of the afternoon. He had only arrived with the reinforcement, and as he did not know exactly what had happened, I related to him the incidents of the afternoon, in which he was deeply interested. "What a beastly thing it is that they wont fight a little," he said. "There will be no fun at all, after our long march through the desert. I had hoped they were going to oppose the passage of the river, and after the affair of Sheik-Arik, they might have given us an infinite deal of trouble; but they let us pass without striking a blow. And see what a defence they might have made here in those gardens, they could pick us off from behind every wall and canal at short range, where their arms would be as good as ours; and yet we pass along here as safely as though we were riding along the Nevsky in St. Petersburg. *C'est dégoûtant!*"

We arrived at camp at dark, and it was not until next day that I learned that the officer whose pocket-flask I so unceremoniously helped to empty was Prince Eugene of Leuchtenberg. I knew he was with the expedition, but had not yet made his acquaintance, so that I had entered into conversation with him without in the least suspecting who he was. I felt at first some embarrassment, when I remembered the cool manner in which I had made away with his sherry, but soon found I had no occasion for it. Both he and the Grand Duke Nicholas were very simple and unassuming in their manners, and were on even terms of good-fellowship with everybody.

CHAPTER V.

HAZAR-ASP.

GENERAL KAUFMANN decided to march against Hazar-Asp next day, as a sufficient number of the troops had now passed the river. He had, besides, news from General Verevkin, the commander of the Orenburg detachment, who had taken Kungrad, and was now marching upon the capital.

General Kaufmann related to me a very curious anecdote about the way in which he received General Verevkin's letter, which is very characteristic of the place and people. The three Kirghiz djigits or guides, to whom the letter had been intrusted, were captured by the troops of the Khan, and the letter seized, together with some Russian paper money. The messengers were brought before the Khan, and the chief dignitaries of state, to be questioned. When asked why they were going towards the Russians, they replied, that they were on the way to Bokhara, to collect the money for sheep they had previously sold. But as they could give no satisfactory explanation of the way in which they came by the papers, they were thrown into prison, and a grand council of war was held over the captured documents.

These nobody, of course, could read. So a certain

Khivan merchant, who had been in Russia, was called in to see if he could give any opinion as to the contents of the papers. He, although unable to read, judged rightly that the letter was some important correspondence between the two advancing armies, and determined to get the papers into his own hands. After examining them very intently for some minutes, he gravely assured the council that the letter was nothing at all—a bit of worthless paper; but that the bank-notes of ten and twenty-five rubles were most important documents, and should be carefully kept until some one could be found to read them. Having thus succeeded in withdrawing attention from the letter, he slily slipped it into his khalat, when nobody was watching, and made off with it. Before it had been missed, he had sent it with a trusty messenger to General Kaufmann, then crossing the Amu. This incident illustrates forcibly Eastern ignorance and cunning. Nobody but an Oriental, under such circumstances, would have ever thought of the ingenious device of making anybody believe that bank-notes were valuable state documents.

We marched next morning at sunrise for Hazar-Asp. Taking our way over the road we had traversed the day before, we soon arrived upon the scene of the previous day's engagement. The body of the dead Turcoman was still lying in the mud beside the road, where we had seen it yesterday. Apparently the enemy had not been here since, they would certainly not have left the body of their dead comrade here without burial. When we arrived at the place where they had shown themselves the day before in such force, we found it deserted. They had retired, we supposed, into the fortress of Hazar-Asp. This fortress was reported as standing in the middle of a large pond;

as having only one gate, and as very strong. It was thought the enemy would make a stand here, if they meant to fight at all.

IRRIGATION WHEEL.

We had reached about halfway, when we met two ambassadors coming to meet us. They were very humble in their demeanour, dismounted from their richly-caparisoned horses, and took off their hats as they met the advance-guard. They were sent on to General Golovatchoff, who heard what they had to say, and in his turn sent them to Kaufmann, but continued the march. They had

been despatched by the Governor of Hazar-Asp, Said
Emir Ul-Umar, an uncle of the Khan's, to offer their
submission, and surrender the fortress. The Governor
himself had gone to Khiva. Their submission was accepted; but Kaufmann, accustomed to all the tricks and
wiles of Central Asian warfare, nevertheless omitted no
precaution to prevent a surprise.

The morning was bright and warm; the orchards and
gardens through which we were passing green and
fragrant with the odour of many blossoms, and the march
seemed more like a holiday excursion or picnic than the
iron tread of grim-visaged war. Some of the houses
along the road we found abandoned; but at others the
inhabitants were quietly sitting on the ground before
their doors, and rose and bowed to us gravely as we
passed.

About ten o'clock we came in sight of the fortress,
which, as seen through the trees at a distance, with
its high battlemented walls and buttresses, crooked and
irregular, and the water that surrounded it, presented
a noble appearance, not unlike that of Windsor Castle.
We halted a few minutes, as some men were seen on
the walls; and, in spite of the fortress having already
been surrendered, General Kaufmann was not sure
that there was not some mischief preparing. The
proper dispositions having been taken, the army again
moved forward, and entered a long, narrow, covered
street, with a single line of houses or shops on each
side, which, leading over the water, served as a kind
of causeway and entrance to the fortress. We filed
through this crooked, irregular street, not without some
apprehensions of an ambuscade; and making two or
three short turns to the right and left, found ourselves

in front of the main entrance. It was a heavy, massive, arched gateway, with flanking towers, built of brick, and plastered over with mud. The gates were pierced in one or two places with holes, evidently made by cannon-balls in some old siege.

Kaufmann rode in, followed by his staff, and a couple of companies of infantry; made the circuit of the inside of the fortress; and, winding about through several very narrow, crooked streets, at last dismounted in a small court. Entering by a succession of small, dark corridors and rooms, we found ourselves in the principal court of the palace of Hazar-Asp. It was only about thirty by fifty feet, and the southern side was entirely taken up by the great hall of state, which is simply a high portico, opening into the court towards the north. Around this court were disposed the different rooms of the palace, the harem, and stables. Here General Kaufmann received the chief dignitaries and mullahs of the place, who came to treat with him. He told them that if they quietly submitted, without resistance, their lives, property, and women would be respected; that he had not come to conquer Khiva, but only to punish the Khan. They received these communications with every mark of satisfaction, and then withdrew.

Thus Hazar-Asp, really a stronger place than Khiva, surrendered without striking a blow. Most of the officers, and the Grand Duke especially, were dissatisfied with this result, but they consoled themselves with the hope that a desperate resistance would be made at Khiva.

Hazar-Asp is a place of about 5000 inhabitants. It is a mud-built town, entirely encompassed by the walls of the fortress, a rectangular structure, inclosing about three acres, to which a kind of addition or wing has been built. The fortress is nearly surrounded by a wide

15

but shallow pond, and is about ten miles from the
river, and forty from Khiva. It is regarded as a place
of great importance in the Khanate. The inhabitants
were very timid at first, and did not feel at all sure
they were not to be massacred on the spot. They soon
regained confidence, however, and in the course of the
day the bazaar was opened. Many of the surrounding
Uzbegs, supposing probably that the place would be
defended, had assembled within the walls, with their
goods and chattels, they now returned to their houses
in the environs. The houses in the town were poor and
miserable, and displayed far less pretentions than the
heavy, roomy country houses of the Uzbegs.

Five or six cannons were found, probably the same
that had been engaged in the affair of Sheik-Arik, together with a number of falconnettes, and a large quantity
of very good powder, which was left lying around in a
very careless manner.

After resting a couple of hours, Kaufmann left a small
garrison here, under command of Colonel Ivanoff, who with
Colonel Weimarn, had arrived the day before from Khala-
ata; and then returned about halfway back to the river,
and camped in the gardens. His intention was to wait
for the whole detachment to come up before making the
final attack upon Khiva.

Our camp here was pleasant enough, situated in the
gardens, and among the fruit-trees and the elms, with
streams of fresh water all around us; we considered
ourselves in a veritable paradise.

The houses in the immediate vicinity of the camp
were all abandoned, and we found nothing in them in the
way of household goods, but a few cooking utensils and
earthen jars In nearly every one, however, was a room

or two full of silkworms; many thousand of the little spinners, I am afraid, were starved to death, as there was nobody to feed them.

One day I mounted my horse and rode to Hazar-Asp, where I was hospitably entertained by Colonel Ivanoff. While taking dinner with the Colonel, an orderly came in, and informed him that a woman was waiting outside, asking permission to lay a complaint before him.

The Colonel turned to me and said, " Come along now, and you will see something curious."

As the regular course of justice had been interrupted by the flight of the Governor, the people of Hazar-Asp, it seemed, came to Colonel Ivanoff, who was then the supreme power, to have their wrongs redressed, and their quarrels settled. So we now went out into the great porch, which I have spoken of as the hall of state, or audience chamber. Here we sat down on a piece of carpet, and the Colonel put on a grave face, as befitted a magistrate in the administration of justice. The woman was now led into the court, which was some three feet lower than the floor of the porch on which we were seated. She came in, leading a lubberly-looking young man about fourteen, and bowing almost to the earth at every step, and addressed the Colonel, whom she took for General Kaufmann, as the " Yarim-Padshah," or half-emperor, which title the Colonel accepted with grave composure. She was an old woman, and was clad in the long dirty-looking tunic of the Khivans. The only article of dress that distinguished her from a man was the tall white turban worn by all the Khivan women. She brought in a little present of bread and apricots, which she handed to the Colonel with many profound bows, and then proceeded to state her case.

"Her son," she said, pointing to the gawky boy who accompanied her, "had been robbed of his affianced wife."

"By whom?" asks the Colonel.

"By a vile thieving dog of a Persian slave. My own slave, too; he stole my donkey, and carried the girl off on it; may the curse of the Prophet wither him."

"So then he is three times a thief. He stole the donkey, the girl, and himself," said the Colonel, summing the matter up in a judicial way. "But how did he steal the girl? Did he take her by force?"

"Of course; was she not my son's wife? How could a girl run away from her affianced husband with a dog of an infidel slave, except by force?"

"Who is she? How did she become affianced to your son?"

"She is a Persian girl. I bought her from a Turcoman who had just brought her from Astrabad, and I paid fifty tillahs for her. The dog of a slave must have bewitched her, for as soon as she saw him she flew into his arms, weeping and crying, and said, 'he was her old playmate' That was nonsense, and I beat her for it soundly. The marriage was to be celebrated in a few days; but as soon as the Russians came, the vile hussy persuaded the slave to run away with her, and I believe they are as good as married."

"Well, what do you want me to do about it?"

"I want you to give back my son's wife, and my donkey, and my slave."

The Colonel told her, with a smile, that he would see about it, and motioned her to retire from the presence. She withdrew, walking backwards, and bowing to the ground at every step, in the most approved and courtier-

like manner. Evidently it was not the first time she had
pleaded her own cause.

But her son never got back his wife, nor she her slave
or donkey.

During the three days we lay encamped at Hazar-Asp,
Kaufmann was busily engaged in collecting horses and
carts for transport, in the stead of the camels sent
back for the troops left at Khala-ata and Alti-Kuduk.
By this time the whole of the detachment had arrived;
news had been received from General Verevkin, who had
already taken Kungrad, and was rapidly advancing upon
the capital.

We broke up camp on the morning of the 8th of June,
and the evening of the 9th had reached a point about ten
miles from Khiva. All the way, the people came out
to meet us in groups of twenty and thirty, tendering
Kaufmann their submission, and making him peace-
offerings of bread, apricots, and sometimes a lamb or a
sheep.

Kaufmann had not been all this time without news of
the Khan. Three or four times since reaching the river he
had received messages and letters, in which the Khan professed the greatest astonishment to hear that the Russians
were invading his domains. He furthermore required to
know the meaning of these proceedings, and requested
the invaders to withdraw immediately.

We had just camped on the evening of the 9th, when
Kaufmann received a last letter from the trembling
potentate, in which, humbly proffering his submission, he
professed his readiness to surrender at discretion, and to
throw himself on Kaufmann's mercy. I must now go
back a little to explain the events, which had brought
the Khan to this humble frame of mind.

CHAPTER VI.

THE ORENBURG AND KINDERLY DETACHMENTS.

ALTHOUGH the campaign against Khiva was not decided upon in St. Petersburg until towards the end of December, General Kaufmann had really been two years preparing for it; and when he went to St. Petersburg to obtain permission of the Emperor to attack the Khanate, everything was ready in Turkistan for the instant opening of the campaign.

But there were several aspirants to the honour of conquering the one little spot in Central Asia that had successfully defied the Russian arms ever since the time of Peter the Great. And as the difficulties of the campaign were considered very great, nobody being able to say to a certainty which route offered the most chance of success, the Emperor decided to send four expeditions, in order to insure against failure One was to start from the Caucasus, under Colonel Markosoff; another from Orenburg, the direction of which was to be left to General Krysanovsky, the governor of the department, who confided the expedition to General Verevkin; one from Kinderly Bay, under Colonel Lamakin; as well as the one from Turkistan, prepared by General Kaufmann himself.

As Markosoff's expedition never reached Khiva at all, I

will dismiss it at once with a very few words. The base of operations was Chikishlar, in the Valley of the Attrek; and not Krasnovodsk, as originally intended. This line was chosen on the supposition that camels could be more easily obtained; but the change proved disastrous to the expedition, on account of the great increase to the length of route. By the time the column reached the well of Bala-Ishem, the troops were suffering fearfully. The heat was terrible—as much, it is said, as 149° Fahrenheit; the wells few, and the men almost dying of thirst. The camels and horses were completely exhausted by the long and rapid march, and began to die by the hundred. They were still 120 miles distant from Khiva; and this was the severest part of the route. There were but few wells on the way; and the camels were utterly unable to carry sufficient water for the troops. So on the 4th of May, just when Kaufmann was at Khala-ata, and Verevkin had reached the western shores of the Aral Sea, Colonel Markosoff found himself compelled to retreat.

An account of the Orenburg and Kinderly expeditions will come in the more fitly here, because, as will afterwards be seen, it was they who did the greater part of the fighting, and it was by them Khiva was really taken. To the presence of these columns in his territory is also to be attributed the fact that the Khan made so slight a resistance to the advance of Kaufmann.

These detachments had already arrived before the walls of Khiva, while Kaufmann was still some ten miles distant; and it is not the least remarkable part of this remarkable campaign, that four different columns, starting from as many different points of the compass, more than a thousand miles apart, should, nevertheless, have arrived before Khiva within a day of each other.

The facts relating to these expeditions I have obtained from different sources; partly from Lieutenant Count Shuvaloff, who commanded a company in General Verèvkin's detachment, and who was deputed by that officer to give me the necessary information; partly from Colonels Skobeloff and Lamakin; and, finally, from Lieutenant Stumm, a German officer, who accompanied in the first instance the Kinderly, and afterwards the united Kinderly and Orenburg columns, and who was the only foreigner beside myself that succeeded in reaching Khiva. Lieutenant Stumm has since published his experiences in an accurate and highly-interesting work, which has been of considerable assistance to me.

General Krysanovsky, the governor of Orenburg, only received the order to organise the Orenburg expedition during the first days of January; and the fact that everything was ready—transport, armaments, forage, provisions, tents, and clothing for the coldest of winters, and a march of 1100 miles through an entirely unknown country—by the 27th of February, shows with what rapidity the Russians can prepare for war when occasion requires.

The troops of this detachment were assembled at three different points, Orenburg, Uralsk, and Orsk, and commenced the march about the 27th of February, to unite at the fort on the Emba river. This is the Russian advance post in the Kirghiz steppes, and is a distance of about 400 miles from the different points mentioned.

The difficulties and hardships of this march were terrible; the cold attained a severity of 25° Réaumur; and the troops were harassed by storms such as are only known on these open level plains, where the wind finds not so much as a stone to obstruct its passage for hundreds of miles, and by the snow, which very often reached a depth of ten feet.

In spite of all these difficulties, which would appear insurmountable to any other troops but Russians, the three detachments formed their junction towards the last of March at the fort of the Emba, with transport, munitions, and provisions. This was not accomplished without the proper precautions having been taken. The soldiers were provided with furs, and heavy furred boots; felt tents, or kibitkas, had been placed along the road at intervals of a day's march; wood for fires, and hay for the horses and camels had been collected; and every precaution which experience had taught them had been taken to avoid a similar disaster to that which befel Perovsky in 1840. The result was that the detachment arrived at Emba without the loss of a single man, although, owing to the extreme cold, this was the most difficult part of the whole march. There were thus assembled at Emba nine companies of infantry, about 1600 men; nine sotnias of Cossacks, 1200 men; together with eight pieces of flying artillery, a battery of rockets, and four mortars, provided with three times the ordinary supply of ammunition. The train consisted of 5000 camels, collected among the Kirghiz, at a hire of £3 a month for the winter months, and £2 8s. for the summer. The soldiers only received their ordinary rations: two pounds of black bread and half a pound of meat a day, tea and sugar morning and evening, two glasses of vodka a week, besides vegetables, cheese, vinegar, and other things of antiscorbutic nature. Supplies were taken for two months and a half, and felt tents, each affording room for twenty men, were provided for the whole detachment.

On the 7th of April the column left the Emba, marching

southward, and struck the Aral Sea on the 2nd of May, after a march of twenty days, and continued its course along the western shore to the Gulf of Aibugir on the south. The Gulf of Aibugir, marked on all the maps, and which did really exist fifteen years ago, Verevkin found perfectly dry. The Kara-Kalpaks had even commenced to cultivate its ancient bed. The march of Verevkin was very remarkable, in being one of the longest probably ever recorded in history—over 1000 miles.

He arrived at Yani-Kola, in the Khanate of Khiva, on the 14th of May, while General Kaufmann was still at Alti-Kuduk, on the other side of the river, with the most difficult part of the way before him.

On the 1st of June Verevkin entered Kungrad, which the Khivans had already abandoned.

The march of the Kinderly detachment was likewise one of the most remarkable ever made by any army in any time. The distance was great; the road lay through a desolate desert, in which there was scarcely a well; and the means of transport were utterly disproportionate. And, by a strange want of foresight, but few skins, or vessels of any other kind, had been provided for carrying water.

This column was intended to meet the column from Orenburg at Lake Aibugir. The Orenburg detachment had already started fourteen days when the Kinderly column begun its march. Colonel Lamakin, the commander, was assisted by Lieut.-Colonel Pajaroff, Captain Ali-Khan, who had volunteered for the expedition, Lieut.-Colonel Skobeloff, Major Navrodski, and several other officers. This force was composed of twelve companies of infantry, one sotnia of 150 Cossacks, and two sotnias of the mountaineers of the Caucasus, each containing 120 men—in all about 1800 men. There were ten cannons, and a battery of rockets.

It was calculated that 1300 camels would be required; but the number obtained was far below this. The Kirghiz of Mangischlak refused to supply the 600 required of them, and Major Navrodski had to be despatched to seize them. After a pursuit of some days and a small skirmish, the Major succeeded in capturing 380 camels, 110 horses, and about 3000 sheep and goats. Thus, with a very small supply of camels, with many even of this supply daily dying, the journey through the waterless desert seemed a journey to certain destruction.

During the first five days of the march, the troops had a foretaste of the horrors of the desert. The heat was excessive, and the sand blinding and scorching. The wind, instead of alleviating the heat, only added to it, for it came against the face like a blast from a furnace From such an enemy the soldier had no protection; the sand and heat penetrated through the tents. Want of water soon began to be felt. The few wells that were found on the way were brackish, muddy, and full of insects. The soldiers bore all these hardships with cheerfulness; and although the camels and horses died by the hundred, the health of the men remained good.

Kaundy was the first place where a halt of any length was made, and this was reached by the advance on the 26th April. The journey from this to Senek, a distance of sixty miles, tried the soldiers greatly; for the heat was terrible; there was scarcely any water, and the men eagerly drank a few drops, black as ink, nauseous and stinking. Sickness began to attack the column, principally the infantry. The cavalry gave up their horses to the invalids; and a worn-out Cossack had occasionally to lead his worn-out horse, burdened with a sick foot-soldier. In one afternoon, and in one company, no less than 150 camels either died or became incapable of proceeding farther. Sunstroke, dysentery, and general debility were the principal forms of illness. Fever was so common that it was scarcely minded. Some of the officers on the staff had gone through three or four attacks in the march from Kinderly to Senek.

On May 2nd, Bish-Akti was reached. This station is about ninety miles from the Caspian Sea, and is situated in the midst of a sandy desert, and surrounded by low limestone hills. It has six wells. A small fort was built here, being so constructed that it included the wells within it.

The journey from Bish-Akti to the second fort at Ilte-Idshe, and, indeed, all the way to Kungrad, was rendered extremely difficult by the sand and wind. At one time there was almost a hurricane, so that the tents could not be raised at night. The order of march was as follows: a sotnia of Cossacks formed the advance-guard, and on each side, at a distance of about 3000 feet, there was a patrol of two horses. Then came the staff, with an escort of a company of cavalry, four horses acting as a patrol on either side. A sotnia followed, also protected by flanking patrols. The rear was protected by a company of infantry, under whose charge were twenty camels loaded with the forage for the horses of the staff. The main body of the army followed at some distance behind. In this way from twenty to thirty miles were travelled daily. The march used to begin at five or six o'clock in the morning, and was continued until noon. From twelve till three there was a halt; for during that time the heat was so great that it was impossible to attempt any movement, even the erection of a tent. At three the march was resumed, and was continued to ten or eleven, or sometimes even two o'clock in the morning. The horses were fed and watered once a day; sometimes they had to remain even thirty hours without water.

The 9th and 10th of May were days of terrible suffering. It seemed almost as if the whole column were about to die of thirst. The well of Kol-Kinir, at which it arrived on the evening of the 9th, was so deep that water could only be obtained very slowly, and thus but a small portion of the detachment could be supplied. It was now evening, and the troops had had no water since mid-day; nor was any to be obtained until they reached Alpai-Mass, a distance of thirty-five miles. On the evening of the 9th and the morning of the 10th, both the soldiers and the beasts had to remain without water. Under these circumstances the march to Alpai-Mass began. By mid-day of the 10th, when the heat was most violent, the horses commenced to sink, their riders hung on to them helplessly, and even the officers of the staff were losing hope; for Alpai-Mass was still about fifteen miles distant —that was, a march of four hours.

Colonel Lamakin ordered a halt, and everybody, even the officers with their horses, sank down helplessly into the burning sand. Not a drop of water was left in the column; round about, as far as the eye could reach, there was nothing but the white sand. Lieutenant Stumm, in describing the scene to me, said that at this moment his senses were beginning to reel and the fever to mount to his brain. While all were still in this miserable condition, two wild forms were suddenly seen on a sand-hill far away in the distance. Colonel Lamakin had found a dried-up channel, and sent forward two Kirghiz, who discovered a small well—the Kuruk—at the distance of about a mile to the north.

Just as the men, with the staff, had refreshed themselves, news came that the portion of the troops which had been left behind under Lieutenant Grodikoff, three miles and a half from Ilte-Idshe, were unable to proceed any farther, and were now lying exhausted on the sand. At once every animal which could be ridden was sent back, with every and any sort of vessel that would hold water; and it was only after the troops had been thus relieved that they were able to resume their march, after a narrow escape from death.

About one o'clock on the night of the 14th the well of Kyzil-Agir was reached, and as it was expected the troops would come to Bei-Shagir the next day, and would thus be quite close to the frontiers of Khiva, a council of war was held. It was agreed that the advance-guard, under Skobeloff, should go forward to Lake Aibugir; but as General Verèvkin could scarcely reach that place before five or six days, a reconnoitring diversion was to be made towards the south as far as Kuna-Urgench, which town was, if necessary, to be taken. In the meantime the main body would remain at Lake Aibugir until the General arrived.

On the 16th news came from General Verèvkin which modified this plan. The General's messengers stated that fifteen days before he was but two marches from Lake Aibugir, and that he hoped on the 18th of May to reach Urga, on the Aral Sea. Colonel Lamakin was ordered to proceed, not in a southerly direction towards Lake Aibugir, but towards the north, so as to meet Verèvkin in Urga. The two columns would proceed together thence through Lake Aibugir to the fortified town of Kungrad.

On receipt of these orders, Colonel Lamakin sent messengers to recall Skobeloff. He, however, received the message too late, for, on the 17th, he had had an engagement with a considerable body of Turcomans, who were on their way to Khiva with a large caravan. In the attack which ensued several were killed, fifteen were taken prisoners, and 150 camels, with a large amount of provisions, were captured. Skobeloff, however, with another officer, and several of the Cossacks, were wounded.

The column was now marching northerly towards Urga; but on the 7th another message came from Verevkin, with the news that the General had already left the place, and was on his way to Kungrad, whither Lamakin was to follow. Thus once again the line of march was completely changed. Colonel Lamakin now came to the conclusion that, if he were to bring any assistance to the General before meeting the enemy, he should march very rapidly. He resolved, therefore, to go forward with the staff and the cavalry only, leaving the main body to follow under Pajaroff, and to make straight for Kungrad by forced marches, whether there were wells or no wells on the way.

The three days' march that followed were the severest the expedition passed through. There was no water the whole time, the only well on the road having been poisoned by the Turcomans, who threw the corpses of putrefying animals into it. On the night of the 22nd, an attempt was made to continue the march, so as to arrive at Kungrad a day earlier. But so dense was the darkness, that the troops, in spite of a number of torches, were continually going astray. So the army had to halt, and pass the night, without food, without water, in the middle of the desert.

On the morning of the 23rd of May the bed of the
Aibugir was reached; and during the course of this day the
first kibitkas of the Kungrad Kirghiz were met, and the
Khivan territory for the first time entered.   The morning
of the 24th of May was a joyful one, for on that morning
flowery meadows, green pasture lands, and flowing and
really fresh water were met with for the first time for two
months.

The same day they reached Kungrad, which they found
occupied by a strong body of Cossacks.   These had been
left behind by General Verevkin, who had the day before
taken up his march for the capital.

Both town and fortress were in the greatest state of
decay and desolation, caused by the continual wars of
rival Khans, and especially by a siege sustained some
fifteen years ago, when the town was in rebellion against
Khiva.   Kungrad has several times had a Khan of its
own, and more than once dictated laws to Khiva.   It is
now, however, almost depopulated, and will probably never
again lift its head in defiance of its victorious neighbour.

Up to this point neither General Verevkin nor Colonel
Lamakin had met any formidable resistance from the
Khivans.   They had shown themselves several times, but
had never offered any serious opposition.   They had simply
contented themselves with sending more or less insolent
messages, requesting the Russians to return to their
homes at their earliest convenience, under pain of the
extreme displeasure of the Khan.   General Verevkin
generally sent the messenger back without an answer.
There was one of these messages so curious and so illustrative of the extreme naïveté of the Khivans, that it deserves
especial notice.   The day before Verevkin entered Kungrad, he received a message from the governor, with the

very extraordinary request that the Russians should wait three days until his cannon could arrive; he would then be ready to give them battle. But if they blindly persisted in pushing forward before he was ready to meet them, he would simply refuse to fight! As the Russians blindly persisted, he was as good as his word, and abandoned Kungrad without striking a blow.

Soon after leaving Kungrad, however, the Turcomans commenced showing themselves in considerable numbers, and from this time forward, not a day passed without a skirmish, nor a night without an alarm. Sometimes they hung on the flanks of the army all day, uttering their wild cries, making feigned and real attacks on the train, firing from behind walls and trees, sometimes on the rear-guard, sometimes on the advance-guard, and harassing the troops from morning until night, and from dark until daylight.

The continual night alarms were especially harassing, for they kept the troops always on the alert, and prevented them from getting any rest. These night attacks I afterwards found in the campaign against the Turcomans to be something terrible, and their horror can only be understood by those who have experienced them.

About two o'clock the cavalry went on from Kungrad towards the south, and at last at nine o'clock on the same evening, after an uninterrupted march, reached General Verevkin's column. The staff had thus marched continually, without feeding or watering the horses, without halting or resting the men, and under a scorching sun, from five o'clock in the morning till nine in the evening.

Meantime the main body of the expedition, consisting almost entirely of infantry, under the command of Lieutenant-Colonel Pajaroff, had followed the staff and the

16

cavalry, enduring privations as great, if not greater, with the same heroic patience. Pajaroff divided his troops into two bodies, one of whom, under Major Avarsky, followed the same route as the staff. Pajaroff himself, after a day's rest at the well of Alan, started thence on the 20th of May, at two o'clock in the morning. For the first day his troops had nothing but brackish water, almost undrinkable. On the second day, the wells being poisoned by the corpses of animals, he had to rely on the very small quantity of water he had been able to carry along in vessels. At two o'clock on the morning of the 22nd he started from Kara-Kuduk, arriving at seven o'clock in the evening of the same day at the west shore of Lake Aibugir. During this journey of thirty miles he did not find a single well.

At two o'clock on the morning of the 23rd he started from Aibugir, reaching Irali-Kotchkan at three o'clock in the afternoon. During this march also, which was twenty-one miles in length, he found no well, and thus the troops travelled about fifty miles in thirty-seven hours, absolutely without water the whole time. The supply of water which he was able to bring along in vessels seems to have been wholly exhausted during the first two out of the five days of the march. Even during these two days the quantity of water was ridiculously out of proportion to the wants of the soldiers, and yet the infantry had heroism enough to give some of their water to the artillery.

This is one of the most remarkable marches on record

CHAPTER VII.

THE MARCH OF THE UNITED COLUMNS.

WHILE the events I have just related were transpiring, Captain Sitnikoff—the Admiral of the Aral fleet, whose name probably has not been forgotten by the reader—was sent from Kazala with a flotilla down the Aral Sea to the mouth of the Oxus. He was to ascend the river as far as it was possible and co-operate with the land forces as occasion might require.

In the beginning of May, the flotilla attacked and destroyed a well-fortified Khivan fort, called the Ak-Kala, on a branch of the Oxus called the Ulkun-Darya, with a loss of four killed and three or four wounded. Subsequently it went forty miles up the Amu. Here a Khirgiz came and informed Sitnikoff that he had seen General Verevkin's detachment and was willing to act as guide, in case Sitnikoff wished to communicate with him. One officer and eleven sailors were despatched to the General with letters, the Kirghiz acting as guide.

On the morning of the 17th, the troops of General Verevkin found, near the town of Kungrad, the corpses of these twelve Russian marines, without clothes and arms, and with their heads cut off. The Kirghiz messenger had been an agent of the enemy, and had probably decoyed the Russians into an ambuscade. Here ends the history of the operations of the flotilla during the campaign. Owing to obstructions placed in the river by the Khivans, it was unable to ascend high enough to render any assistance to the land forces.

On the 24th of May, the united columns of General Verèvkin and Colonel Lamakin took up their march. By this time General Kaufmann had reached Uch-Uchak.

At five o'clock on the morning of the 26th the troops had arrived at Kara-Baili, and at about twelve, a halt was made by the side of a small river; and here it was intended to make a two hours' stay for breakfast. Scarcely, however, had the troops stopped, when several shots were heard in the distance. Shortly afterwards a Cossack brought the news that an officer, who had gone forward with an escort of eight or ten Cossacks for the purpose of reconnoitring, had been attacked by a largely superior number of the enemy. Two sotnias of cavalry immediately rushed forward; but the Turcomans had already disappeared, having captured several horses, killed one Cossack, and wounded several others. Quick as had been their flight, they had found time to cut off the head of the Cossack whom they had killed. The cavalry pressed forward at full gallop for about half an hour, but no sign of the enemy was to be seen. Just as they returned, shots were heard on the flank of the column, where the enemy, whom they had just endeavoured in vain to catch, had now made an attack. Here, too, the enemy had succeeded in killing two camels and two men. The chase was renewed. This time the enemy collected themselves in a body, and were awaiting an attack. Several horses were taken, some prisoners made, and many of the Turcomans killed or wounded. One of the wounded Turcomans, who had received no less than five shots in the hip, and who bore his sufferings with the most wonderful fortitude, was induced, after much persuasion, to give some information. From him it was learned that a body of Turcomans, 400 or 500 strong, was around the army—a detachment from a force of 6000, mostly cavalry, which the Khan had sent forward, under the command of his brother, to defend the town of Khojali. This force was awaiting an attack before the town, and the Khan was resolved to defend himself to the last extremity.

Shortly afterwards the enemy appeared in force. At first it looked as if they were about to attack, but afterwards they halted, apparently awaiting an assault. The cavalry were sent forward with a rocket battery, and having fired some shots, the enemy retired.

After an hour or so they again appeared in force, but after they had advanced within 2000 or 3000 feet of the Russians, they halted, and began to retire slowly on Khojali. A few grenades hurried their retreat, and soon they entirely disappeared, with the exception of some scouts.

The advance on the town was then commenced. For a while the enemy continued to ride before the troops, sometimes coming up quite close, but soon they disappeared behind the gardens of the town, and then were seen no more.

When the army had approached within 500 yards of the gate of the city, a numerous deputation of the elders of the place came out and, promising submission, begged for mercy. They at the same time gave up a Kirghiz, whom the General had a month before sent with despatches to Kaufmann, and who had been taken by the Khan and imprisoned.

The troops remained for two days before the town, during which time their intercourse with the inhabitants was quite friendly. On the second day all the shops and the bazaar were opened, and trade with the soldiers in full swing.

Having resumed their march, the troops, on the 31st of May, saw for the first time the waters of the Amu-Darya.

On the morning of the 28th, a few shots that were fired by the Khivans proved the prelude of a general engagement.

The enemy was found assembled in force in a plain covered with reeds and tall grass. They had taken position on a number of sand-hills before the town of Manghit, towards which the Russian troops were advancing. The moment the Khivans caught sight of the army, their hosts of cavalry rushed upon them with wild cries. Spreading themselves out into a line seven or eight miles long, they attacked the Russians on all sides, but directed their principal efforts against the train of camels in the rear.

General Verévkin, who occupied the centre, brought four cannons to bear upon the enemy, and sent three others to the left flank. Nevertheless, the enemy continued to attack desperately, time after time, the cavalry, and at one moment actually approached within 200 yards of the staff of General Verevkin himself.

The cavalry on the right flank, under Colonel Leoncheff, was at one time very hard pressed, nor could it succeed in keeping back the advance of the enemy. Sweeping past him, they attacked the rear-guard, which they expected to find weak, imagining that all the cannon were at the head of the column. The vigorous resistance which they met there thoroughly took them by surprise, and their confusion was increased by seeing the main part of their own forces retreat over the heights of Manghit. After doing as much injury as they could to the camels, they, in their turn, followed their companions in flight.

Soon again the enemy renewed the attack. They followed the same tactics as before, but soon had to retreat before the well-directed fire of the artillery and the advance in force of the cavalry. They retired behind the town of Manghit, and then wholly disappeared. The troops then advanced and burnt the village just occupied by the enemy. After a short halt, the army advanced at three o'clock to the town and immediately occupied it. As they marched through, some of the enemy, who had taken refuge in the houses, fired on the troops; enraged by this, the soldiers reduced the town to ashes and slaughtered every man, woman, or child they could lay hands on. The losses on the Russian side on this day were one captain and eight men killed, about ten men severely and several slightly wounded.

The losses of the enemy must have been very large, and from this time forth they seemed to have lost all hope. Their resistance became feeble, and their operations, losing all unity of plan, degenerated into a mere guerilla warfare. If the Khivans had only properly understood their own advantages, they might have, with little trouble and no cost, placed insurmountable obstacles to the march of the Russians on their capital—possibly they might have even blocked up the road to Khiva. They could have destroyed all the bridges; and the column, which carried with it only a bridge with at most a span of forty yards, would have been unable to cross the canals, which were often forty to a hundred feet broad, and were for the most part very deep and swift. Hitherto, however, the troops everywhere found the bridges untouched, and so strong that it only required a few trunks of trees to make them fit for bearing heavy cannons. Now, however, the enemy for the first time resorted to the plan of burning the bridges. At first they caused much embarrassment to the advancing Russians, but after a while the cavalry, who now always were sent forward, succeeded in reaching the bridges just after they had been set on fire, and immediately put out the flames.

During the next few days several skirmishes took place, the enemy as usual attacking the rear, where the camels and forage waggons were.

The army continued its march through an extremely fertile country. One day, while the troops were passing through a network of thickly-grown gardens, mud buildings, and countless streams and canals, they were suddenly attacked from all sides. Their position, in the midst of a thickly-built Uzbeg village, was at first very critical. But after several mud walls had been knocked down, the infantry were able to get some cannon into position, and the enemy were defeated with great loss. The Russians only had one non-commissioned officer and one man severely and three men slightly wounded.

As the troops went on, the inhabitants came out from several villages, often with bleeding heads. Their own countrymen, they said, had ill-treated and plundered them, and they besought protection and help. The losses of the Khivan troops they declared to be enormous; and they told the horrible story that many, in terror of the shots of the advancing Russian infantry, had taken refuge in houses, and had there been burnt alive by the troops, who were quite ignorant of their being inside.

A message came in the mid-day of the 4th from the Khan, begging for an armistice. General Verevkin of course at once saw that the sole object of the Khan was to gain time, and rejected the proposal.

The letter of the Khan was a curious production, and excited much merriment in the Russian camp. It began by saying that a document of a similar import had been forwarded to General Kaufmann. He asked the Russian commanders, in the most naive and friendly manner, to be kind enough to become his guests in Khiva. He himself had always entertained the most friendly feelings towards the Russian troops, and it would be particularly agreeable to him to be allowed to receive and entertain them splendidly in his capital. He asked three or four days, that he might be able to make the festal preparations on a proper scale of magnificence. Repeatedly he assured the Russian commanders of his friendliest feelings, and begged them, above all, not to confound his attitude with that of the plundering and barbarous Turcomans, who had recently, in a thoroughly unjustifiable manner, had the criminal presumption to oppose the Russian troops. With these robbers and waylayers he had nothing to do: on the contrary, he regarded them as his worst enemies

On the 7th of June the column reached the extensive gardens of a country palace of the Khan, Shanah-Tchik, and were thus within two miles and a half of the northern gate of the city. There a stay of three days was made, during which there were several engagements—great and small—with the Khivan troops. In one of these the enemy lost between 400 and 500 men.

No news had recently come of the advance of General Kaufmann . a report, on the contrary, was current that he had been obliged, from want of provisions and waggons, to return to the Oxus, and that he was now sixty-five miles from Khiva. These facts, together with the harassing effects upon the men and horses of hourly encounters with the enemy, and the report that the Khan was preparing for a great battle before the walls of the town, convinced General Verevkin that he would not be justified in any longer delaying an attack on Khiva.

Accordingly, on the evening of the 8th, the proper dispositions were made for reconnoitring the city on the following day.

On the morning of the 9th of June, an advance was made, General Verevkin, as usual, with his staff, leading the head of the column. The enemy occasionally appeared in large masses, but made no attempt at an attack. After a while, the troops found themselves in a narrow road, not more than four yards wide. The road was inclosed by walls; and all around there was an impassable network of houses, gardens, and canals.

They proceeded along this narrow path silently and cautiously, raising a cloud of dust so thick that no man could see his neighbour. Suddenly broke upon their ears, like a thunderclap, a crash of musketry and the roar of artillery, followed by a volley of bullets that went shrieking overhead, and the heavy thud of round shot striking in the mud walls beyond them. It was a surprise, almost an ambuscade. Owing to the trees, the walls, and the clouds of dust which enveloped them, they had approached within 200 yards of the walls of Khiva without being aware of it; and the Khivans had opened on them at point-blank range.

Discharge after discharge followed, but, fortunately for the Russians, the aim of the Khivans was too high, and the greater part of the bullets passed overhead. The men began to fall, however, and it became necessary to act at once.

Retreat would have been impossible, had it been desirable. The only course open to them was to advance towards the walls under a fire which at every step became more destructive.

General Verevkin gave the order, and the troops started forward at a run. In a moment they found themselves in an open field before the walls of the city, in front of one of the gates. Right in front of them, at the distance of 100 yards, and the same distance from the walls, was a kind of earthwork thrown up across the road, defended by four pieces of cannon. The artillery was ordered to advance; but, in the meantime, the fire from this battery proved so galling that General Verevkin determined to capture it. Two companies of infantry, under Major Burovstoff, were ordered out for the attack. The next moment they rushed forward along the dusty road with a shout. But a few yards in front of the breastwork they found a deep, wide canal, over which was a narrow bridge. This bridge the enemy had, strangely enough, not destroyed. They dashed over it, under a terrible fire from the walls and gates of the city, as well as from the breastwork itself, leaped over the obstructions with a yell, and bayoneted the gunners. They had virtually possession of the guns, but so many obstructions were in the way, and the fire of the enemy was so deadly, that it was difficult to drag them off. They were obliged to take shelter behind the banks of the canal; and here crouching, returned, as best they could, the fire from the walls. Their bullets took little effect on the Khivans in their protected position. Had they but had scaling ladders, they might have found it less dangerous to storm the walls than to retire. The Russian artillery had now got to work; and the storming party, placed between two fires, heard the solid shot of the Khivans and the shells of the Russians pass shrieking over their heads so low as to almost touch them.

This continued for a quarter of an hour, and then the Russian artillery, having for a moment silenced the fire of the enemy, ceased, in order to give the storming party a chance to retreat. They seized the opportunity, laid hold of the guns, and commenced dragging them off. But the Khivans instantly reopened their fire, and the Russians were obliged to haul the guns off one at a time over the narrow bridge and then along the straight road 200 yards before they reached shelter. They only succeeded in dragging off three of the guns, and were obliged to leave one behind.

In the meantime General Verevkin had been wounded. He received a shot just over the left eye, which well-nigh proved fatal. After giving orders for planting a battery to breach the walls, he retired, and surrendered his command to Colonel Saranchoff.

A regular bombardment was now opened under the direction of Colonel Skobeloff, which was continued until four o'clock.

Then a messenger arrived from the Khan, asking for a suspension of hostilities, and begging that the bombardment might cease, in order to negotiate terms of capitulation.

Colonels Saranchoff and Lamakin granted a suspension

of hostilities for a few hours; but the messenger had scarcely left the camp, when the Khivans again opened fire. The Russians immediately recommenced the bombardment.

Again a messenger arrived from the Khan, assuring the General that he was not responsible for the firing, which was continued contrary to his orders and wishes by the refractory and intractable Turcomans. As this was regarded as an instance of the impudent effrontery of the Khan, the bombardment was continued. It turned out, however, that the Khan was in earnest, and that he had no control over the Turcomans.

About sunset, orders came from Kaufmann, with whom communication had been established, to stop the bombardment, which order was obeyed somewhat reluctantly. Thus ended the affair of the 9th of June.

CHAPTER VIII.

THE ENTRY INTO THE CITY.

The Khan's letter to General Kaufmann, of which I have spoken in a previous chapter, proffered his submission, and begged that the bombardment of the city might cease. Kaufmann, it will be remembered, was still ten miles distant from the city. He immediately despatched a courier with instructions to General Verevkin to stop the bombardment. He likewise wrote a letter to the Khan, telling him to ride out the next morning, before the gates of the city, with 100 followers, and there the terms of surrender would be dictated to him.

The next morning at sunrise we were again on the march, but the wildest rumours were afloat about what had passed at Khiva during the night.

The people along the road, who came flocking to meet us in great numbers with their peace-offerings, informed us that the Khan had been driven out by the enraged inhabitants when they heard of his meditated surrender, that his brother had been chosen in his place, and that they were going to resist à outrance. It was another 4th of September, in short, arranged after the latest French style, as well as we could make out, and it was even said that Rochefort and Cluseret had arrived, and declared the

Commune. Upon tracing the latter part of this story to its source, however, I found it had originated with the Grand Duke Nicholas, who recounted it with the gravest face imaginable. The joy expressed throughout the detachment at the prospect of a fight was unbounded, but it was soon clouded. About three miles from Khiva we were met by a delegation, headed by Said Emir Ul-Umar, the old uncle of the Khan before mentioned, Governor of Hazar-Asp. He came to surrender the town, and informed General Kaufmann that the Khan, instead of being driven out by the people, had run away of his own accord. He had left instructions for his wives and slaves to follow, but the people had prevented the women from leaving the palace, and kept them prisoners in their own rooms, as an acceptable peace-offering to General Kaufmann. His flight had occurred in this wise.

It appeared that the Turcomans were determined to fight to the last. Despite the Khan's orders to the contrary, they kept firing upon General Verevkin's troops, who were before the walls. To this fire the Russians, of course, replied, and the fight was renewed in a desultory way. The Russians, at last, recommenced the bombardment of the city, which they kept up at intervals during the night. Some of the shells had even fallen into the palace, and one was afterwards picked up in the stables by the Russians, which had not exploded. This continued bombardment the Khan had become frightened at, and he had fled with a few hundred Turcomans to Imukchir, near Iliah. But the people of the town, so far from wishing to continue the fight, were ready and willing to submit.

Said Emir Ul-Umar was about seventy years old, very feeble, and with a perfectly idiotic expression of face, caused by a hanging lower jaw and open mouth, said to be the result of opium eating. He was not so imbecile as he looked, however, and had proved the soundness of his judgment by advising the Khan for years to accede to the demands of the Russians, and thus prevent an invasion. He had long been in disgrace on account of his pacific views with regard to the Russians. But it was because of these same views that he was now charged by the Khan to surrender the city and to intercede for him. He was dressed in a bright green khalat, the tall black sheep-skin hat of the Khivans, large boots made of unblacked leather, pointed and turned up at the toes, and garnished with high narrow heels.

Kaufmann related to me that Said Emir Ul-Umar had at one time persuaded the Khan to accede to the Russian demands, but that Mat Murad, another of the Khan's counsellors, had dissuaded him from it by the following argument:—" When I was a boy," he said, " very young indeed, I remember hearing it said that the Russians were coming—but they did not come. And since then there has been a report nearly every year that they were coming. Now I am an old man, and still the Russians have not come, and I do not believe that they ever will come." This argument proved conclusive, and the Khan only discovered its fallacy when the Russians were thundering away at his capital. A younger brother of the Khan, Atta-Djan, who had been in prison for the last two years, and who had just been liberated, accompanied Said Emir Ul-Umar, and, as it soon appeared, was a candidate for the throne. General Kaufmann received him kindly, and promised that if the Khan did not return, he would set him up in his place, but not otherwise. Atta-Djan is a tall, rawboned, rather lubberly young man, and does not look as though his was just the hand to take the helm of state. He is said to be more clever than he looks, however, and is much liked by the people.

It was now about nine o'clock in the morning, and the column resumed its march, old Said Emir Ul-Umar and Atta-Djan riding along with the staff. The day was growing hot, and the dust becoming awful; it rose up around us in a thick cloud, so dense that at times you could not see the man riding next you. At ten o'clock we were within a mile and a half of Khiva, and were met by a part of Verevkin's detachment in full uniform, drawn up to meet us. The troops exchanged hearty cheers, as they met each other for the first time after their long march from almost different quarters of the globe; but General Verevkin was not there to receive Kaufmann, and we soon learned that he was not able to leave his tent.

Kaufmann turned off the road, under some trees, to hear the story of the Orenburg detachment. During this time several reports of cannon were heard, which was rather extraordinary, considering that the city had already capitulated. I did not receive the explanation of this circumstance for several days afterwards, as for some unaccountable reason all the officers in our detachment tried to keep it a secret from me. It was only upon meeting some of the officers of the Orenburg troops that I heard the story.

The explanation was this. The Turcomans, not at all satisfied with this tame ending to the war, were resolved to fight awhile longer. General Kaufmann had advanced by the road from Hazar-Asp, towards the Hazar-Asp gate, whereas General Verevkin's attack of the day before was

on the northern or Hazavat gate, about half a mile distant.
The Turcomans, in spite of the fact that Said Emir
Ul-Umar was surrendering the city on the Hazar-Asp
side, still kept up an irregular fire on Verévkin's troops,
against whom they seemed to have a grudge. I cannot
help expressing my admiration for these people. Long
after the Khan and all the other inhabitants of the oasis
had given up the struggle, they continued it, if all the
people of Khiva had shown their courage and pluck, the
result of the campaign might have been very different.
The Russians would undoubtedly have taken the place, but
with such great loss as to have rendered their position
for the moment a very precarious one.

The command, when General Verevkin was disabled,
had devolved upon Colonel Saranchoff, a somewhat fiery
officer, who was as much disposed to fight as the Turcomans. And he was surrounded by several spirited
young officers, such as Colonel Skobeloff and Count
Shuvaloff, who were only too glad of the pretext thus
offered them.

In spite of the fact that Kaufmann was making a
peaceable entry on the other side, they, chafing under
the fire of the Turcomans, determined to take the town
by storm.

Accordingly a few shells were thrown against the Hazavat
gate, which was soon battered down, and Colonel Skobeloff and Count Shuvaloff, at the head of about 1000 men,
rushed to the assault, under a lively fire of small arms
from the walls. As soon as the Russians got possession
of the gate, the Turcomans retired from the walls into
the streets and houses, and still kept up a discharge of
small arms. The Russians cleared the streets before them
with rockets, and thus advanced in a kind of running

KHIVA AND THE HAZAR-ASP GATE.

From a design by Capt. Feodoroff, of the Turkistan Sharpshooters.

fight, into the city, until they reached the palace of the Khan.

They had scarcely been here five minutes when the Tashkent detachment was reported entering by the Hazar-Asp gate, in grand state, with music and flying colours. Skobeloff instantly gave the order to retreat, and retired by the gate by which he had entered. In this affair Count Shuvaloff received a severe contusion from a falling beam, from which he had not yet recovered when he left Khiva, while some fourteen soldiers were wounded.

In the meantime we on the other side of the city had been awaiting the result of the negotiations with Said Emir Ul-Umar. Everything having been satisfactorily arranged, General Golovatchoff moved forward. Two companies of infantry led the head of the column, followed by four pieces of cannon, after those two more companies, and 200 Cossacks.

It was now about noon, and in ten minutes we were within sight of the renowned city. We did not see it until we were within less than half a mile, owing to the masses of trees everywhere that completely hid it from our view. At last it broke upon us, amid the clouds of dust which we had raised. Great, heavy mud walls, high, and battlemented with heavy round buttresses, and a ditch, partly dry, partly filled with water, over which we could see the tops of trees, a few tall minarets, domes of mosques, and one immense round tower that reflected the rays of the sun like porcelain. We were before the gate of Hazar-Asp. A heavy arched and covered gateway, ten feet wide by twenty deep, arched over with brick, and flanked by heavy towers with loop holes—a little fortress in itself. Through this gate, which had been opened to receive us—in a cloud of dust so dense and thick that I, at times, could not see my horse's head—we marched with flying colours, a military band from the Orenburg detachment playing the national Russian air, "Bodje Tsaria Haranyie." As we passed through the long arched gateway we left the dust behind us, and emerging from this, found the city before us.

I think every one of us experienced a feeling of disappointment. We had not expected much in the way of architectural display or of imposing beauty; nevertheless we looked for something striking and picturesque, and in this we were disappointed. There are points of view in Khiva which are very picturesque, but this was not one of them, and the great porcelain tower, the most striking object, now that we were near it, was hid from view by intervening walls or trees. Immediately before us, along the interior of the walls, was a wide open space, with a few trees here and there, then a few mud houses and sheds, not more than ten or fifteen feet high; a little to the right a great number of round semispherical tombs— there is a cemetery almost in the middle of the city— farther on more mud houses, taller and more pretentious, with high porches, trees here and there among them; then the mud walls of the citadel, behind which arose a minaret or two. Here there was no soul to greet us, but as we entered a long, narrow, winding street, built up of bare, black, hideous mud walls, we began to see small groups of men in the lateral streets, in dirty, ragged tunics, and long beards, with hats off, bowing timidly to us as we passed. These were the inhabitants, and they were not yet sure whether they would all be massacred or not. With what strange awe and dread they must have gazed upon us as we passed, dust-covered and grimy, after our march of 600 miles over the desert, which they had considered impassable. Grim, stern, silent and invincible. we must have appeared to them like some strange, powerful beings of an unknown world.

Then we came upon a crowd of Persian slaves, who received us with shouts, cries, and tears of joy. They were wild with excitement. They had heard that wherever the Russians went slavery disappeared, and they did not doubt that it would be the case here. Some had already liberated themselves, and I saw several engaged in cutting the chains of three or four miserable beings, shouting the while, and laughing and crying all at once in the wildest manner.

I may as well state in this connection that my people, curiously enough, found the young Kirghiz whose mother had come to me in Bey-Tabuk's tent, and begged me to have him set at liberty. They found him heavily loaded with irons for attempting to run away, but they soon set him at liberty, to his great joy and satisfaction. I afterwards saw him gaily equipped in a red tunic, provided with sword and gun, and mounted on a horse he had probably taken from his master.

We passed through the narrow, dusty, crooked street until we came to the citadel, which we entered by a long, heavy, arched brick gateway. As soon as we were through this gateway we had a nearer view of the large tower, which now came out in brilliant colours of blue, green, purple, and brown. Taking a narrow street, not more than ten feet wide, leading directly towards this tower, we soon arrived upon a square about fifty by seventy-five yards, which proved to be the great square before the palace of the Khan. One side of this square was taken up by the palace, a huge, rambling structure, with mud-battlemented walls about twenty feet high; opposite was a new médressé not yet finished; the other two sides were filled up by sheds and private houses, while at the south-eastern angle of the palace rose, beautiful and majestic, the famous sacred tower of Khiva.

It was about 30 feet in diameter at the bottom, and tapered gradually to the top, a height of about 125 feet, where it appeared to have a diameter of 15 feet. It had neither pedestal nor capital, nor ornament of any kind—a plain, round tower—but its surface was covered with burnt tiles, brightly coloured in blue, green, purple, and brown on a pure white ground, arranged in a variety of broad stripes and figures; the whole producing a most brilliant and beautiful effect. The tower is likewise covered with verses of the Koran, and is held in great reverence by the Khivans; from its top may be heard, every evening at sunset, the shrill, piercing voice of a mullah calling the people to prayer.

The tops of the two towers flanking the palace gate were embellished in the same way as the large tower, and parts of the façade of the new médressé opposite, not yet finished, were evidently to be decorated in like manner. Near the middle of this place was a hole about ten feet square and six deep, which, I afterwards learned, was the place where criminals were executed.

We rode into this square, and formed around it to await the arrival of General Kaufmann. He soon rode in, followed by the Grand Duke, Prince Eugene, and the staff, and was greeted with cheers. We all then alighted, and entered the gateway of the palace, which was partly obstructed by a heavy brass cannon. Having passed this, we came into a long, narrow, irregular court. To the left it branched off, and led to the stables; to the right was a pair of high heavy wooden doors, leading to the harem,

THE GREAT SQUARE IN KHIVA.

On the left the Great Tower, and the Medressé of Kuli Khan. In the centre the Khan's Palace. *From a design by Capt. Feodoroff.*

and right in front a mass of low, irregular, mud structures. These we entered by a dark, narrow corridor, first into a dark room about eight feet by sixteen, then into another room, nearly the same size, lighted by a hole in the roof, then into another dark corridor, from which we emerged into the grand court of the palace. It is about forty feet square, paved with brick, only shaded by a small elm-tree growing in one corner, and shut in by walls twenty feet high, over which, on the northern side, rose the square mud tower of the harem. On the southern side was the grand hall of state, or audience chamber of the Khan.

Imagine a kind of porch entirely open to the court, thirty feet high, twenty wide, ten deep, and flanked on either side by towers ornamented with blue and green tiles, in the same way as the large tower on the square; a floor raised six feet above the pavement of the court, the roof supported by two carved, slender, wooden pillars, the whole resembling much the stage of a theatre, and you will have a very good idea of the grand hall of state, wherein the Khan of Khiva sits and dispenses justice. We all mounted the steps leading up to this kind of stage, Kaufmann, Golovatchoff, the Grand Duke Nicholas, Prince Leuchtenberg, staff officers and all, and threw ourselves down to rest, while the band struck up an air from ' La Belle Hélène,' followed by another from 'Bluebeard.' As the old familiar music broke upon our ears, and the whole absurd farce of Offenbach appeared to our mind's eyes, we of the younger part of the company set up a shout of delight that made the old palace ring.

Old Jakub Beg, one of the Khan's ministers, brought us in some ice-water, a thing we had never hoped for in Khiva, with wheaten cakes, apricots, and cherries, with which we merrily proceeded to refresh ourselves. The Khan, Said Muhamed-Rahim-Bogadur-Khan, had fled; the Russians were in possession of his palace and his harem: and so fell Khiva, the great stronghold of Islamism, in Central Asia, after a succession of disastrous expeditions extending over a period of 200 years.

CHAPTER IX.

PREVIOUS EXPEDITIONS AGAINST KHIVA.[*]

IT may not now be without interest to take a retrospective glance at the previous expeditions that were directed against Khiva.

The first of these was undertaken by the Yaik, or Ural Cossacks. It was organised, set on foot, and carried out by a famous Cossack chieftain, and was simply a freebooting expedition on a large scale. He actually succeeded in conquering the Khanate. Probably finding the Khan unprepared for war, he drove him out, took possession of his capital, and seized his treasure and his wives. He then declared himself Khan, and governed the country, it is said, for two or three months, during which time he converted the Khan's favourite wife to Christianity and married her. At last, finding he could maintain himself no longer, he determined to retreat, and started back to the Ural, loaded with booty.

The Khan having, in the meantime, assembled a large force, pursued the invaders hotly, with projects of direst vengeance, and overtook them at last. A great battle was

---

[*] The account of these expeditions I have obtained principally from translations of Russian papers, kindly furnished me by Mr. Michell, of the India Office.

fought, in which the Cossacks were completely routed and cut to pieces. Only five or six escaped to tell the tale The Cossack leader, seeing escape hopeless, killed his newly-converted bride, that she might not fall a victim to the vengeance of the enraged Khan, and died, sword in hand, with a hecatomb of slain Mussulmen around him.

Some years later, another expedition of Cossacks made a dash upon Kuna-Urgench, captured about a thousand women whom they wanted for wives, and retreated across the desert, laden with spoil. The Khan again pursued, overtook, and slaughtered them nearly to the last man. Another Cossack expedition proved equally disastrous. They did not even reach the oasis, but were met halfway by the Khivans, and overpowered by superior numbers.

The next expedition undertaken against Khiva was that of Beckovitch-Cherkassky in 1717, under Peter the Great. In the year 1700, Peter had received an envoy from the Khan of Khiva, Shah-Niaz, who, finding it somewhat difficult to maintain his authority against his rebellious subjects, sought the powerful protection of the Russian monarch. Shah-Niaz begged Peter to accept the submission of the Khanate. Peter, although incessantly occupied with his project of connecting Russia with Europe, never abandoned the idea of increasing the commercial relations of his empire with Asia. Accordingly he intimated in a letter to Shah-Niaz his acceptance of the submission of Khiva.

But no further steps were taken to conclude the agreement thus entered into. At length, in the year 1714, a Turcoman, Hofa-Nefes by name, who had been to Khiva, in an interview with Peter, asserted that in the country bordering the Amu gold sand was to be found, and that the river, which formerly flowed into the Caspian, and which, in fear of the Russians, had been diverted into the Aral Sea by the Khivans, might, by destroying a dam, be made to run again in its old channel. In such a work, the Russians would receive the willing assistance of the Turcomans.

To determine the truth of these statements, Peter sent Prince Beckovitch-Cherkassky to explore the shores of the Caspian, and to see what were the prospects of sending an expedition along the supposed ancient bed of the Oxus to Khiva. Beckovitch spent three years on his task; exploring the eastern shores of the Caspian, and building forts to protect the country of which the Russians took possession there; and he also satisfied himself that, as reported by the Turcoman, the Oxus had formerly flowed into the Caspian. Having reported these results to Peter, the Tsar determined to send an expedition to Khiva to assert the claim, which he founded upon the submission of Shah-Niaz, seventeen years before. A force for the purpose, composed of about 4,000 regular and irregular troops, was organised by Beckovitch.

This expedition left Gurieff, on the mouth of the Ural, in the beginning of June. They marched around the northern shores of the Caspian until they struck the old caravan route to Khiva, where they started across the desert. Undertaken during the summer heat, the march proved a terrible one. By the time they had reached Khiva, one fourth of their entire forces had died. They traversed in sixty-five days 900 miles of the barren and waterless desert, during the very hottest season of the year, and arrived about the middle of August upon the delta of the Oxus, within 100 miles of Khiva.

Before reaching this point, Beckovitch had sent a letter

to Khiva, in which he assured the Khan that he was not going to make war, and that he came on a friendly mission from the Tsar, which he would explain on arriving. By this time the Khan, Shah-Niaz, had died, and had been succeeded by Shir-Gazi, a Khan, whose views with regard to the Russians were very different from those of his predecessor. The messengers of Beckovitch, on their arrival in Khiva, were thrown into prison, and the Khan hastened to assemble a numerous army of Khivans, Turcomans, Kirghiz, and Kara-Kalpaks, resolved upon offering resistance.

On the day when the Russians reached the oasis, the Khivan cavalry appeared in sight, and without any preliminary parley, bore down on the Russian camp. The battle, thus begun, lasted till nightfall, when the Khivans withdrew. Foreseeing a fresh attack, Beckovitch fortified his camp during the night, and placed his six guns in position. The fight was renewed next morning, and continued for two days longer, when the Khivans, finding that they were unable to beat back the Russians, resorted to negotiations. A messenger came from the Khan to say that the attack on the Russians had been made without his orders, and that, if Beckovitch had really come as a friendly envoy to Khiva, he had no cause to fear the enmity of the Khivans. Negotiations were now entered into, and soon resulted in a preliminary treaty, which was confirmed by oath; the Khan kissing the Koran, and Beckovitch the cross.

The Khan then invited Beckovitch to accompany him into his capital, and, having accepted the offer, Beckovitch, leaving the main body of his army under Colonel Frankenburg, with instructions to follow him at an easy distance, marched forward with a body of 1000 men.

Two days' march from the town, Beckovitch halted; and here he had a long talk with the Khan. In this interview, the Khan represented the difficulty of finding quarters and provisions for the large body of Russians in the capital, and suggested to Beckovitch that he should divide his own escort and the column behind into several small parties, which could then be distributed among the towns nearest the capital.

Beckovitch might have been expected to have viewed with suspicion so extraordinary a proposal. But his mind had unquestionably become affected by this time. On the very day he started from Astrakan, his wife and two daughters were drowned; and this, together with the fatigues of the journey across the desert, the losses of his troops, and the terrible anxieties of his position, had almost reduced him to madness. In place of showing any suspicion of the Khan's intentions, he immediately sent back orders to Colonel Frankenburg to divide his troops, as had been suggested; and when that officer refused three times to obey these orders, he despatched a fourth messenger, once more repeating his command, with the threat of a court martial in case of disobedience. Frankenburg accordingly divided his troops into five parts, and allowed them to be distributed according to the Khan's instructions. Beckovitch reduced his own escort to 200 men.

He had scarcely made these dispositions, when he was surrounded and attacked by the Khivans. Some of his troops were cut down, some secured as prisoners. He and his officers were then thrown into prison, and, after undergoing various tortures, were beheaded. At the same time, upon a preconcerted signal, the whole Khivan population rose and slaughtered the small bodies of Russians in detail. Of the whole 4000 men who started
18

for Khiva, only forty escaped. These, having been retained as prisoners for a long time, were at last released, upon payment of a large ransom. Curious to say, two of Beckovitch's brothers were among those who were allowed to escape. So ended the fourth expedition against Khiva.

During the next 120 years, the Cossacks and the Khivans changed *rôles*. The Cossacks, who had formerly attacked and plundered the Khivans, were now themselves attacked and plundered. Caravans, on their way to trade in Central Asia, were daily seized, and thousands of Cossacks and other Russian subjects were captured and kept in slavery in Khiva.

In 1839 these forays had reached such proportions as to be no longer tolerable. Several attempts were made to induce the Khan by negotiations to put a stop to these depredations. All these attempts failing, the Russians determined to send an expedition against Khiva.

The expedition was organised by General Perovski in Orenburg. After a year's preparations, a body of about 5000 men, with twenty-two guns and a transport train of 10,000 camels, started from Orenburg about the 1st December, 1839. It was supposed to be impossible to cross the desert in summer, on account of the scarcity of water; and it had, accordingly, been decided to attempt the march in winter.

By the middle of December, the thermometer (Réaumur) marked thirty-two degrees below zero, and the mercury was congealed in the glass. The troops, nevertheless, reached Emba in good condition; not a man having died from cold or exposure. But the winter proved to be an exceptionably severe one. Snow had already fallen to a depth that had seldom been seen before, even on the steppe. From this time forward, the camels began to die rapidly, and before the troops had reached halfway to Khiva, the number of the animals had been reduced by death and exhaustion to 5000, instead of the 10,000 with which the expedition had started. The hardships suffered by the soldiers were terrible. In order to spare the camels as much as possible, the infantry had to march in front of them in four files, so as to make a beaten track for them to advance upon. Where the snow was very deep, the cavalry were made to pass and repass several times over the same ground, and in some places the infantry had to shovel away the snow, the object still being to make the road easy to the camels. But notwithstanding all these precautions, the animals continued to die daily in large numbers.

The fall of a camel, besides it own loss, caused a serious amount of inconvenience to the army. The load of the animal had to be taken off, then transferred to another; and afterwards the body had to be removed out of the way, before the column could proceed The men, sinking to their knees, and sometimes to their waists in snow, exhausted their strength in labour of this kind. In some places, the snow, hard as ice, was able to support any weight, but in other places, it was soft, and then the men had to use incredible exertions to extricate the horses, camels, and guns. Some days, after all this fatigue and struggle, a distance of but two and a half miles was made.

During the terrible "Burans" or snowstorms, it was impossible to advance; and, while one of these lasted, the soldiers had simply to camp, and wait until it was over. The cold became more and more terrible every day. Even the night halt brought no relief: 19,000 packages had, whenever the troops made a stop, to be unloaded; and before a fire could be lit, the roots and shrubs from which it was made had to be dug out of the hard, frozen ground. It had then to be cleared of snow for the horses and camels; and it was not till eight or nine o'clock in the evening that the soldier could obtain a little repose. At two or three o'clock next morning, he was obliged to rise and recommence the march. In such cold weather it was impossible to wash linen or pay any attention to personal cleanliness. Many men did not once change their linen, or even take off their clothes during the whole campaign. Thus, covered with vermin and dirt, and weakened by fatigue and hunger, they soon were stricken by disease.

By the 1st of February, the expedition had reached the spring of Ak-Bulak, on the edge of the elevated plateau of Ust-Urt, nearly halfway to Khiva. General Perovski found at this point that his camels were dying at the rate of 100 a day; that less than 5000 only were left out of 10,000; and that those which remained were now able to carry but one-fourth of their original burden. As to the soldiers, the sick list was increasing at a terrible rate. 236 men had died; 528 were under treatment; while a great number had been left behind as a garrison at Emba. Deducting all these, the effective force only amounted to about 2000 men. And there was still a distance of 500 miles before the inhabited portions of Khiva could be reached. General Perovski decided to retreat.

During the march back, the same difficulties had to be encountered; the cold continued with unceasing severity, the thermometer ranging from fifteen to twenty degrees below zero (Réaumur). There were, besides, high winds and little water; and, as before, the only fuel was small plants and roots, which had to be dug for in the snow. The march back was thus attended with the same difficulties and sufferings as the advance; and there were besides the discouraging influence of a retreat. The roads were strewn with the bodies of the camels they had left behind; and the carcasses were by this time devoured by the wolves and foxes, who had gathered among the prey in great numbers. The sick-list increased terribly; scurvy began to spread among the officers as well as men. At last, the number of invalided reached the extraordinary figure of 3000 out of 5000. Haggard, dispirited, and utterly worn out, the troops reached Fort Emba on the 20th of February, and here awaited the return of spring.

Such was the fate of the fifth expedition against Khiva. That organised by General Kaufmann was the sixth.

CHAPTER X.

IN THE PALACE.

GENERAL KAUFMANN remained in the palace of the Khan
about two hours, and then, accompanied by the Grand
Duke and Prince Eugene, rode out to the camp of the
Orenburg detachment, in order to see General Verevkin,
who, as will be remembered, had been wounded in the
affair of the day before. General Golovatchoff remained
in the palace with three or four companies of troops, part
of whom were camped in the court, and a part on the
square before the palace.

After a nap of a couple of hours—which I obtained
stretched out on the floor of the great hall of state—a
cup of tea, and some brown wheaten cakes, I commenced
looking about the palace. The afternoon was now well
advanced, and the heat, which had been so oppressive
during the day, began to abate.

The palace, as I have before stated, was a large irregular structure, consisting of a mass of low mud
buildings, enclosed by a heavy mud wall, twenty feet high,
a rather fine gateway, and two or three watch-towers.
To the left, upon entering, were the stables, which we
found empty. On this side were also several suites of
rooms or dwellings, each composed of a small court, sur-

rounded by walls ten or fifteen feet high, and a number
of small rooms that opened into it. On one side of this
court there was always a high open porch, very lofty,
facing to the north—a peculiarity of Khivan archi-
tecture.

The rooms were dark, generally receiving no light nor
air, except through the door, or sometimes a little square
hole in the wall or ceiling; and although they may
have been not at all uncomfortable when furnished with
bright-coloured rugs, bed-covers, and cushions, they
now, bare and naked, presented, with their mud walls and
uneven floors, an appearance rather suggestive of cow-
stables than anything else. We found a few bedclothes,
carpets, and cooking utensils in some of them, which,
scattered about as they were, gave token of the hasty
flight of their late owners I am not sure, however,
whether the inhabitants of this part of the palace had
had time to carry off their most valuable effects, or
whether the people had got in after the flight of the
Khan and plundered the place.

Directly in front of the main entrance, at the distance
of forty feet, was a high, strong, double door, leading into
the harem, and a little to the left of this, the low corridor
before spoken of, which led to the principal court of the
palace. In the rooms immediately surrounding this court
lived the principal officers of the Khan's suite. The room
immediately forming the back of the great porch, or hall
of state, which I have described as resembling the stage of
a theatre, was the Khan's treasure-room.

In the course of the afternoon, General Golovatchoff had
this place opened. It was a low, vaulted room, the same
size as the porch; the walls and ceilings were covered
with frescoes, representing flowers and vines in the crudest

and most unmatched colours it is possible to imagine. On one end of it, set up on a kind of platform, was a large square old chair, broad and low-backed, and covered with leather. This was the Khan's throne. The chair was of superior workmanship, and was quite a curiosity. It showed some very skilful carving and incrusting; and reminded one somewhat of the old throne of the Russian Tsars shown in St. Petersburg. On the upper part of the back there was an oval silver plate with the inscription, "In the time of Mahomed Rahim Shah of Kharezm in the year 1231. Done by the unworthy Mahomed." At the other end of the room were three or four iron chests, with heavy locks. These were open and empty, all but one, which contained, perhaps, thirty pounds' worth of Khivan silver. In another were a saddle, bridle, and harness, all covered with gold plating and set with rubies, emeralds, and turquoises, which, though for the most part of an inferior quality, produced in the sunlight a very brilliant effect.

Precious stones in this country, so far as I had occasion to observe, though often large, had many blemishes. Although there were some very big emeralds and rubies, they were full of holes, or the colour was so pale as to make them valueless.

Leaning up against the wall, or lying on the floor in heaps, were arms—swords, daggers, guns, pistols, and revolvers of almost every conceivable shape and description. There were several splendid old matchlocks, with their crooked stocks and long, slender, tapering barrels, beautifully inlaid with gold, together with a good many guns of a more modern style, and one beautiful English double-barrel breech-loading hunting rifle, No. 12 or 16, with a good supply of cartridges, percussion caps, moulds for round shot, and instruments for refilling the cartridges.

This rifle, as we soon learned, was a present from Lord Northbrook. Close by, was found the letter written by the Viceroy of India, in September, 1872, to the Khan, in reply to his demand for help against the Russians, besides a field-glass and a music-box, and several other little things presented by Lord Northbrook.

Then there were pistols of all kinds, from the old-fashioned flint-lock to something resembling a Colt's revolver; and even one very bad Russian imitation of the Smith and Weston cartridge-revolver, which showed at least that the Khan knew something of the perfection of modern firearms. There were swords of all sorts. Two or three sabres of English manufacture; a number of the broad, beautiful, slightly-curved blades of Khorassan, inlaid with gold; several slender Persian scimitars, with scabbards set in turquoises and emeralds; short, thick, curved poignards and knives from Affghanistan, all richly mounted and provided with sheaths set in precious stones. Beautiful carpets, coverlets in silk of the brightest colour, cushions, pillows, khalats, and a number of fine Cashmere shawls were scattered about in the greatest confusion, and gave evidence of the hurried departure of the Khan.

At the end of this room was a little stairway, leading up into another room, the floor of which was about six feet higher than that of the first one. It was low and small, and served, apparently, both as the library and the lumber-room of the Khan. About 300 volumes of books, with all sorts of old lumber, chain armour, plated armour covered with rust and dust, half a dozen old telescopes—one of a very large size—pottery, bows and arrows, old iron, and pig-lead were found in this room.

Many of the books, as I was informed by Mr. Kuhn, the Orientalist of the expedition, were very curious and valuable. They were all written by hand, many of them beautifully; for the most part, they were bound in leather or parchment. Among them were a history of the world and a history of Khiva from the beginning of time. They have all been sent to the Imperial Library of St. Petersburg.

Of the armour, there were several very fine suits, beautifully inlaid with gold, that possibly found their way here through the Saracens and Crusaders. On one beautiful pair of gauntlets was traced in gold a lily and near it a crescent of a later and much ruder workmanship. Possibly it had been lost and won in some desperate hand-to-hand fight, when some noble French knight, whose name has long since passed into oblivion, fell beneath the sharp scimitar of the Saracen.

While thus viewing the interior of the palace, I had a curious example of the dexterity of the Persian slaves in stealing. Two or three of them, who had helped to open the doors of the strong room, came in with us, unnoticed. Just before we were going out, preparatory to shutting up the place again, I observed one of these Persians deftly slip a beautiful dagger under his long loose khalat. He did this unperceived by anybody but myself, although there were a dozen officers in the room at the time. I kept my eye on him, and after a moment saw him go quietly out into the court, linger about a few minutes, and then move off with an assumption of indifference that was amusing. I followed him until he got into the outer court, where there were no officers, and then stopped him, making a significant gesture, with the single word "bir!"—"give." He pretended not to understand at first, and opened his khalat to show me he had nothing. As I remembered the story of a certain well-known "heathen Chinee," however, I simply laid my hand on my revolver, with a scowl, whereupon he immediately produced the dagger from his sleeve. I then majestically motioned him away, and he glided out with a scared face, glad to get off on such easy terms. My object in allowing him to escape unpunished was two-fold. First, I did not want to have the poor devil shot, as he would inevitably have been, had I denounced him; and secondly, I wanted the dagger myself. Ill-gotten goods, I soon learned, however, do not profit the getter the dagger was stolen from me before two weeks, probably by the same dexterous hand, along with the valuable little Kirghiz horse of which I more than once spoke in the account of my travels in the Kyzil-Kum.

My only revenge was in devoutly wishing and praying that my acquaintance was among those unlucky Persians who, falling into the hands of the Turcomans on their way home to their native land, were murdered.

It was now near dark, and I commenced looking anxiously around for my people, whom I had not seen since our entry into the city. I could not find any of them, and was beginning to grow uneasy, when something else arrested my attention, and drove all thoughts of them out of my head. The gates of the harem, before which two sentinels had been placed, had been partly opened, and behind them I beheld crowds of women and children, clamouring and weeping as though they were just on the point of being led out to execution. There were women of all kinds—old and young, pretty and ugly, infants and adults, sweet young girls of fifteen and old toothless hags, apparently a hundred and fifty, and all were

crying and wringing their hands in the most despairing
way. As it was difficult to make out what they wanted,
the officer in command of the palace was sent for, who
soon arrived on the spot with an interpreter. It appeared
that they simply wished to leave the place and go into
the town, pretending they were afraid to remain where
they were. The officer having refused to grant this
request, they next said they had nothing to eat or drink.
The officer immediately ordered an immense quantity of
pilaoff to be made; and sent them in word that if they
would bring pails and jars to the door, he would have
water brought. They seemed to be satisfied with this;
and the water and pilaoff having been sent in, they
retired, and the doors were shut. The officer then gave
orders that no one be allowed to enter, and moved off to
place sentinels for the night.

Among the crowd of weeping and distracted women,
there was one who had remained calm. To her the others
paid the greatest deference and obedience, and to her
they seemed to look up for protection. She was about
eighteen, of medium size, had a clear rosy complexion,
showing her Caucasian origin, broad low forehead, round
face, black hair, and large dark eyes. Her quiet firm-
ness, tranquil air of authority, and noble appearance,
convinced me, in spite of the old ragged khalat she wore
over head and shoulders, that she was the sultana of the
harem. She spoke to her half-demented companions in
an authoritative, motherly manner, and conferred with the
officer in a straightforward sensible way, that impressed
us all very favourably. She turned her eyes towards me
several times in a half-imploring way, as though she
would have spoken to me. I never in my life before so
much regretted my ignorance of an unknown tongue. I

looked again for my servants, with the intention of having Ak-Mamatoff speak to her, and ask her if I could do her any service; but he had disappeared, and, as it turned out, had followed Kaufmann to the Orenburg camp, supposing I would be there.

The dark eyes of this woman haunted me after she had disappeared. I could not forget her calm, majestic figure, as she stood in the midst of the enemies of her race and religion, with weeping women and children relying upon her for protection, and I determined to communicate with her and help her, if possible. Unfortunately I had never seen the officer in command of the palace before, and did not like sounding him, for fear of arousing his suspicions Again and again I cursed old Ak-Mamatoff for not following me, as he had been ordered; but as it was pretty clear that he was not in the palace anywhere, I determined to try what I could do alone.

CHAPTER XI.

AN ADVENTURE IN THE HAREM.

I BEGAN to look about for another entry to the harem. I found one leading out of the principal court, but this, like the other, was guarded.

After rummaging about a good while, passing through two small courts and suites of rooms directly behind the great court, I at last came upon a narrow, dark, and steep stairway, leading upward. I ascended, and found myself on the top of the exterior wall of the palace. The latter was built square up against the inside wall of the citadel, and upon looking over between the mud battlements, I found they had a height here on the outside of forty feet. Along the parapet I took my course, in the direction of the great square tower seen in the picture, which was within the walls of the harem.

I soon reached a point overlooking the main court, and gazed down on General Golovatchoff sleeping the sleep of a tired soldier. I was on a shoulder of the tower, which formed a platform about ten feet wide, nearly on a level with the high walls of the citadel.

Listening attentively, a low murmur of voices came to my ears from above. There were sentinels up in the tower.

It was now near midnight, and the silent, sleeping city lay bathed in a flood of glorious moonlight. The place was transformed. The flat mud roofs had turned to marble; the tall, slender minarets rose dim and indistinct, like spectre sentinels watching over the city. Here and there little courts and gardens lay buried in deepest shadow, from which arose the dark masses of mighty elms and the still and ghostly forms of the slender poplars. Far away, the exterior walls of the city, with battlements and towers, which in the misty moonlight looked as high as the sky and as distant as the horizon. It was no longer a real city, but a leaf torn from the enchanted pages of the Arabian Nights.

I peered down into the harem, and saw a large court, half of which was lighted up by the moon, and the other half covered by a dark, cranelated shadow. Suddenly I saw a female figure come out of the shadow, flit across the moonshine, and disappear on the other side, while a light could be seen glimmering in one of the rooms that were dispersed around the court. I entered the tower, and found a door which was locked by a padlock; but the posts were so loosely set in the wall, that I had no difficulty in taking them down without noise. Here there was a stone stairway, without balustrade, leading down into a little moonlit court, only separated by the wall of the harem from the one in which General Golovatchoff was camped. Into this I descended, and found two passage ways, one leading to the main entrance, where were stationed the sentinels, and the other apparently into the interior rooms of the harem. This latter, after much deliberation and listening, I entered—not without a beating heart, however, for it was dark as pitch, and I had not the most remote idea of what the place was like, of the intricacies in which I might find

myself involved, or of the pitfalls into which I might
stumble. I might meet with armed men, still in hiding
here, determined to guard the honour of the harem, and
I knew what I might expect in that case; or I might
simply lose myself and be unable to find my way out
until morning, to be then discovered by the Russians—a
by no means pleasant ending to my adventure.

Taking my revolver in one hand, and feeling my way
with the other, I entered the corridor, which at first
seemed to lead me in the direction of the large court,
where I had seen figures flitting in the moonshine.

Fifty feet of darkness, and I come to a door, which
swings easily open, and I suddenly find myself out again
in the moonlight. It is another very small court, and a
corridor runs around it, which is separated from the court
by a small partition, covered by a projecting roof, fifteen
or twenty feet high. I proceed around this little court,
keeping well in the shade, until, reaching another corridor,
I enter, and find myself in a high room, into which a little
moonshine penetrates through small square holes near the
top. Here are five or six doors, leading in as many different directions I choose one, but must have lost all
idea of direction in my various turnings and windings, for
I am soon involved in a hopeless labyrinth of intricate
passages and small rooms, which seem interminable. I
had taken care to provide myself with a small piece of
candle and with matches, and I lighted one occasionally
to aid me in my search. It was without avail. Only the
bare mud walls and floors, without a vestige of anything
to indicate the presence of man or woman.

The rooms were from eight to fifteen feet square, and
must have been perfectly dark, even in daytime, as I
could see no sign of window or any aperture by which the

fight might have penetrated. Dungeons I would have believed them, had not the thin mud walls precluded that idea. A search afterwards made by Kaufmann proved that there were no dungeons in the palace of the Khan, the truth being that imprisonment as a punishment is a refinement of cruelty unknown at Khiva. They cut off people's noses, ears, and heads, whip them, stone them to death, but never imprison them. There is not a building in Khiva capable of holding a prisoner twenty-four hours.

Once I stumbled into a large, low room, where there were five or six old-fashioned ovens of mud, such as may be seen at almost any farmhouse, several great iron kettles, each mounted on a little furnace, with various cooking utensils scattered about. This was probably the kitchen of the palace.

Shortly afterwards I again found myself in a small room. The floor, I observe, is wet and muddy. I strike a match, and, to my horror, I find myself on the verge of a deep well, with a very low curb.

Thoroughly frightened, I light my short piece of candle, determined to rather face any danger from concealed enemies than incur the risk of being precipitated into some horrible hole or pit. The well appeared to be about fifty feet deep, and contained water, as a bit of earth which I dropped into it proved. The room was small, close, and low, with a smell somehow suggestive of a charnel house, and I thought it was a strange place of all others for a well.

The silence became oppressive, even fearful, and I began to have a strange feeling as if everything around me were unreal I was evidently far away from the inhabited portion of the harem, and I had lost all idea of its

19

direction. I rose and again commenced the search, this
time taking my lighted piece of candle. But I soon had
reason to doubt whether light was not more dangerous
than darkness. I enter a small room, and, looking round,
perceive in one corner a pile of black earth, which somehow excited my curiosity. Following a kind of blind
impulse, I stoop down and pick up a handful; but I drop
it in terror—it is gunpowder. Quickly retreating through
two or three rooms, until I have put a safe distance
between me and the dangerous compound, I lean against
a wall, weak with fear. I think of the carelessness of the
Khivans in handling powder, as shown in the way in
which large quantities of it were left lying around in the
palace of Hazar-Asp; and here I had been wandering about,
striking matches, and throwing down the still burning
ends, for an hour. There was enough powder in that
little room to blow the whole palace to atoms. And then
the thought occurred to me that the Khan might have
laid a plan for blowing up the place, as is often done in
these countries. I thought of the last Chinese governor
of Kuldja, who, foreseeing that the Mahomedhans would
soon take the city by storm, assembled all his household,
councillors, ministers, wives, and children, to debate upon
what was best to be done, and who, while the discussion
was at its hottest, hearing the shouts of the victors
entering the city, gently laid down his pipe on the floor
by his side, firing a train of powder connected with the
magazine below, and putting an end to indecision and
debate. At that moment this seemed to me the most
uncomfortable story I had ever heard; I began to look
upon my adventure as the most absurd, foolish, and
ridiculous thing I had ever attempted, and to wonder
how I could have ever been so idiotic as to undertake it.

Once more I took up the light, and commenced trying to find my way out, resolved to let the dark-eyed beauty of the harem take care of herself. I had, as it seemed, narrowly escaped death twice, and that was enough for one night. Getting out was not so easy, I found, as getting in. I wandered about for half an hour longer in the labyrinth of rooms without finding any outlet, and just began to think I was lost for good, when I suddenly came out into a wide corridor. I turned to the right, determined, if I did not find the outlet here, to explore the other end, and in no case again involve myself in the intricacies of the small rooms. I soon came to the end of the corridor, and found a door, which was closed.

Just as I was on the point of opening it, supposing I had at last found my way, I was arrested by a sound of voices on the other side. I instantly blew out my light, and set myself to listen with feelings of curiosity, possibly not unmixed with fear. The voices were plainly those of females, and, after listening some minutes, I concluded there was no man among them. I had evidently reached the court of the harem just when least expecting it, and I was only separated from it by a thin wooden door.

What surprised me, however, was that these voices were chattering and laughing in the gayest manner, although in suppressed tones: one would have thought it was a bevy of schoolgirls having a surreptitious midnight party unknown to the matron. The women who appeared at the doors in the early part of the evening were weeping and wringing their hands in the most disconsolate manner, and apparently with such good reason, that I was not all disposed to doubt the sincerity of their grief. These, on the contrary, were seemingly in the gayest and the merriest of humours. This puzzled me for a while; but concluding that as they had at first expected to have their heads cut off, and had since been assured that they would not be harmed in any way, this gaiety was not, after all, so unnatural.

I softly found the iron handle of the door, and tried to pull it open, without success. I then attempted pushing it, with the same result; it was evidently fastened on the other side.

I at last decided to knock.

Those inside were apparently so occupied that they did not at first hear me, and I was obliged to repeat the knock several times before I succeeded in attracting their attention. Then the voices suddenly ceased, and there was a silence.

I repeated the knock softly.

In a moment I heard them whispering behind the door, and easily distinguished one or two suppressed giggles. Again I knocked, and this time there was a voice in answer —a soft, girlish voice that went rippling over the smooth syllables of the Tartar tongue like a brook over stones.

I could not understand a word; but it was not hard to suppose she was asking who was there. I answered, "*Aman*"—"peace," or "peace be with you"—the universal salutation in such cases, inwardly consigning Ak-Mamatoff to the lowermost regions of the Inferno, for having disappeared when I needed him most. There was another smothered laugh, and then the same word, "*Aman ?*" "*Aman ?*" repeated in an interrogatory manner, as though wishing to be assured of my peaceful intentions. Again I repeated the talismanic word, and then there was a rattle of bolts, the light door swung open, and I was greeted with a peal of laughter.

I was never more astonished in my life. I had expected to see them all fly in terror, upon perceiving who I was, and that I would have all the difficulty in the world to reassure them. So far from manifesting any sign of fear, they acted, I thought, as though they expected me. There were six or eight of them; some old and ugly, some young and pretty, grouped around the door in their strange costumes, and among them I noticed the one that had particularly attracted my attention at the gates of the harem.

It was she who opened the door, and now stood holding a heavy stone lamp overhead, which cast a fitful light over the scene. She looked at me intently with her great dark eyes, and only smiled gravely when the others laughed.

As soon as I recovered from my astonishment, I laughed in my turn, uttered a " salaam," and then asked for " *chai*"—tea. They instantly understood, and the one I have spoken of as queen, stepped forward, took my hand in hers, and led me into a very small court, about eight feet square, and out of that into the moonshine, followed by the whole of the company, chattering in an excited manner. We were in the grand court of the harem.

It was very large for Khiva—about 150 feet long by 40 wide. There were a succession of great high porches, such as I have already described, all along the southern side, and dispersed along the centre three or four very large kibitkas or tents, set on circular platforms of brick. The scene was strange and beautiful by moonlight.

I had only time to glance at these things, for my fair conductress led me into one of these porches, and, opening a door, ushered me into a large room behind it.

She motioned me to a pile of cushions, and proceeded to light five or six lamps of the same kind that she carried, which were disposed in niches around the walls. Then taking a teapot, she ran out with it, giving at the same time some orders to the other women, some of whom went out with her, while others came in, sat down, and looked at me, exchanging remarks seemingly about my personal appearance.

For my own part, I sat and looked around me, lost in astonishment. The room in which I found myself was ten feet wide, twenty long, and twelve high: parts of the ceiling were painted in a variety of rude designs, in crude colours, like the treasure-room of the Khan. One wall was entirely covered from floor to ceiling with shelves of fanciful woodwork, which were stocked with cups and bowls of all sizes and colours, pots, teapots, and vases. As I learned on the morrow, these were, for the most part, specimens of the finest old china porcelain, and they were ranged side by side with the cheap, showily-gilded ware of Russian make, which, in the eyes of the women of the harem, was in all probability equally valuable.

The room presented an appearance of the greatest disorder. The floor was strewn with carpets, cushions, coverlets, shawls, robes, and khalats, thrown about in confusion, together with many household utensils, some arms, another English double-barrelled hunting rifle, with empty cartridges, percussion caps, and two or three guitars. All of these things, seen by the light of the lamps disposed around the wall, presented a curious spectacle. Everything showed preparations for flight, and that the most valuable effects had already been removed.

While thus looking about, trying to assure myself that

it was not all a dream, my hostess returned with a steaming teapot, which she put down on the floor before me. Some of the other women brought in bread, apricots, and sweetmeats. She then asked me by signs if I wished to wash my hands, and led me to the other end of the room, where there was a square hole sunk in the floor, forming a kind of basin Taking an elegantly-shaped pitcher or ewer, made of copper, without a handle, but with a long slender curved spout, she poured water on my hands, and afterwards gave me a towel to dry them—all this in the most kindly, officious manner. Cups were taken down from the shelves, and she poured out tea, first for me and then for everybody else, herself included, and watched me while I drank it with a strange, eager interest. I began to think my first supposition that she had some favour to ask of me was right, and, as the sequel proved, I was not mistaken.

Looking around on the group, I found it composed of eight in all. Of these three were horribly ugly old hags, three moderately good-looking middle-aged or young women, and one very pretty one, besides my hostess, who was by far the most interesting, from her superior intelligence, exquisite grace of movement, and that undefinable air of superiority which distinguished her from the ordinary beings around her. She wore a short jacket of green silk, embroidered with gold thread, a long chemise of red silk, fastened on the throat with an emerald, slightly open on the bosom, and reaching below the knees, wide trousers, fastened at the ankles, and embroidered boots. She wore no turban, and her hair was wound about her well-shaped head in heavy glossy braids. Curious earrings, composed of many little pendants of pearls and turquoises, hung from her ears, and heavy, solid silver bracelets without joint or spring, of a construction I never saw anywhere else, encircled her wrists. They were of solid silver traced with gold, about an inch wide and a quarter of an inch thick, the shape of a letter C, with the space of half an inch between the two ends. As I afterwards learned, they are slipped on the wrist by a tedious and sometimes difficult operation.

She now half-knelt, half-sat on the ground before me, watching me with her brown eyes in a way that was exceedingly embarrassing, while I sipped my tea and disposed of a large quantity of sweetmeats What was going to happen next? What should I do in the almost utter impossibility of talking to them? were the questions I was turning over in my mind. Judging by the eager manner in which my fair friend watched me, she was thinking of the same thing, and was trying to hit upon some plan of communication; while the others sat around and watched us, as though expecting to hear us commence a fluent and familiar conversation.

At last I thought of the device of asking them their names as a means of starting it. "Fatima?" I asked, pointing to her. She understood instantly, shook her head, then pointed to one of the old women, by which I understood the latter's name was Fatima. She then said, "Zuleika," pointing to herself. In this manner I learned the name of each of them in turn.

Having got on so well thus far, I decided to launch out into a more general conversation. *"Urus ma Yakshe?"* I ask. "Are the Russians good?" " *Yoke— yoke — yoke* " — "No—no—no—" -- with gestures of dislike.

I was somewhat taken aback by this, imagining that

they did not know I was not a Russian, and thinking that as I was their guest, it was pretty plain speaking.

However, I determined to remove at once that unfavourable impression, if it existed, and continued: "*Min Urus yoke*"—"I am not Russian"—to which they eagerly answered, "Yes, yes"—"we know," "we know."

This again astonished me, and for a moment I did not know what to make of it.

I may as well remark here, that the presence of a stranger was soon known to the Khivans; and I afterwards learned that I was suspected by them of being an English agent, sent out by the English government, as Lieutenant Shakspeare was in 1840, during the expedition of General Perovsky. This fact accounted for my reception this evening. The Khan had fled, they had been prevented from leaving the palace by their own servants, and the poor things now looked to the stranger for protection.

I gave them to understand, as well as I could, that they had nothing to fear from the Russians; and after a conversation, principally in signs, which lasted about two hours, I left them, giving each a small present as a token of remembrance, and then withdrew.

They conducted me to the door by which I had entered, and when I made them understand that I could not find my way out alone, my hostess conducted me to the little court into which I had first descended from the large tower. Here I took leave of her, and mounted the stone stairs. I turned around at the top, before entering the tower, she kissed hands to me, and then disappeared in the dark corridor.

I found my way back into the court, where General Golovatchoff was asleep, and throwing myself on the floor of the porch, on a piece of carpet beside an officer, was soon sound asleep.

The next morning, when food was sent into the harem for its inhabitants, it was found to be empty. The women had escaped !

CHAPTER XII.

THE HAREM BY DAYLIGHT.

NATURALLY, I did not think it necessary next day to report my adventure to General Kaufmann, and he will now learn of it probably for the first time. I hope he will excuse my not having made my report earlier, in consideration of the peculiar circumstances of the case.

"The women have escaped!" were about the first words I heard upon opening my eyes next morning. The officer in command of the palace, Captain Reisveh, had only learned the fact upon sending a quantity of pilaoff into the harem for breakfast. A cordon of Russian soldiers around, the doors all guarded; how, asked, everybody, had the women managed to escape? Conjecture was rife, of course, I was no more able than anybody else to give the proper explanation. The report of the affair, presented to Kaufmann, suggested that they had got out through a sewer; a task somewhat difficult of accomplishment, seeing that no such thing as a sewer is known in Khiva.

In the course of the day, old Said Emir Ul-Umar, the Khan's uncle, reported that the women had taken refuge with him; and as there was no particular reason for keeping them prisoners, Kaufmann allowed them to remain there.

Several of us now went into the harem, to make a formal investigation of its contents. We enter, by the heavy gates before spoken of, into a high, wide corridor. The walls are of mud, and light wooden beams support the flat roof, which is made of small sticks of wood laid closely together, and covered with earth. After various twists and turns, we emerge into the large court of the harem. Very different it looked now, in day-time, from what it did in the pale white moonlight of the night before. Then it had been just such a picture as one might have conjured up from reading 'Lalla Rookh;' now it was a shabby-looking, dilapidated, miserable court, surrounded by heavy mud walls, that one shower of rain, such as we often have in Europe, would reduce to a heap of earth.

We enter the room where I had been so handsomely entertained the night before. Everything is in much the same condition in which I left it. We visit the rest of the rooms in succession. They are like the first one, except that there is less pretension about them. A heap of khalats, bed-coverlets, womens' clothing, cooking utensils, household implements, water-cans, ewers of copper and brass, of a very elegant shape, perhaps a guitar, with brass strings, and a spinning-wheel or two, all tumbled in confusion about the floor, is what usually meets our gaze.

Upon searching closely, we found many little toilet articles of the women, although they had probably carried most of these things off with them. There were small looking-glasses, with the mercury half rubbed off; coarse wooden combs; small phials of henna, and perfumery with a strange penetrating scent, unlike anything we meet in Europe; and pots of *hash-heesh*. Then again there were storerooms, in which all these things were heaped up in great quantities; and in one of them were several small iron chests, provided with heavy solid locks, in which were probably kept the jewels of the women. They were now open and empty. In short, the appearances were that everything of any great value had been removed. The Khan must have foreseen the fall of his capital several days before it really took place, and therefore had plenty of time to remove and secrete his money and jewels. I am only surprised that he left so many valuable effects. For instance, there were two fine double-barrel English hunting rifles, and some music-boxes that were probably highly prized by the women, one of which, by-the-way, played an air from the 'Belle Hélène.' I can only account for this, and the fact of his having left his women here a prey to the conqueror, on the supposition that he had decided to remain in his palace and throw himself on Kaufmann's mercy, until, panic-stricken by General Verëvkin's bombardment, he had fled, without taking time to look after either the one or the other.

Besides a number of Cashmere shawls, the most valuable thing we found was a fine collection of old China porcelain, numbering about a thousand pieces. The collection consisted of bowls and cups, varying in size from that of a large teacup to that of a large bowl holding a gallon. They were all of the finest kind, mostly blue and white, but some few were flowered in a beautiful red and brown. They were heaped up indiscriminately with cheap but showily-gilded ware of Russian make.

It was a pity to see all this fine porcelain—the pride

and joy of the women of the harem, the hoarding, probably of generations—turned over to the soldiers to be broken and lost. Many of them, it is true, found their way into the hands of the officers, who knew their value, and I confess to having bought several fine specimens that Ak-Mamatoff had found—where they were not lost

An inventory was taken of everything else; and carpets, khalats, coverlets, clothing—everything of the slightest value, found here or in other parts of the palace, was seized to be sold for the benefit of the soldiers. Only a few old rugs, carpets, and clothes were left lying about the court, which presented but a sorry spectacle; and then the doors were locked, and we left the harem alone in its desolation.

A day or two afterwards, the palace and town were definitely abandoned, except by a small body of troops that remained in the palace to guard it and preserve order.

Kaufmann pitched his camp in and about a large garden belonging to the Khan, a mile from the city.

This garden is the summer residence of the Khan. It is about six acres in extent, and is inclosed by a heavy mud wall some fifteen feet high. It is planted with apricot, peach, and plum trees, and, besides, boasts several very beautiful elms and two fine avenues of young poplars. A number of little canals that run through it irrigate the ground, and afford a regular supply of fresh water to the trees, and feed two or three little ponds under the elms. The summer palace is in one corner, and is far more comfortable than the one in town.

Imagine a large rectangular structure, a hundred yards long by fifty wide; the tops of the walls surmounted, like a feudal castle, by battlements. You enter from the garden by a narrow door cut in the wall, and find yourself in a large court or yard, in the middle of which are four large elms, whose roots are bathed by a little pond of water. On the right, a high porch, opening to the north, behind which is, as usual, a cool dark room, very pleasant this hot weather. Above this porch is another, and above that still another, into which the elms extend their long arms.

Behind this series of porches and rooms there is another and smaller court, with its little pool of water and two large elms. This is the court of the harem, and a very pleasant place it is. There are small suites of rooms around three sides of it. On the fourth, which is the sunny side, tall elms just outside the wall lift their huge cloud-like masses of green, affording a cool, luxurious shade. Each of these suites of rooms is composed of an apartment below and two above, with a little porch or balcony looking out on the court. In the railing and woodwork of these balconies we saw the work of the Russian prisoners, who were principally employed about this palace and garden.

The Grand Duke Nicholas took up his residence on one side of this court; Prince Eugene on the other. Outside of the palace in the garden were two small summer-houses, each in the shade of a clump of elms. These were occupied by General Kaufmann and General Golovatchoff; the rest of the officers pitched their tents wherever they could find room for them beneath the fruit-trees.

My comrade Chertkoff and myself decided to take rooms in the palace, and accordingly installed ourselves in a porch on the second story, where we found two very dark, cool rooms; while the porch itself was shaded by the thick foliage of the elms. Here we put down our carpets and our pieces of felt, arrange a few coverlets our people have found in the other palace for our beds, and make ourselves at home. In these quarters we had all the advantage of any air that might be stirring, while we were protected from the sun by the thick shade of the elms. By stepping up into the porch above, some forty feet from the ground, we had a splendid view of the city and of the surrounding oasis; beyond which, over the thick foliage of the trees, we could see the yellow gleaming sands of the dreary desert.

The only drawback to this palatial residence was the stairway. I do not think that even in its palmiest days it would have compared favourably with that of the Tuileries or St. James's. It was built of mud, purely and simply, which, whatever may be its other qualities, is not a durable material when subjected to the trampling of many feet. The steps were nearly worn out, and some of them had entirely disappeared when we took possession. In two or three days there was nothing left of them, and the descent from our rooms down a very steep and dusty inclined plane became a matter of considerable peril and difficulty.

As for food, Ak-Mamatoff did our cooking; and chickens, mutton, melons, apricots, grapes, and peaches were to be had in abundance. Every morning hot wheaten cakes and fresh milk were brought us, and even ice. The Khivans store a large quantity of ice every year, which they seem to appreciate at its proper value, judging from the price they asked for it. It will be seen that we were by no means so badly off in Khiva as might be at first supposed.

For a day or two Kaufmann heard nothing from the

Khan. At length information was obtained that he had fled to Imukchir with his faithful Turcomans. Kaufmann instantly wrote him a letter, informing him, that if he would return to Khiva and surrender himself, he would be treated with all the honours due to a sovereign; but that if he declined this invitation, somebody else would be made Khan in his stead. As it was not in the views of Kaufmann to permanently occupy the country, he wished to re-establish order and tranquillity as soon as possible.

In the meantime Atta-Djan, the Khan's youngest brother, who had been in prison for the last year, was a candidate for the throne, and had already pleaded his claim to Kaufmann. Had the Khan not acted upon the hint conveyed in Kaufmann's letter, and returned, there is little doubt that the Russian General would have dethroned him.

20

CHÁPTER XIII.

KAUFMANN AND THE KHAN.

On the 14th of June the Khan came back to Khiva accompanied by his followers, and was conducted into the presence of the conqueror.

Kaufmann received him under the elms before his tent. Here there was a raised platform of brick, on which carpets were spread, and tables and chairs set. On this platform took place the first interview between Kaufmann and the Khan.

As soon as the latter's arrival was announced, we all gathered around Kaufmann, curious to see the despot about whom we had heard so much. He rode humbly enough now into his own garden, with about twenty followers; and when he reached the end of a short avenue of young poplars, leading up to General Kaufmann's tent, dismounted from his richly-caparisoned horse, and came forward on foot, taking off his tall sheepskin hat, and bowing low as he approached. He ascended the little platform, where he had probably often received the respectful homage of his own subjects, and knelt down before Kaufmann, who was seated on a camp-stool He then retired a little further on the platform, which was covered with probably one of his own carpets, and remained

MUHAMED RAHIM BOGADUR KHAN. *From the 'Graphic.'*

kneeling. It should be observed, that the Khivans do not
sit cross-legged like the Turks, but in a kind of half-
kneeling posture, like that of the Kirghiz, which I have
already described, and that it is in this posture they eat,
talk, and confer. In kneeling, therefore, the Khan did
not adopt a posture of humility, but simply one of respect.

A man about thirty, with a not unpleasant expression
of countenance, when not clouded by fear as at present,
large fine eyes, slightly oblique, aquiline nose, a very thin
black-beard and moustache, and a heavy sensual mouth.
Physically he is decidedly powerful, fully six feet three
inches high, broad-shouldered in proportion, and weighing, I should say, between 250 and 300 pounds. He was
dressed in a long khalat, or tunic, of bright blue silk,
and the tall sheepskin cap of the Khivans. Humbly
he sat before Kaufmann, scarcely daring to look him
in the face. Finding himself at last at the feet of the
Governor of Turkistan—the famous Yarim-Padshah—
his feelings must not have been of the most reassuring nature The two men formed a curious contrast;
Kaufmann was not more than half as large as the Khan,
and a smile, in which there was apparent a great deal of
satisfaction, played over his features, as he beheld Russia's
historic enemy at his feet. I thought there never was a
more striking example of the superiority of mind over
brute force, of modern over ancient modes of warfare,
than was presented in the two men. In the days of
chivalry, this Khan with his giant form, and stalwart
arms, might have been almost a demi-god; he could have
put to flight a regiment single-handed, he would probably
have been a very Cœur de Lion, and now, the meanest
soldier in Kaufmann's army was more than a match for
him.

"Well, Khan," said Kaufmann, smilingly, "you see, I have come to see you at last, as I wrote you I would, three years ago."

KHAN. Yes; Allah has willed it.

KAUFMANN. No, Khan, there you are mistaken. Allah had very little to do with it. You have brought it upon yourself. If you had listened to my counsel three years ago, and acceded to my just demands, you would never have seen me here. In other words, if you had done as I advised you, Allah would not have willed it.

KHAN. The pleasure of seeing the Yarim-Padshah is so great, that I could wish nothing changed.

KAUFMANN (with a laugh). The pleasure, I assure you, Khan, is mutual. But now let us proceed to business. What are you going to do? What do you wish to do?

KHAN. That I leave to you to decide in your great wisdom. If I could wish for anything, it would be to become a subject of the Great White Tsar.

KAUFMANN. Very well. You shall not be his subject, but his friend, if you will. It only depends upon yourself. The Great White Tsar does not wish to deprive you of your throne. He only wishes to prove to you, that he is too great a Tsar to be trifled with, which I hope he has shown to your satisfaction. The Great White Tsar is too great a Tsar to take revenge. Having shown you his might, he is ready to forgive you, and let you retain your throne under conditions, which you and I, Khan, will discuss another day.

KHAN. I know I have done very wrong in not granting the just demands of the Russians, but I was ignorant and ill-advised; I will know better in the future. I thank the Great White Tsar and the illustrious Yarim-

Padshah for their great kindness and forbearance to me, and will always be their friend.

KAUFMANN. You may return now, Khan, to your capital. Re-establish your government, administer justice, and preserve order. Tell your people to resume their occupations and their work, and they will not be molested Tell them that the Russians are neither brigands nor robbers, but honest men; that they have not come to carry off their wealth, nor violate their women.

After mutual questions about each other's health, and wishes for each other's prosperity, expressed in the most flattering language, the Khan retired. He then returned to the city, and resumed his ordinary occupations. He did not, however, take up his residence in the palace—which was, to tell the truth, scarcely habitable—but passed his nights with Said Emir Ul-Umar.

The first visit was followed by several others during the next few days, at one of which the Khan assisted, with a younger brother, at the review of the Russian troops. It was amusing and interesting to watch the curious and astonished expression with which he looked at the filing-past of the Russian troops. Their solid, regular tramp, and the short, quick, shout which they uttered without turning their heads, when addressed by Kaufmann, gave them to his eyes a something mysterious and diabolical. He reminded me of a half-frightened, half-curious child, watching some strange thrilling Christmas pantomime. These then, he must have thought, are the men, who are conquering Central Asia: before a handful of whom, whole Mussulman hosts went down at Samarcand like grass before the scythe; these the devils, twelve hundred of whom took Tashkent, a town of a hundred thousand inhabitants by storm with a loss of half their number,

before whose unholy breath the religion of Islam is disappearing from the earth.

Under Kaufmann's instructions, a divan or council of
state was formed to discuss ways and means for raising
money for the payment of a war indemnity which Kaufmann
proposed to levy.   This council was composed of the Khan,
and three of his ministers, together with three Russian
officers, among whom was Colonel Ivanoff.   This council
was not only to find ways and means for providing the
war indemnity, but to advise the Khan on the general
government of his kingdom.   The Khan entered into these
arrangements with great interest, and showed much zeal
in carrying out the necessary measures.

The truth is, he had very little experience in affairs
of state, and the subject had for him all the charm
of novelty.   He had been in the habit of leaving the
direction of state affairs to one of his ministers, Divan-
Bégi Mat-Murad, of whom more hereafter.   He displayed
a childish eagerness in the execution of Kaufmann's
orders, that sometimes seriously compromised their effect.
Kaufmann related to me an anecdote about him which
illustrates this.   Having decided to emancipate the
slaves, he wrote the Khan a letter one day, informing
him of his decision, and requesting him to issue a proclamation to that effect.   The last part of the letter contained
advice and counsel as to the best means of carrying out
the measure, and among other things, requested the Khan
to make arrangements with the governors of the different
provinces to have the proclamation read all over the
Khanate the same day, in order not to give the Uzbegs
an opportunity for maltreating the Persians.   The Khan,
however, having read the first part of the letter,
immediately, without stopping to finish it, wrote out a

proclamation, and ordered it to be proclaimed through the streets next day by a herald, and then went to Kaufmann, with childish eagerness, to tell him what he had done, and show him how prompt he was to obey his wishes.

"But," said Kaufmann, "did you not read the last part of my letter?" "No," said the Khan, "I did not know it was necessary." "Why, yes," said Kaufmann, "with us the last part of a letter is often the best. In it I advised you not to issue your proclamation for a few days yet."

"Oh," replied the Khan, "I did not know that; I will go back, read the letter through to the end, and give orders not to issue the proclamation until the time you have fixed."

He soon got accustomed, however, to Russian ways of doing business, and manifested a great deal of intelligence and good sense in the direction of affairs. It is probable that having once tasted of the delights of governing, he will not again readily yield up his authority to another man.

Little satisfactory information has I believe been obtained as yet by the Russians, regarding the administration and revenues of the Khan's government, or the resources and population of the country. One peculiarity in the administration of the government is that, with the exception of the Mullahs, and a small police force, employed to preserve order and to punish offenders, few of the officers and functionaries of the government receive regular pay. They all, from the highest to the lowest, make their living out of the perquisites appertaining to their offices, a system which of course gives rise to a great deal of corruption and thieving on the part of officials.

The whole financial department of the Khan's government seems to have been in the most inextricable and

hopeless confusion According to Mr. Kuhn, who devoted a good deal of time to investigating the affairs of
the Khanate, the whole revenue of the state was about
90,000 tillas, or £45,000 English money; but the accounts were in such hopeless confusion, that it was impossible to form anything like a correct estimate of the
amount of taxes really collected. Nor was it ascertained
what portion of the revenue fell to the Khan himself.
Judging by his simple, frugal manner of life, I should
say he received but a small portion of it. In his way
of living, he could not have spent the tenth of this
sum; and although he has a large household, and three
or four hundred slaves, he has a great deal of land which
probably brought him in a large revenue. Luxury, in
our sense of the word, is unknown to him. The only
expensive luxury he could well indulge in, was a stable full
of fine Turcoman horses, and an occasional new wife.
He did not, I believe, keep a standing army.

This revenue, whatever it may have been, was raised
by the imposition of several different kinds of taxes.

First among these was the *ziaket*, or customs duties,
which was collected by Mat-Murad.

As nearly as could be made out from Mat-Murad's
books, the duty on Russian imports, at $2\frac{1}{2}$ per cent., produced about £2750; and those from Bokhara and other
countries, about £2150; £4900 in all. Only half this
sum was turned over to the Khan. Whether Mat-Murad
simply pocketed the other half, or whether it was allowed
him by the Khan for farming the revenue, and the
expenses of collecting it, is not known. It is, however,
highly probable that Mat-Murad simply stole this sum
from the government.

In addition, a tax was levied upon the interior trade of

the country, which was likewise collected by Mat-Murad. This tax was simply assessed upon the shopkeepers in a general way, according to the size of the shop and value of the wares it was supposed to contain, and varied from a shilling to £2 or £3.

Next was the *salguit,* or tax upon land and houses, which was collected by two ministers of the Khan, called the Mekhter, and the Kush-begi. It was levied at the rate of 2s. per acre.

The Kara-Kalpaks paid at the rate of a sheep in every hundred, a bullock in every twenty, and a camel in every six. The Kirghiz who came to the bazaar were charged for every camel a shilling, and the same amount for every ten sheep.

In addition to these there was what might be called a harvest tax. The government assessors went around just before harvest, and agreed with the proprietors on the amount of tax each field should pay.

It was as impossible to determine the exact population of the Khanate as to get the truth regarding other matters connected with it. And it will probably be some time before the exact number is known. Even in Central Asian towns, long under Russian rule, it has been found impossible to get a correct census, owing to the suspicious nature of the people. Taking the census would drive them to revolt when nothing else would. The general impression was that the whole population of the Khanate was about 500,000, exclusive of the Kirghiz of the Kyzil-Kum, over whom the Khan exerted an uncertain sway.

The roads and canals are kept up by the government A part of the land tax is put aside for that purpose. The land tax may be worked out instead of being paid in money.

The tenure of land in Khiva is much the same as in all Mahomedan countries. The land is supposed to belong to the state, or rather to the Mahomedan religion, and is not held as freehold. Believers cannot, however, be easily deprived of the land they hold as long as they pay their taxes, and cultivate it But if the land should remain unoccupied for three years, it may be seized by the first comer, whose claim is then nearly as good as that of his predecessor. But if the previous owner should appear within a reasonable time, and offer to pay for growing crops and improvements, the owner *de facto* is obliged to give him possession. The reclamation of wild lands, is however, considered of such importance in Central Asia to the general weal, that a freehold may always be acquired by irrigating any uncultivated, unproductive ground, and planting it with trees.

CHAPTER XIV.

AN INTERVIEW WITH THE KHAN.

LIEUTENANT SEROVATSKY, the astronomer of the expedition, finding the garden in which the troops were encamped unfavourable for astronomical observations, requested leave to occupy a room in the palace of the Khan in the city. Having obtained permission, he visited the palace twice a day, and passed the night there. The Khan manifested considerable curiosity about the instruments, and, Serovatsky having promised to explain them, the Khan appointed a day for his reception. Serovatsky invited me to accompany him.

Having first sent in a present of a carpet and a revolver, the Lieutenant had his instruments removed into an inner court. Here we found the Khan on the stage-like platform, of which I have already spoken. The stage was uncarpeted. The Khan, I fancy, had few carpets left, and perhaps took a grim pleasure in thus displaying his poverty to the Russians. We ascended the steps, and he motioned us to sit down, and offered us melons, bread, and tea. Then he intimated his desire to see the instruments. A large telescope was first shown him, but as we were completely shut in by the surrounding walls, it was impossible to observe anything with it, except the sun. A darkened glass, and an eyeglass of sufficient power to show the spots on the sun, were put in. The Khan looked through the telescope, while Serovatsky explained the phenomena shown by the instrument, but this did not seem to interest the Khan, who probably would have been more pleased if the glass had been directed against terrestrial objects. Serovatsky next endeavoured to explain the use of the quadrant and mercurial horizon, but his explanation seemed to bewilder the Khan to an alarming extent, although he evidently did his best to understand. He became much more interested when Serovatsky went on to explain that, although he were led blindfold to any city in the world, he could, if placed in a little court from which he might see the sun, tell with the quadrant what that city was. " I will tell you," said he, "that I am in Khiva, and not in Bokhara, or in Bokhara, and not in Samarcand." The Khan opened his eyes wide with astonishment, and seemed to regard the astronomer from this moment, as a magician or a sorcerer. At the same time he must have inwardly cursed Serovatsky as the dog of an unbeliever, who had, by his devilish arts, shown the Russians the way to his city of Khiva, which everybody had told him was inaccessible. The barometer seemed to interest him very much. When Serovatsky showed him his chronometers, large and small, the Khan took out his watch, a gold one, which he had received from Lord Northbrook, and compared the time. Although it was now about noon, the Khan's watch only marked six o'clock in the morning. Serovatsky having examined the watch, told him that it was a very good one The instruments explained, the Khan began to exhibit considerable curiosity about me. Upon more than one occasion I observed that he looked towards me in a peculiar and marked manner, and I was not surprised to find that he afterwards intimated a desire to have a second interview with me.

At this interview he began by asking from what country I came.

"America," I replied.

"Are you not English, then," he asked, with apparent astonishment—a question which confirmed my suspicion that his interest in me came from his supposition that I was an English agent.

"No," I replied; "my country is much farther away."

"How far?"

"It is away over a great sea, 400 days' march of a camel."

In amazement he asked how I managed to cross so wide a sea.

I asked him if he had not seen the *Perakhote*—the steamboat of the Russians on the Lower Oxus. He said he had heard of it, but had not seen it. I told him that a *perakhote* would cross this sea in ten days; and that they travelled just forty times as fast as a camel. I proceeded to inform him that it was my countrymen who had invented the *perakhote;* and that they had likewise invented a rapid system of sending messages, so that you could despatch a message from Khiva to Bokhara in five minutes. This statement appeared to him too amazing to be believed, and I think he looked on me as a great liar.

It is only since the fall of Khiva that the telegraph has been brought to Tashkent, and it is an invention of which very few Central Asiatics know anything.

I next told him that it was the Americans who had invented the breech-loading rifles of the Russians—hardly a gracious thing to do, seeing how severely he had suffered from the effects of these same weapons. The Khan received this information with apparently great interest. He went on to ask me, if the Americans made many rifles? what they cost? and whether it would be difficult to get some. Having given him the required information on these points, he next began to put me many questions about Frenghistan (France) and England.

I drew a rough map on a piece of paper, showing the relative positions of France, Germany, England, Russia. and India, and this he examined with minute attention. I told him that there had been a great war between Frenghistan and Germany, in which Frenghistan had been beaten, and obliged to pay a great sum of money This touched him nearly, and he seemed to readily perceive the analogy between this case and his own. He asked if such were the way people made war in the West. I assured him that it was, and that besides, they did not kill their prisoners, nor treat them with cruelty, nor sell them into slavery; and that they did not burn nor pillage their enemy's country. They had a more effective way of accomplishing the same end. When I told him that the people of Frenghistan counted 40,000,000, and the people of Germany about the same, and that each had an army of 1,000,000 in the field, he seemed amazed beyond expression; and doubtless it was some consolation for him to find that a country as large as Frenghistan could suffer humiliation as well as himself.

He now asked me if Russia was a very great country. I told him that Russia was larger than England, France, Germany, and India put together; and that the Russians numbered twice as many as the English, or the French.

What seemed to astonish him most about America was, that the Khan only reigned for four years, and that another Khan was then elected in his place.

"Why does the Khan allow another man to be chosen in his stead?" he asked with surprise.

"Because the law commands it; and if he did not submit, the people would compel him." I added that even I might, on my return home, be chosen as Khan.

He looked at me with an incredulous air, as if this eventuality, at least, was one not likely to happen. He then asked me if the English and the Russians were good friends. I assured him that they were; and that the Great White Tsar had just betrothed his daughter to the son of the Queen of England; and that the English Lion and Russian Bear now lie down together like lambs. I permitted myself this little stretch, because I knew it would be impossible to explain to the Khan that there could be any diversity of interest between two countries with such a bond of union between them.

The Khan is by no means unprepossessing in appearance. He has a pleasant, genial expression of face, and nothing whatever of a blood-thirsty, or cruel look. I found him courteous and affable. At the same time he has something of a royal air—a quiet self-possession, and a tranquil air of authority which shows the man accustomed to implicit obedience; and he had an off hand way of dismissing you that would have done credit to the Great White Tsar himself. On the whole, I should say he is disposed to act kindly. The Russian prisoners gave him a very good character. He would stop and speak to them pleasantly, when he passed them at work, and often enter in conversation with them. But, unquestionably, he showed himself during the present campaign both cowardly and ungrateful. He never commanded his forces in person; he fled at sight of the Russians; and he showed the basest ingratitude toward the Turcomans; as will afterwards be seen.

During the whole time of my interview with him, an attendant brought in a pipe every five minutes. He took one whiff, and then handed it back again; when the tobacco was renewed, and the pipe once more handed to him. I learned that he continued smoking in this way the entire day. While the Russians were at Khiva, he passed his time in the following way. In the morning he rode to the Russian camp, where he held a divan or council of state, presided over by Colonel Ivanoff. Here he passed an hour or two, in discussing affairs of state. He then returned to his palace, and breakfasted, after which he administered justice for two or three hours. He heard all kinds of cases, from the most important questions of property, down to a trivial quarrel between man and wife. In the afternoon, when he had taken tea, he retired to the harem to sleep. When evening came, he again rode out, sometimes paying a visit to General Kaufmann, and sometimes going into the country, being generally accompanied by three, or four, and sometimes by as many as twenty of his followers. He was always careful to return any salutes that were given him; and I never saw him neglect to acknowledge one, whether it came from a Russian, or from the humblest of his own subjects.

The Khan has only four wives; but he has, I believe, about a hundred slave women; he seems to have some from each of the races that are found in his dominions. The exact number I did not ascertain; the Khan himself one could not ask, as it is considered extremely unpolite, in Central Asia, to make any mention to a man of his wife, or wives. The womens' way of life is very simple and frugal. There is no rivalry between them about dress; and even civilised women might take a lesson from them in more respects than one. They spend most of their time at home, and pass nearly all the day in making clothes, beds, and carpets, for the family, and in their household work.

There were several ministers of state: Mat-Murad, Mat-Niaz, Jakub-Bei, and the Khan's uncle, Said Emir-Ul-Umar. Mat-Murad had been an Affghan slave, and had belonged to the old Khan, by whom he was very much esteemed. He ingratiated himself into the favour of the young Khan, and when he came to the throne, succeeded in becoming his chief counsellor. He had a strong hatred of the Russians; and it was by his advice that the Khan refused to accede to the Russian demands. He led the Khivan troops at the battle of Sheik-Arik; and when the Khan fled, accompanied him in the flight. Kaufmann asked Mat-Niaz if his fellow minister, Mat-Murad, were able. "He is cunning, but not clever," was the reply. As soon as the Khan gave himself up, Mat-Murad was seized, separated from his master, and never allowed to see him again. He was afterwards sent to Kazala, where he still, I believe, remains in prison.

Mat-Niaz, as well as Said-Emir, belonged to the peace party. He was a small, rather ugly man, with round, sharp eyes, thin beard, and a turned-up nose. He seemed very friendly towards the Russians; and it was from him Kaufmann obtained the most trustworthy information respecting the Khanate. He was about forty-five years of age. Jakub-Bei, is an old man, about sixty apparently. He is stout, and strongly-built, with a heavy, bull-dog face, and a short, thick nose, and is blind of an eye. In some of his features he resembled the Turcomans, probably having some of their blood in his veins. Said-Umar I have already described.

The Khan had two brothers; one he greatly loved, the

other as cordially detested. The latter had aspirations to the throne; after the flight of the Khan, he offered himself, as will be remembered, to Kaufmann, as a candidate for the place vacated by his brother.

I was told by some Russian officers that some Khivan merchants at Kuna Urgench said the Khan used to obtain a large quantity of wine from Russia every year, and that he was in the habit of getting very drunk. As no wine-bottles were found in the palace, however, and as the story itself seems very improbable, there can be little doubt that it was a pure fiction.

CHAPTER XV.

THE CITY OF KHIVA IN THE YEAR 1873.

THE exterior view of Khiva, from certain points, is striking and peculiar. High walls, with battlements and
towers; a covered gate, with its heavy towers of defence;
the domes of the mosques and minarets, rising above the
walls of the town; these things seen against the western
sky in the light of the setting sun, are very beautiful and
picturesque; but the agreeable impression made by its
exterior disappears on entering the town itself. There
are only three or four buildings in the whole place that
make any attempt at architectural display; the rest are
all of clay, and present but a miserable appearance.

There are two great walls; an exterior and an interior one. The interior wall, with the part of the
town it incloses, forms the citadel, and is a mile long by
a quarter wide. Within this wall are the palace of the
Khan, the great tower, several medressés, and, in fact,
most of the public buildings. The wall is protected by
three or four towers. It is of much older origin than the
exterior one; indeed, nobody seemed able to say at what
precise date it was built. Probably it inclosed the whole
town of Khiva at one time. The exterior, on the contrary, dates from a year so recent as 1842. In that year

the reigning Khan, Allah-Kuli, was engaged in warfare
with Bokhara; and built this wall as an additional
defence to his capital. The diameter of the outer wall
varies; for in shape it is somewhat like an oyster-shell,

VIEW OF THE CITADEL.
(From a design by Feodoroff.)

with the narrow end elongated and squared. The diameter
at longest is a mile and a half; and at shortest a mile.
In height the wall is, on the average, twenty-five feet,
but in many places higher; and it is twenty-five feet
thick at the bottom, and only two or three at the top.
Round about the city is a ditch, some twenty or twenty-

five feet broad. I saw this ditch quite full of water in some places—a regular canal, in fact; in other places it was quite dry. In the course of my narrative, I have already spoken at length of two of the gates, by which the city is entered. Besides the Hazar-Asp and the Hazavat gates, there are five more.

The space between the exterior and interior walls is at one place almost completely occupied by tombs. This is not the first time I have observed on the curious habit of the Khivans to place the dwellings of living and dead close beside one another. I remarked the same thing in Khala-ata, Hazar-Asp, in fact, in every part of the Khanate.

In another place, the interspace between the citadel and outer wall is taken up with gardens. This—the western part of the city—is by far its pleasantest quarter. There are numbers of elms and fruit trees, and many little canals; so that this quarter has the air partly of an agreeable country suburb, and partly of a small Dutch town, where every street has its canal. Here I should mention that the water supply comes principally from two canals: the Chingeri, in the northern, and the Ingrik, in the south-western part of the town. Inside many of the courts of the houses, as already more than once remarked, there is a little pool of water for the use of the household; these pools are supplied from the canals.

It is not to be inferred, because the houses are of mud, that they are so very miserable in anything else but appearance, or that they are so very uncomfortable. They are, on the contrary, very well adapted to the country and climate; and although not corresponding to our ideas of luxury, afford, with their cool dark rooms, a welcome retreat from the sultry heat; and they are often fitted up

with a degree of comfort that contrasts pleasantly with
their shabby exterior.

The plan of a Khivan house is generally as follows.
There is a large court to which admission is gained sometimes by a small narrow door, sometimes by one large
enough to admit a cart. Around this court are disposed

A VIEW INSIDE THE EXTERIOR WALL.
(*From a design by Feodoroff.*)

the rooms of the dwelling, all opening into it, and rarely
having any other communication with each other. On
the south side, and always facing the north, is a high porch,
whose roof usually rises some eight or ten feet above the
surrounding walls ; and serves to catch the wind, and bring
it down into the court below on the principle of a windsail
aboard-ship. A gentle circulation of air is thus kept up,

conducing greatly to health and comfort in summer, whatever may be its effect in winter.

The interior of the rooms are fitted up in very much the same manner as those of the harem of the palace, which I have already described, but usually with less luxuriance.

It is needless to say that such things as chairs and tables are unknown, carpets, felts, cushions, pillows, and coverlets, all made up of various bright coloured stuffs, taking their places. Window-glass also is unknown, and in summer at least is little needed, as heat and light are almost inseparable, and the half-obscurity that reigns in the rooms, even in daytime, is far more conducive to comfort and repose than the broad glare of daylight.

As there is no attempt at architectural display in the houses—no windows, and few doors in the principal streets—a walk about Khiva presents about as much variety as would a walk between two mud walls, varying in height from ten to twenty feet, anywhere else. The streets are from ten to twenty feet wide, and of course very dusty this time of year, and you see but the bare mud walls everywhere, cut here and there by an occasional cross street, with nothing whatever to relieve their muddy monotony. Occasionally you catch a glimpse through an open door of a dark interior, and see a woman or two, hastily scurrying into their rooms, to escape the prying glance of the hated "Urus" Sometimes you come upon a group of little girls, five or six years old, who, already taught to avoid the glance of a man, scatter and hide like young partridges; or you meet a woman, closely veiled in the horrid horsehair veil, who cowers along the other side of the street, as though your eyes were sufficient to blast her; or simply turns

her back to you, and waits until you pass. The boys,
however, are not in the least afraid, and like boys

A STREET.
(*From a design by Verestchagin.*)

everywhere else, are rather disposed to be troublesome
and inquisitive, though ready to hold your horse, or do you
any other little service.

Khiva possesses seventeen mosques and twenty-two medressés. A medressé has some resemblance to a Catholic monastery; it is a place where the mullahs or priests are supposed to spend their time in leading holy lives and acquiring religious knowledge. I visited several of these one day, in company with Baron Kaulbars. We first called on the Khan, whom we found in the Divan or council, which was held in a kibitka in a garden outside the walls. He readily gave us a guide, and seemed pleased that we should take such interest in the medressés.

The most beautiful, and at the same time the most sacred structure in Khiva, is the mosque Palvan-Ata. It is rather prettily situated back in a small garden, and with its tall dome, presents a very fine appearance. It is built of kiln-burnt brick. The dome is about sixty feet high, is covered with the same kind of tiles as those of the great tower already spoken of, burnt a brilliant green, and is surmounted by a gilt ball. The general appearance is not unlike that of a Russian Church. It was built in 1811, by Mahomed-Rahim-Khan, and contains the tomb of Palvan—the patron saint of the Khivans.

The appearance of the interior of the dome is very beautiful and striking. It is covered from bottom to top with tiles, which are adorned with a delicate blue tracery, interwoven with verses from the Koran. These tiles are so closely fitted together that the joints cannot be seen, and the whole appearance is that of an immense inverted vase of Chinese porcelain.

This dome, owing to its construction, has peculiar acoustic properties, to which the Khivans attach a superstitious importance. The prayers, uttered in a loud tone of voice, and by many persons together, are caught up

and echoed with considerable distinctness; and, doubtless, this is sufficient to convince the simple minds of the
Khivans that Allah is not deaf to their prayers.

Inside are the tombs of the Khan's predecessors. The
tombs are placed in a niche in the wall, and are protected
by a copper lattice-work. In this part of the mosque
three Khans are buried: Muhamed-Rahim, Abul-Gazi,
and Shir-Gazi. It may be understood that the Russians
looked with not a little interest on the resting-place of
Shir-Gazi; for he is the Khan, it will be remembered, who
treacherously put Prince Beckovitch-Cherkasky to death,
and murdered nearly all his expedition.

There are two rooms off the apartment I have just been
describing. In one is the tomb of the Khan, Allah-Kuli,
who died in 1843, and who, as I have already stated,
built the outer wall of the city. In the other room is
the tomb of St. Palvan himself. The room is small, low-
roofed, and square. It is almost dark, being lit by
one small window only. The walls are made of dark
grey tiles, and so is the tomb. The tomb lies in the
middle of the floor; is seven feet long, four wide, three
high; and the tiles, of which it is made, are so closely
fitted together that it looks like one block of grey
marble.

Behind the mosque is a kind of mud structure, containing a number of rooms occupied by the blind. We visited
several of these. They were the merest cells, sometimes only four feet by six, and the furniture consisted of
a few cooking utensils, a sheepskin thrown on the floor,
with a coverlet or two for a bed, and a stone water-jug.
Small as the place was, a miniature chimney in one corner
offered conveniences for the blind " student," as he is called,
to cook his food and make his tea. There was something

considerable distance, and, doubt-
less, meant to convince the people minds of the
that Allah is not deaf to their prayers.

Here are the tombs of the Khans, too. The
bodies are placed in a niche in the wall, and are protected
by copper lattice-work. In this part of the mosque
three Khans are buried: Muhamed-Rahim, Abul-Gazi,
and Shir-Gazi. It may be understood that the Russians
looked with not a little interest on the resting-place of
Shir-Gazi, for he is the Khan, it will be remembered, who
treacherously put Prince Beckovitch-Cherkasky to death,
and murdered nearly all his expedition.

There are two rooms off the apartment I have just been
describing. In one is the tomb of the Khan, Allah-Kuli,
who died in 1843, and who, as I have already stated,
built the outer wall of the city. In the other room is
the tomb of St. Palvan himself. The room is small, low-
roofed, and square. It is very dark, being lit by
one small window only. The walls are made of dark
grey tiles, and so is the tomb. The tomb lies in the
middle of the floor; is seven feet long, four wide, three
high, and the tiles of which it is made, are so closely
fitted together that it looks like one block of grey
marble.

Behind the mosque is a kind of mud structure, containing a number of rooms occupied by the blind. We visited
several of these. They were the merest cells, sometimes only four feet by six, and the furniture consisted of
a few cooking utensils, a sheepskin thrown on the floor,
with a coverlet or two for a bed, and a stone water-jug.
Small as the place was, a miniature chimney in one corner
offered conveniences for the blind "student," as he is called,
to cook his food and make his tea. There was something

A DERVISH. *From a design by Verestchagin.*

touching in the scrupulous cleanliness with which every thing was kept; and the neatness and order displayed in the arrangement of their poor simple effects, appealed directly to one's sympathy, in showing the same characteristics in these people that distinguish the blind of our own race.

There were fifteen or twenty blind persons here. They informed us that they receive tea, bread and rice every day, and meat two or three times a week, besides little presents of fruit, melons, and sugar from the people, when they go through the bazaar. The place is partly supported by a donation from the founder, St. Palvan, partly by the present Khan. That such an institution should exist here in Khiva, shows that these people are not such barbarians as might be supposed.

We then mounted by a narrow, crooked stairway to an upper story, or platform, where, disposed around the central dome in an irregular way, was a jumble of little cells, and rooms inhabited by the mullahs. These rooms were usually arranged in suites of two and three, scarcely larger than those of the blind students, and situated on the south side. Though exposed to the sun, the dark little room itself, when the door was shut, was not uncomfortable; and we threw ourselves willingly enough on the floor, while the mullah prepared us tea and pilaoff.

From here we went to the medressé, built by the present Khan, on the square before the palace. This medressé is a new edifice, constructed of excellent firebrick, and making considerable pretensions to architectural display. It appeared to be built upon the plan of a Persian caravansary, and the design was probably furnished, and the work done by Persian slaves. It is about 100 feet square, two stories high, and presents a very handsome façade, with an elevated portal about fifty feet high, and, when finished, will be ornamented with the blue and white tiles so often spoken of.

Inside is a large, well-paved court, which gives access to all the rooms. The rooms are ranged around the court in two stories. Each mullah has two rooms; one for the kitchen—the mullahs and students all do their own cooking—and the other for a sitting-room and study. The larger is about six by eight, and is provided with a fireplace, sewer, and other conveniences, all on a miniature scale, that reminds one of a children's play-house. No light gets into the rooms, except through a crevice over the door, and they are consequently rather a dark place, one would think, to study. There is series of cells on the second story, opening on a long balcony on the façade, and looking out on the square and the palace of the Khan, which are very pleasantly situated. This medressé affords ample accommodation for 100 people, with Khivan ideas of room, but it was now almost entirely unoccupied. It is surprising that the Khan should have built a medressé instead of a palace, for his present one is far inferior, in point of taste, solidity, and comfort, to this medressé.

Quite close to the Khan's palace is the medressé, built by Mahomed Emir Khan in 1844. This, which will be seen in the illustration, is the most important medressé in the city; and consists of a large quadrangular building, surrounding a spacious paved court.

It is built on exactly the same plan as the one I have described; and it supports 300 scholars, who are super-intended and taught by four teachers. Each scholar receives yearly fifteen bushels of wheat, fifteen bushels of djugera, and from £3 to £4 in money. At the corner

of this medressé stands the large tower, the most prominent object in Khiva.

There are twenty-two mosques and medressés in Khiva. Of these, only four or five are built of brick, the rest are of clay, and there is little to distinguish them from the surrounding houses.

These mullahs are an extraordinary set of men. Lean and withered, long-bearded and sunken-eyed, they go prowling about, with benumbed and stupid faces, which are only lighted by the fires of bigotry and fanaticism.

Years passed in their close, dark, little cells, learning the Koran by heart, without even understanding it, poring over the same theme, to the exclusion of every living human interest, reduces them to this state of semi-idiotcy. As an illustration of their ignorance and stupidity, as well as their capacity for some kinds of mental labour, General Kaufmann told me that when in Samarcand, he heard of a young mullah there who was very famous for his piety and his knowledge of the Koran Upon expressing a desire to make his acquaintance, the young mullah called upon him. Kaufmann found he actually knew the Koran by heart in Arabic, and could commence at any part, and recite it right through to the end. When, however, asked to translate a chapter, he expressed astonishment at such a request, and declared that he did not understand a word of Arabic. And yet the poor fellow had spent the best years of his life in this parrot's occupation. Is it wonderful that after such a course of study he should not only look, but be stupid?

But, apart from the kind of life they lead, the head-gear of these mullahs would be sufficient of itself to benumb their brains, and deprive them of the last spark of intelligence left by their severe course of religious training. Imagine an ordinary sheepskin, with the wool on, made up into a high conical cap, weighing seven or eight pounds; around the base of this, twenty-five or thirty yards of white muslin, wound in guise of turban, and you will have some notion of this monstrous hat. It is worn in the hottest weather, and the sight of one of these mullahs plodding through the dusty streets in the broiling heat of a noon-day sun, supporting this monstrous superstructure on his head, is enough to make one shudder at man's inhumanity to himself. Their object in wearing the sheepskin hat, especially in hot weather, when only the turban is required by the Koran, is not easily understood.

The influence these priests exert in keeping alive the spirit of intolerance, bigotry, and superstition, among the people, in hindering progress, and promoting vice and ignorance, by confining all knowledge to the Koran, is very great indeed. And the superior honesty, virtue, tolerance, and kindliness of spirit of the Kirghiz, as compared with the people of the towns, may, I think, be in great part attributed to the absence of mullahs from among them.

CHAPTER XVI.

THE BAZAAR.

It is about noon one day as I leave my quarters in Khiva, to take a view of the bazaar. The streets are hot and dusty; the sun is shining fiercely; the grey mud-walls receive and again throw out the heat, so that walking through the streets is like walking through a baker's oven.

Out of this blinding glare you gladly step into the cool dark shade of the bazaar. A pleasant compound scent of spices, and many other agreeable odours, greet your nostrils; the confused noise and hum of a large crowd assail your ears, and an undistinguishable mass of men, horses, camels, donkeys, and carts meet your eyes. The bazaar is simply a street covered in, and it is altogether a very primitive affair. The roof is formed by beams laid from wall to wall across the narrow street, supporting small pieces of wood laid closely together, and covered with earth. It serves its purpose very well, however, and keeps out the heat and light.

With delight you breathe the cool, damp, spice-laden air, and survey, with watering mouth, the heaps of rich, ripe fruit spread out in profusion. There are apricots peaches, plums, grapes, and melons of a dozen different species, together with an indescribable array of wares only

to be seen in Central Asia. Properly speaking, there are
no shops; an elevated platform runs along one side,
and men are seated among heaps of wares, with no
apparent boundary line between them. On the other
side there are a few barbers, butchers, cobblers, and
smaller traders.

You push your horse with difficulty through the crowd
for about fifty yards, until you come to another street,
likewise covered in, which cuts this one transversely
Turning to the left, you enter a heavy arched gateway of
brick, with massive wooden gates, and now you are in the
Tim," or bazaar proper. In this bazaar is transacted
the principal retail business of the city. It is a double
arcade or passage, 100 yards long, by forty feet wide;
and is built of brick, in a succession of arches. The roof
is some forty feet high, and each arch ends in a kind of
dome-funnel, with a round hole in the top, which serves to
light and ventilate the place. In the middle is a dome
higher than the rest, which is not wholly without aichi-
tectural pretensions.

The shops here are the merest booths or stalls, six or
eight feet square, with one side open to the passage,
displaying the most incongruous assortment of wares it
is possible to imagine. Tea, sugar, silks, cotton-stuffs,
khalats, boots, tobacco, everything, in short, found in
Central Asia you will see displayed in one of these stalls.

You take your seat in front of these booths, indulge
your taste for fruit to its utmost on water-melons, cool
and juicy, and peaches, rich and luscious, or grapes that
make you think what a pity it is there is no wine. Or if
you want to make a more substantial meal, a pilaoff with
hot wheaten cakes, will be brought you in a twinkling;
and you sit down there in the midst of the surging crowd,

... ... Properly speaking, there are
... ... platform runs along one side,
... ... of wares, with no
... ... On the other
... ... barbers, butchers, cobblers, and
... ...

... ... with difficulty through the crowd
of ... ... until you come to another street,
likewise covered in, which cuts this one transversely.
Turning to the left you enter a heavy arched gateway of
brick, with massive wooden gates, and now you are in the

Tim ... bazaar proper ... this bazaar is transacted
the principal retail business of the city. It is a double
arcade or passage, 100 yards long, by forty feet wide:
and is built of brick in a succession of arches. The roof
is some forty feet high, and each arch ends in a kind of
dome-funnel, with a round hole in the top, which serves to
light and ventilate the place. In the middle is a dome
higher than the rest, which is not worth without architectural pretensions.

The shops here are frequently ... or stall six or
eight feet square, with one side open to the passage,
displaying the most incongruous assortment of wares it
is possible to imagine. Tea, sugar, silks ... stuffs,
khalats, boots, tobacco, everything, in short, found in
Central Asia you will see displayed in one of these stalls.

You take your seat in front of these booths and fee
your taste for fruit to its utmost on melons, cool
and juicy, and peaches, rich and luscious, grapes that
make you think what a ... it is there ... wine. Or if
you want to make a more substantial ... a pilaf with
hot wheaten cakes, will be brought you in a twinkling;
and you sit down there in the ... surging crowd,

and quietly enjoy your meal.   The tea used here, by-the-
way, is the green, and is the only import, the supply of
which is monopolised by the English.

AN UZBEG.

You may stretch yourself out on a piece of carpet in
some nook or corner, and watch the ever-varying group

and the succession of strange, wild faces for hours with unflagging interest. Representatives of all the peoples of Central Asia may be found in the motley crowd. Here is an Uzbeg, in tall, black sheepskin hat and long khalat, with the thoughtful face and dignified bearing of his race. He is one of the landed aristocracy of Khiva, the descendants of the conquerors of the country, and stands in the same relation to the rest of the Khivans as do the descendants of the Norman-French to the masses of the English people. Tall and well-formed, with straight nose, even, regular features, heavy beard, and pensive expression, you might take him for a European, but for his swarthy complexion, and a certain lean and sinewy appearance, and hardness of face that marks the Oriental, of whatever race or country. He may well look pensive now; the domination of his race here is past, and Muhamed-Rahim-Bogadur-Khan is the last Uzbeg that will rule in Khiva. Here is a Kirghiz, mounted on his camel, his broad, flat, stolid, but good-natured face wearing a look almost of comic bashfulness He hears himself execrated by various persons among the crowd, whom his camel has pushed aside, and the butt for divers observations, probably of a very personal and not flattering nature, from all sides. The highly-educated and refined people of the towns look down with a great deal of contempt on the simple nomads, who do not enjoy the advantages of a great metropolis. The Kirghiz has probably come thirty or forty miles to sell a couple of sheep, to buy a little tea and sugar, or perhaps a new khalat and a few beads for wife or daughter.

This man, with a white turban and the many-coloured robe, that flashes out in the sunshine like a bed of brilliant flowers, is a Bokhariot merchant, who has come here upon a mission of cheating his confrères of the, to him, provincial town, and perhaps to pick up a few slaves. The latter part of his mission at least is a failure.

Next comes one with a swarthy complexion, almost black, thick lips, heavy, beetling brows, short, thick, upturned nose, and fierce black eyes. He has an easy, independent air of self-confidence, verging upon insolence, and he urges on a large, fine horse upon which he is mounted through the crowd, without seeming to care a pin whether he rides anybody down or not. There is no jeering at him, nor witticisms at his expense, which you may think surprising, as he has done far more to merit them than the timid Kirghiz. There is a reason for this respect This individual is good at repartee, and, if anything, a trifle more ready with his sabre than his tongue. He is a Yomud Turcoman, of whom we shall hear more anon.

He is followed by a Persian; erewhile a slave; with sharp, hatchet face, and agile, cat-like motions, who glances at you with a quick movement of his ferret eyes. And now you prick up your ears at the sight of a tall, white turban, which you have learned belongs to a woman, in the hopes of feasting your eyes on a female face once more. But no. Enveloped in her long, ragged robes, a dirty khalat thrown over her shoulders, and the horrid, black horsehair veil covering her face like a pall, you can only catch the occasional gleam of a bright eye as she glides past. The women, when they go out, put on the raggedest and dirtiest clothes they can find, making themselves look like beggars, in order to escape notice. This becomes, after a while, one of the most disagreeable features of Khiva. Men's faces, nothing but men's faces for weeks and months, until you long for the sight of a woman's face as you do for green grass and flowers in the desert.

While the "Tim" is the mart of the retail trade, most of the wholesale is transacted in the caravansary.

This caravansary, I learn from Russian sources, was erected in 1823, by Khan Muhamed-Rahim, after the plan of all such buildings in Central Asia. It is a square building, with a large, quadrangular paved court, about fifty by sixty feet. On each of the four sides are a number of cells, that serve as shops, none of which are more than eight feet square. The booths have arched ceilings, front towards the court, and receive light through the doors only. In these booths are stored away the wares of the rich merchants of Khiva, who traffic with Russia and Central Asia.

I have seen it stated in a Russian journal that a church official, armed with a whip, visits the bazaar several times during the day, in order to decide the complaints concerning weights and measures. He is also answerable, according to the same authority, that nobody sleeps during the hour of prayer. Those who offend against any of the regulations of the place, are punished on the spot; and the official is accompanied by assistants, who inflict the punishment prescribed. But, possibly on account of the general disorganisation, I saw nothing of all this. The weights and measures are Russian, and so are the reckoning boards, on which the merchants make their calculations. The standard of money in Khiva is the silver kokan, or tenga, which is worth twenty kopeks. Nine kokans make a tilla, a gold coin, worth one ruble and eighty silver kopeks, or two paper rubles. There are also double tillas, equal to three rubles and sixty kopeks. There is a small copper coin, the pul or cheka, sixty of which are equal to one tilla: a pul having the value of one-third of a silver kopek.

Here also is the slave mart. The kidnapping of Russian and Persian subjects, and their sale as slaves in Khiva, had gone on for a long time. In the first half of this century, the number of Russian slaves was large; there being, according to the authority I have quoted above, before the expedition of General Perovsky, 2000 in Khiva. But during the campaign of this General, in 1839-40, the greater part of them were set at liberty and sent to Orenburg. In the treaty which Colonel Danilewsky made with the Khan, after the ill-fated expedition, the Khivan ruler pledged himself to deal no more in Russian prisoners. In spite of this treaty, and that which was subsequently concluded with the Khan in 1858, the commerce in Russian slaves still continued, though less extensively. Russian prisoners were sold in the Khivan market in recent years for 100, and even 200 tillas; the Persian men at seventy, and the women and young boys at from sixty to 300 tillas. The Russian prisoners were dearer than the Persians, because they worked better; and the Khan generally kept them for himself. Some even attained a certain rank, becoming chiefs in the army, and artillery instructors.

Persia, however, furnished the largest contingent of slaves. The Persian "Shiites," or heretics, were kidnapped by the Turcomans, who captured great numbers of them on the Persian frontier. The treatment of the prisoners by the Turcomans was purposely barbarous. According to Vambéry, they were fed scantily, almost to starvation point, from the fear that if they were better nourished they would escape. Besides being whipped, they were tortured in every possible manner that only

Asiatic barbarity could invent. They were bound at night to stakes so close that they could neither stand nor sit. It is sufficient to say that they arrived in Khiva veritable skeletons.

In the Khanate itself, however, the slaves are not, so far as I could learn, treated so badly. They get enough to eat and drink; and as to their clothes, there is no difference in this respect between the master and his slave. They would not seem to have been overworked, for many of them were able to purchase their liberty by doing extra work.

Afghans were also captured; but, according to the law of the Koran, they could not be sold as slaves, as they are orthodox sunnites, and not heretics. But the avaricious Turcomans and Khivans forced the Affghans, by whipping and other tortures, to acknowledge themselves "shiites," whereupon they were sold as slaves for having renounced the true religion. Jews are never made slaves, owing to the contempt in which they are held by the Mahomedhans. The Russians were captured by the Turcomans for the most part on the east coast of the Caspian Sea; the Kirghiz making prisoners of the Russian fishermen along the northern coast of this sea, and also on the Orenburg and Siberian frontiers.

The Persian and other slaves hailed with wild delight the approach of the Russians; for the emancipation of the slaves has always followed the occupation of any place in Central Asia by the Russians.

After the occupation of Khiva, open war arose between the slaves and their masters. The Persians commenced robbing the Khivans, and then the Khivans came to the Russians in crowds, and besought protection from the fury of the Persians. To put an end to this disorder, strict measures were taken, and two Persians, proved guilty of robbery, were condemned by court-martial to be hanged. I saw their dead bodies hanging to the beams in one of the bazaars, where they remained for several days. I may mention that many of Kaufmann's officers strongly condemned this act, thinking that the Persians had too much reason for taking some vengeance on the masters, to be thus severely treated. The punishment, however, had the double effect of cowing the Persians and of encouraging the masters to punish them severely for the use they had made of their liberty. Several poor fellows came into our camp and showed us gashes in the soles of their feet or in the calves of their legs, in which was strewed cut horsehair.

It was on hearing of these cruelties that General Kaufmann ordered the Khan to issue that proclamation abolishing slavery with regard to which the Khan made the laughable mistake, of which I spoke in a previous chapter. This proclamation was issued on the 24th of June; and the public criers proclaimed it through the streets of Khiva and in all the important towns of the Khanate.

We could not obtain precise information with regard to the number of slaves. Mat-Murad, when questioned on the subject, said that there were only 3000 or 4000. But Mat-Murad, we found, had 400 slaves himself. From all we could gather, there were about 30,000 Persians in Khiva, of whom 27,000 were slaves. I heard that the Russians for a while entertained the project of dividing among the Persians a quantity of unoccupied land in Khiva; but if this excellent idea has come to anything, I have not been informed of it. The Russians determined to send some of the Persians home. Three convoys were formed, of about 500 each; and the Persian Government was asked by telegraph to meet the parties at the frontier. Some of the Persians were sent by Kinderly Bay and Krasnovodsk, and arrived safely at their destination. Others, who went by the Attrek, fell into the hands of the Tekki-Turcomans, and perished miserably. Those who remained in Khiva, though emancipated, are not, I fancy, much better off than before. Some Russian officers seemed to think that three-fourths of the Persians would remain slaves still, and were of opinion that General Kaufmann did not act vigorously enough in this matter. However that be, there can be little doubt that the theoretical abolition of slavery will ultimately result in its practical abolition.

The commerce of the Khanate is concentrated in Yani-Urgench, twenty miles north-east from Khiva. The richest merchants of the Khanate reside there, and do a wholesale business with Russia, Bokhara, and Persia, there being in the capital itself little money or trade. There are 300 shops in Khiva, but the amount of merchandise in them is unimportant, and the greater part of the shops are open but twice a week, on Mondays and Thursdays, which are market-days; on the other days, scarcely any business is transacted.

The following wares are to be seen in the bazaars and shops:—Ripe and dried fruits, wheat, rye, djugera, clover-seed, bread in small rolls, Russian sugar, green tea, which comes from India through Bokhara, domestic Russian and Bokhara stuffs of cotton and silk, bed-covers, boots and shoes, copper-ware, and iron vessels, teapots, teacans, and teacups, which are also brought from Russia.

From this glance it can be easily seen that the greatest traffic is carried on with Russia. There are but two

kinds of English goods to be found—cheap chintz or
calico, and muslin, with the Glasgow stamp.   The Russian
chintz is of a lighter quality, and costs from ten to fifteen
kopeks the yard.

The fruit of Khiva is remarkably fine and abundant,
the dried fruits being a principal export article to Russia.
The melons are of excellent quality, and are sown in
enormous quantities.   They ripen in the latter part of
June, and are, during the summer, a chief article of food.
There are many varieties ; a melon costs about five kopeks.
Water-melons, pomegranates, figs, &c., ripen later.   The
Khivan cucumbers have the form of the melon, and even
the interior of each is not unlike.

A good deal of silk is manufactured in Khiva.   The
whole oasis is planted with white mulberry-trees ; and in
every house throughout the country we found two or
three large rooms full of the busy little spinners, feeding
on the leaves.   And although the whole process of manu-
facture is of the simplest and most primitive kind, silks
of very pretty patterns and of an exceedingly durable
quality are produced.   The whole work of spinning, dyeing,
and weaving is often done in one family by one or two
persons.   The colours are very good, but the people have
little skill in arranging them.   Those wonderful masses of
form and colour that in the sunshine seem to glow and
burn with their own light, for which the weavers of
Bokhara and Kokan are so renowned, are unknown here.
Simple stripes of red, yellow, purple, and brown, is as
far as they have attained in arrangement of colour.

Going along one or two streets in Khiva, you will find
the walls covered with yarn-silk, hung out by the dyers
to dry; and if you do not look sharp, you will find
your clothes bespattered with red and purple, from the

dripping masses over your head. A glance into these factories does not much remind one of the great establishment of Bonnet, at Lyons; but they are interesting in their way, nevertheless, as forming part of the primitive life of this strange, isolated people. The first operation in silk manufacture, that of unwinding the threads from the cocoons, was, however, so much like the same operation in Bonnet's great factory, that if his hands should ever strike, he might easily get workers from Khiva to replace them. You see the same little yellow balls dancing in the basins of hot water, while the thread is wound off on a reel, and your nose recognises the same disagreeable smell. I observed that five cocoons were taken to make up the first thread, just as is done in the Lyons factories. The machinery is very simple. A large wooden wheel, eight feet in diameter, kept in motion by hand, is made to turn a number of little spools, on to which is wound the thread from the cocoons. A reel or two for making the warp comprises all the machinery of the twisting department. The loom is even more simple. There is no mechanical arrangement for separating the warp to allow the passage of the shuttle, and the marvel is how, with such primitive machines, they should still make so much good silk.

CHAPTER XVII.

A DINNER WITH AN UZBEG.

MIRZA HAKIM is the ambassador of Kokan, at Tashkent. What he was while still an untravelled Asiatic, I cannot say; now, at all events, he is a very good fellow. He speaks Russian; has spent a winter in St. Petersburg, and mixed in its fashionable society. He espouses the cause of Patti against Nilsson, drinks champagne, smokes cigarettes, plays cards, and is, in short, quite civilised.

The contrast between him and his royal master is very striking

Khudayar Khan is a fine specimen of the Central Asian potentate. Up to the age of sixteen he was under the tutelage of one Mussulman Kul, who governed in his name, oppressed the people, committed all sorts of atrocities, and carried things with a very high hand. Lest the young Khan should make friends, and thus be able one day to assert his sovereignty, this astute minister never gave him any money, and kept him a kind of prisoner, on a very limited allowance.

At length the continued misrule of Mussulman Kul caused a rebellion The young Khan adopted the rather peculiar plan of joining the insurrection, which was supposed to be directed against his own authority. The

23

rebels received him with open arms; a battle was fought, and Mussulman Kul was overthrown, and captured, with 500 of his followers.

For a period of two months after his accession to the throne, this agreeable young Khan gave a series of very splendid fêtes to celebrate the happy event. He was not revengeful neither, for at every one of these fêtes Mussulman Kul was invited to assist. Each one was rendered picturesque—to Mussulman Kul especially—by the execution of fifteen or twenty of his chief followers. This interesting spectacle was repeated every day for two or three months, and was attended by Mussulman Kul with great assiduity. At last, all his followers having been disposed of, he was invited to exchange his *rôle* of spectator for that of chief actor Saying only, " Allah akhbar "—" Allah is great," he calmly submitted his throat to the executioner's knife.

One day, Mirza Hakim came to me with an invitation to dine with a friend of his, a neighbouring Uzbeg. I gladly accepted the offer. An hour's ride through the gardens brought us to the house of our host. It was a large rectangular structure, of the kind I have already described as belonging to the Uzbegs. A huge cranelated wall surrounded the buildings and inclosed about six acres of ground. This was a very large estate in Khiva, and our host was, therefore, to be considered a wealthy landed proprietor. We first entered a big, rudely-constructed portal, and found ourselves in a small court, around which were a number of stables. Opposite the portal was the entrance to the house itself, before which stood our host, with a number of his people, prepared to meet and welcome us. He did not lead us into the house, however, but took us through a narrow gateway to the left into a garden which surrounded it.   Here a tent was pitched under some elms.   There was a nice plot of grass and a little pool of water, and carpets were spread for us to sit down upon.

No pleasanter spot could have been selected for a meal. The garden, as I have already said, was some acres in extent, and it was planted with fruit-trees, beneath which ran in every direction little canals of clear flowing water.   Towards the further end were two or three small houses resembling summer-houses, in which seemed to live some of our host's people.   Many of these gathered round us, and watched us with curious but respectful gaze; while others helped us to remove our heavy riding-boots and put on the slippers our host had provided.

It was evident that the Uzbeg had made every preparation to make our expected visit agreeable, for he offered us not only Russian cigarettes, but *nalivka*, a kind of gooseberry wine resembling the French *cassisse*, which is much affected by the Russians.   The cigarettes and wine he had obtained from Russian merchants; for scarcely had Khiva been taken, when some ten or twelve, with champagne and other wines, tobacco, and a number of wares, made their appearance—a striking illustration of the enterprise and energy of the Russian trader in extending Russian commerce in Central Asia.

After a while, a cloth was spread on the carpet and dinner was brought in.   In Central Asia, instead of relegating the dessert to the end of the meal, when you have lost all taste and appreciation for it, it is brought in before the solids.   Thus, the first thing we had were fruits—apricots, melons, mulberries.   Then came three or four kinds of sweetmeats much esteemed in Central Asia.

These sweetmeats somewhat resembled toffee, with the addition of the kernels of different nuts; they were of all varieties and colours—red, green, and yellow—and had a very fine flavour. Next came a frothy compound, which was very much like ice-cream without the ice. Into this we dip our thin wheaten cakes, as it is almost liquid and we have no spoons. Then we have various kinds of nuts and *nalivka*, which are followed by the *pièce de résistance* of the meal. The dish now before us is a steaming *pilaoff*, made of great quantities of rice and juicy pieces of mutton, roasted all together in one large vessel. It is not at all a bad dish, and forms the principal part of the Khivan meal.

Large pipes were now brought in, and I began to flatter myself that I was about to enjoy the luxury of a hookah, with something equal, or perhaps superior, to the Turkish tobacco. I was a little disappointed. The pipe consisted of a large gourd, about a foot high. This was nearly filled with water, and on the top was a bowl containing the fire and tobacco, and communicating by a tube with the water. Near the top on either side, just above the water, was a hole, but here was no stem. You simply take up the whole vessel in your hand, and then blow through one of the holes to expel whatever smoke is inside. This done, you put your finger to the hole on one side, and your mouth to that on the other, and then inhale the smoke into your lungs; an operation requiring a certain amount of skill and dexterity, in order to avoid burning your mouth and scorching your eyebrows. Naturally, a very few whiffs were sufficient for me, and I was glad to return to my cigarettes.

We now walked about the grounds, the Uzbeg showing us everything, evidently with great pleasure. There was but little to be seen beyond a wooden plough, probably not unlike the one used by Adam, a few rudely-wrought hoes and rakes, one or two arbas—the wooden car of the country—and two or three scythes. Our host then brought us into his barn, in which there was a considerable store of wheat and barley just gathered in, and of new-saved hay. I was in hopes that he would next take us into his house, and show us its internal arrangements and his wife and children; but in this I was disappointed.

I had afterwards an opportunity of seeing the interior of an Uzbeg house; and I suppose that of my host was pretty much the same. There is little attempt at luxury or taste in the house of even the richest; and in this respect the poorest seems almost on an equality with the most opulent. A few carpets on the floor; a few rugs and cushions round the wall, with shelves for earthenware and China porcelain; three or four heavy, gloomy books, bound in leather or parchment; and some pots of jam and preserved fruit, generally make up the contents of the room. There are usually two or three apartments in the house different from the others, in having arrangements for obtaining plenty of light. In these rooms you find the upper half of one of the walls completely wanting, with the overhanging branches of an elm projecting through the opening. The effect is peculiar and striking, as well as pleasant. From the midst of this room—with mud walls and uneven floor, with the humblest household utensils, and perhaps a smoking fire—you get glimpses of the blue sky through the green leaves of the elm-tree. A slightly-projecting roof protects the room from rain; in cold weather, of course, it is abandoned.

Two or three other rooms are devoted to the silkworms,

the feeding and care of which form the special occupation
of the women.   The worms naturally receive a great deal
of attention, for their cocoons pay a great part of the
household expenses.

To return to my host; the sun had set, and we were
now to be shown the great entertainment of the evening.
We returned to the little grassplot where we had taken our

DANCING BOYS.

dinner, sat down, and resumed our pipes and cigarettes.
Two young boys, the one about eight, the other about ten
years of age, came forward, and, having made a respectful
salaam, disposed themselves to dance.   They were simply
dressed in the long loose khalat of the Khivans, which
reached almost to the heels.   Their heads were shaven,

with the exception of two long black locks, which were behind each ear, and fell over their shoulders. They wore a little conical skull-cap, and their feet were bare. They were very beautiful children indeed, with very large dark eyes and long heavy lashes, and they appeared merry, light-hearted, and well cared-for; and, considering their degrading occupation, I was surprised to find an exceedingly bright intelligent expression in their faces.

A little crowd of people had now gathered—retainers, probably, and servants of the Uzbeg. A ragged-looking musician stepped forward. He had a three-stringed guitar, much resembling those found in the palace of the Khan, which I have already described. Crouching down upon the ground beside a tree, he began to sing, accompanying himself on the instrument. The manner of singing was something like that of the Kirghiz, possessing very little melody, and apparently no musical arrangement whatever; a mere sing-song sort of whine, in a high key, interrupted here and there by exclamatory phrases. The accompaniment on the guitar was, on the contrary, pretty and rather curious. The boys began to dance. For a while their movements were very slow and leisurely. They simply seemed to hop from one foot to the other, keeping time to the music and clapping their hands over their heads, and swaying their bodies in a variety of graceful movements and poses. Soon the music grew more lively, and the boys gradually became excited. They clapped their hands wildly, uttered short occasional shouts, and then began to turn somersaults, to wrestle with each other, and roll upon the ground. This seemed to delight the spectators, who heartily applauded. The Uzbeg himself was greatly amused, laughed very immoderately, and, having picked up the boys, talked to them

caressingly, and gave them refreshments. This perform-
ance was repeated, almost without variation, four or five
times during the evening.

As it grew dark, torches were brought and arranged
around, some being stuck in the ground and some fastened
to the trunks and branches of trees. The prettier of the
boys now dressed himself up as a girl, with little bells to
his wrists and feet, and a very elaborate and pretty cap,
covered with bells and ornaments of silver, and with a
veil hanging down behind. He then danced a new kind
of dance, more quiet and modest than that he had gone
through as a boy. After this had continued for about a
quarter of an hour, the other boy came forward, and,
dancing together, the two enacted a love scene very
prettily. He who did the part of the girl pretended to
be offended, turned his back, and seemed disposed to sulk
and pout. The other boy danced round the apparently-
offended young lady, endeavouring, by all sorts of
caresses, to restore her to good-humour. This failing, he
grew vexed, and commenced sulking in his turn. The
lady thereupon began to relent, and in her turn resorted
to all forms of conciliation. The lover, having for a time
proved inexorable, at last gave in; they then danced
together with great apparent joy and animation, and
then rushed off the scene amid the laughter of the
audience. All this was done very gracefully and with
much seeming intelligence. The actions of the one who
was playing the girl were very pretty and coquettish.
The torches casting a fitful light on the nodding branches
of the trees overhead, the wild faces around, and these
two children enacting a love scene, made up a strange
and picturesque tableau.

It had now grown late. As Mirza Hakim and myself

... ... This perform-
... ... almost without variation, four or five
... ... the evening.

... grew dark, torches were brought and arranged
... ... some being stuck in the ground and some fastened
... trunks and branches of trees. The prettier of the
... dressed himself up as a girl, with little bells to
his ... ... and a very elaborate and pretty cap.
... ... bells and ornaments of silver, and with a
... hanging down behind. He then danced a new kind
... dance more quiet and modest than that he had gone
through as a boy. After this had continued for about a
quarter of an hour, the other boy came forward, and,
dancing together, the two enacted a love scene very
prettily. He who did the part of the girl pretended to
be offended, turned his back, and seemed disposed to sulk
and pout. The other boy danced round the apparently-
offended young lady, endeavouring, by all sorts of
caresses, to restore her to good-humour. This failing, he
grew vexed and commenced sulking in his turn. The
lady thereupon began to relent, and in her turn resorted
to all forms of conciliation. The lover, having for a time
proved inexorable, at last gave in; they then danced
together with great apparent joy and animation, and
then rushed off the scene amid the laughter of the
audience. All this was done very gracefully and with
much seeming intelligence. The actions of the one who
was playing the girl were very pretty and coquettish.
The torches casting a fitful light on the nodding branches
of the trees overhead, the wild faces around, and these
two children enacting a love scene ... up a strange
and picturesque tableau.

It had now grown late. ... Hakim and myself

UZBEG WOMEN. *From a design by Veretchagin.*

had intended returning to the camp before the patrols of the night were placed, we had not received the pass-word. A return would consequently have been somewhat disagreeable; for, to say nothing of the dark ride through the gardens, it would have been difficult to get past the Russian sentinels. We decided to stay all night. Our host, again, did not invite us into his house, but had rugs and cushions spread for us in the tent. Here Mirza Hakim and I threw ourselves down, and went to sleep. We were awakened in the night by the rain beating in our faces. We drew the sides of the tent together, and so managed to pass the night without getting very wet, although the rain was heavy. Next morning, after a hearty breakfast and a cordial farewell from our host, we mounted our horses and rode back to the camp.

CHAPTER XVIII.

A DINNER WITH THE GRAND DUKE NICHOLAS.

A REGIMENT is given to every member of the Russian imperial family on his birth. The regiment bears his name; the soldiers learn to look up to him with personal loyalty and devotion, and he is taught to regard them as specially under his care and protection. These terms subsist frequently for years before the commander and his regiment have ever seen each other. This was the case with the Grand Duke Nicholas Constantinovitch and his regiment. After being quartered in the Caucasus for years, two of its companies accompanied Colonel Lamakin's detachment from Kinderly; and thus the regiment and its commander met for the first time before the walls of Khiva. The Grand Duke determined to celebrate the event by a banquet. The feast took place in the camp of the Orenburg detachment, which adjoined that of General Kaufmann outside the walls of Khiva.

The banquet was spread in the open air, in a garden three or four acres in extent. The place was grandly illuminated, improvised Chinese lanterns hanging from the branches of the peach and apricot trees; and a triumphal arch was constructed from the branches of poplar.

Altogether the appearance was not unlike that of the Jardin Mabille.

Carpets were spread along the ground; and around these were at one end collected the officers, and at the other some 200 or 300 soldiers. When I arrived, the Grand Duke had already made his speech to his men, the dishes were laid, and there was altogether a scene of great animation. The bill of fare was in no way remarkable, but not so the wine list. Besides the inevitable *vodka*, of which there were enormous quantities, several kinds of wine flowed freely. Among the rest, there was a very good supply of champagne; for you will find champagne among the Russians where you cannot get bread. Clear and bubbling the wine flowed, giving beauty and value to the nondescript and decrepit glasses that we held out; we revelled in the possession of the precious fluid, brought from the sunny hills of France over hundreds of miles of burning sand, on the backs of camels, into this almost inaccessible corner of the earth. I should mention that we procured most of our wine from the same indefatigable Russian merchants who had supplied my Uzbeg host the day before with his cigarettes and *nalivka*. We drank the champagne with the greater gusto because it was not dear, it having only cost £3 a bottle.

Dinner passed off with much merriment on all sides, and concluded with a famous bowl of Russian punch. This punch is made of a mixture of vodka, champagne, nalivka, and any other kind of wine that may be at hand. Apricots, melons, and cucumbers are put in to flavour and sugar to sweeten it, and the whole is then ignited, and allowed to burn till it boils. Though palatable and insinuating, it is the most diabolical compound I have ever tasted, for its every drop is laden with headache for a week and dyspepsia for a fortnight.

Dinner over, the real entertainments of the evening commence. First there was a dance of a wild and grotesque kind by the mountaineers of the Caucasus. A circle was formed. Each man got up in his turn and danced to a shrill kind of piping, like that of the bag-pipes, which came from a little flute, the other soldiers meantime clapping their hands to the music. Then came songs in the Caucasian dialect, which raised shouts of laughter among those who understood them. The songs were of an extraordinary character, interrupted here and there by phrases spoken in ordinary tones, and the language itself was full of guttural sounds and clicks, which could only be enunciated by a Caucasian. The Russian Caucasians next danced and sang in their turn Among the rest, they sang a fisherman's song entitled 'Vniss po matushké po Volgé,' or 'Down the Mother Volga,' which was one of the finest things I ever heard.

By this time, under the influence of supper and the libations which so frequently accompanied it, we had all become pretty jolly. Suddenly, to my astonishment, the cry of " Viliki Kniaz !" " Viliki Kniaz !" was raised, and a moment afterwards I saw the Grand Duke seized by his own soldiers in the most unceremonious manner. For a moment he disappears among the surging crowd of men ; the next minute I see him in a horizontal position, ten feet up in the air. He goes down and goes up again, and again up and again down, twenty times at least, being caught each time he descends in the outspread arms of the soldiers, who are laughing wildly all the while. At last, when he must have lost all consciousness of time and place, he is carried almost senseless to his seat at the head of the table. Then there is more dancing, more singing, more-drinking; and another officer is seized and undergoes the same unceremonious treatment. I was somewhat bewildered by all this at first, and began to think that the soldiers, carried away by the excitement of the scene and the vodka they had been drinking, were passing all bounds in treating their officers in so off-hand a way. Just imagine the Prince of Wales tossed ten feet in the air by the privates of the "Black Watch!" I soon learned that this tossing was a mark of particular affection, and that no officer not liked by the soldiers was ever favoured with it.

While I am mentally rejoicing that I do not live in the affections of the soldiers, I hear a cry of "Americanetz!" "Americanetz!" and before I know where I am, I feel a number of rough hands seize me by the arms, legs, and head. The Chinese lanterns, trees, soldiers, and sky suddenly change places and dance before my eyes in wild and inextricable confusion, and the next instant I enjoy a view of the whole scene from an elevated position of ten feet, and look down on a sea of up-turned faces and out-stretched arms. Into these I sink, until I almost touch the ground, and then again I mount to the stars. So, up and down, up and down, till my brain whirls, and my senses become dazed, and everything around is mixed into one confused and blurred picture. At length, after what appears to me an age, I find myself lying on the carpet, among the remnants of the feast, almost senseless and wholly breathless.

"The hug of the Russian bear is rough, but it is hearty," said the Grand Duke, shaking me by the hand and confirming the initiation I had just received at the hands of his men.

It had now grown late, and the Grand Duke began to think of returning to his camp. Everybody opposed his leaving in the most energetic manner; but finding him determined on going, they at last reluctantly consented to his departure. He then shook hands with them all round, the soldiers responding with marks of the greatest devotion and affection. Then they formed themselves into a grand escort, to conduct him back to his camp. We mounted our horses, and every soldier seizing a torch went in front to show the way. In the darkness we followed them through many sinuous turnings, they all the time continuing to shout and sing, and indulge in all the expressions of wild enjoyment.

After a quarter of an hour's march, we found ourselves —exactly where we had started. Our guides professed to have lost their way, and now represented to the Grand Duke the impossibility of reaching home in the darkness.

The Grand Duke, however, was still resolved to return; and once more we started forth with the same escort, the same flaming torches, and amid the same shouts and singing. But again there was a disappointment, for we found the road inundated, so that it was difficult and even dangerous to proceed. The soldiers had let the water in by cutting the banks of a canal, and thus making the Grand Duke a prisoner, obliged him to stay all night with them. He took the joke pleasantly enough, and laughingly consented—when he could have no longer refused—to remain.

After more singing, more dancing, and more drinking, it was decided to retire to rest. The troops and officers here, being for the most part without tents or kibitkas, had constructed very comfortable little houses out of reeds plaited into mats. Into one of these the Grand Duke and I were led. We found beds made for us, the floors carpeted, and every other preparation for passing the night comfortably. We threw ourselves on our beds, and, after such a banquet, sleep came sound and soon.

Nicholas Constantinovitch returned to St. Petersburg soon after, and I have never seen him since. His conduct throughout the campaign was exemplary. Fresh from a life of luxurious ease in St. Petersburg, he showed what stuff he was made of by the way in which he endured the terrible cold of the first part of the campaign, and afterwards the scorching heat at Khala-ata and Alty-Kuduk. Under fire he showed all the coolness and bravery of a veteran.

24

CHAPTER XIX.

TWO RUSSIAN PORTRAITS—ANDREI ALEXANDROVITCH.

ANDREI ALEXANDROVITCH comes of one of the oldest families of Russia. This is saying a good deal, for some of these old Russian families can trace their genealogy back to the eighth century, when they were reigning houses of the then disjointed Muscovite people. In this long descent of a thousand years, Andrei's family has degenerated little; and many of them still retain that physical strength and power of endurance which made their ancestors kings. It is no uncommon thing to find among them, as among many other families of rank, a man who will break a five-franc piece with his fingers with as great apparent ease as if it were lead. The relatives of Andrei retain all their ancient pride of race; and no Hohenzollern glories more proudly in his ancient lineage.

The parents of Andrei Alexandrovitch have a large estate in the environs of Kharkoff, were formerly the owners of several hundred serfs, and are very rich. Andrei's father served with distinction in the wars of Napoleon, attained a high rank, and won several decorations. He not unnaturally wished his son to follow in the same honourable career, and he easily obtained for

Andrei, who was a handsome boy, admission into the corps des pages in the Imperial household at a very early age. Here Andrei was petted by the ladies, and patted on the head by a Grand Duke, or sometimes even by the Emperor. He learned to dance, sing, and fence; to return compliment for compliment, and sarcasm for sarcasm, and all the other accomplishments which are supposed to win the favour of ladies and distinction among men. Having, after a time, entered the military school, he in due course graduated as an ensign, and entered the Guard.

Now the Guard is the rock on which every Russian splits. Everybody in Russia enters the Guard. It is the fashionable thing to do. You will not find a man with the least pretension to respectability who has not been at some time or other in this favoured corps. It is the *corps d'élite* of the Empire, and is the centre of all that wild whirl of dissipation, of extravagance, and folly for which St. Petersburg is so famous. It requires a cooler head and a more phlegmatic disposition than most Russian young gentlemen possess to steer through this vortex of dissipation without suffering financial ruin; and the Guard, it may be safely asserted, is responsible for three-fourths of the wrecked careers of which there are so many in Russian society. This fact does not seem to produce any warning influence on anxious parents; and it produces far less, of course, upon their hopeful sons just entering upon their career. In spite of the hundreds of examples before them, parents exhaust every effort to obtain admission for their sons into the Guard, and look upon a commission in that corps as the most brilliant and desirable start in life. As to the young men themselves, they all evince that faculty for imitation and that lamentable want of originality which have been always regarded as the peculiar characteristics of sheep.

Andrei Alexandrovitch proves no exception to the rule. Three years of life in the Guard suffices to ruin him. In that time he has managed to squander his fortune and his credit, and to get himself, besides, head over ears in debt. He is obliged to leave the Guard, because he can pay his way there no longer, and falls back into a regiment of the line.

Andrei now passes a certain time in what may be called a transition state; dodging his creditors, "doing" landlords and restaurant proprietors, and generally living from hand to mouth by the aid of his wits and his skill in card-playing. But this cannot go on for ever; and Andrei Alexandrovitch at last finds himself compelled to choose one of three different courses. He may marry the daughter of a rich tradesman, and so re-establish his fortunes; he may try his chance in a civil profession; or he may go to Turkistan.

Andrei Alexandrovitch feels no liking just yet for the quiet joys of conjugal existence; he has no taste for a civil career; while in Turkistan there is the still attractive *abandon* of a soldier's life, with double pay and double chance of promotion. For Turkistan has now taken the place of the Caucasus as the refuge of men like Andrei, ruined in fortune, but still hopeful of the future. So Andrei bids adieu to his friends in St. Petersburg, reaches Kazala, and is immediately sent forward to take part in the siege operations against Ak-Mesdjid.

On the day of his arrival he finds everything prepared for an assault, and immediately volunteers to lead the forlorn hope. His bravery wins him a decoration and two grades, and fortune once more seems to smile upon him. But Andrei Alexandrovitch possesses the faculty of defeating his own fortunes faster than a hundred fairy godmothers could mend them.

One morning he takes a walk outside the town, to visit the kibitka of a young lady of the Kirghiz race, whose charms have some attraction for him. In the kibitka he finds his brother officer, Stefan Ivanovitch. Now Stefan Ivanovitch is one of the few men for whom Andrei has no love. Already they have had more than one quarrel in their cups and over the card-table, and Andrei, whose pugnacious disposition is notorious, has been advised by more than one friend to avoid meeting Stefan as much as possible. Andrei had promised to obey the suggestion, but, of course, a meeting so unexpected and in such peculiar circumstances could only end in a duel. The duel comes off, and Stefan receives a bullet through the heart at the first shot. Andrei is brought before a court-martial and reduced to the ranks; for in the Russian army an officer may be, and often is, reduced to the rank of a common soldier. Thus Andrei not only loses all that he had won in Turkistan, but something more.

In Central Asia, however, where more or less fighting is always going on, a brave officer does not long remain without an opportunity of distinguishing himself. After two or three years, Andrei rises to his old rank and gains two or three decorations more. Meantime the Russians have been advancing in Turkistan, and General Tchernaieff has sat down before the walls of Tashkent. Here Andrei has another opportunity of distinguishing himself, and he takes advantage of it in the following manner:—

In the course of the siege operations he becomes

involved in a quarrel with a brother officer, who throws some imputation on his courage. Andrei, without any more ado, proposes to his assailant that they should together make an assault on the walls. Without any orders, the two officers draw up their men in line and rush to the assault. There is a wide and deep ditch to cross, the walls are about thirty feet high, no breach has been battered, and the soldiers have no ladders. The result may easily be imagined. One half of the men are left in the ditch; the other half retreat with difficulty from the impossible and absurd enterprise, under a terrible fire from the walls; Andrei Alexandrovitch himself receives three wounds, and has to be carried off the field by his men; whilst his opponent is left amongst the dead. For this little feat he is once again reduced to the ranks.

During the next few years he has but few opportunities of distinguishing himself; so he leads a listless, careless, vagabond sort of life, which is, in Central Asia, not without its charms. He spends nearly every day in the same round of smoking, drinking vodka, and playing cards, varied only by an occasional hunt for tigers.

Andrei Alexandrovitch was one of the first men who addressed me when I reached General Kaufmann's army; and the acquaintance, thus begun, rapidly ripened into intimacy, and even friendship. At this time, after twenty years' service, he has attained the elevated rank of ensign. This disparity between his age and rank does not, however, strike you as unbecoming; for the fellow seems to have the gift of perpetual youth. Though now close upon forty, he looks scarcely more than twenty, despite the wild, reckless life he has led.

I found him to be the best of good fellows, and generous

to a fault. Utterly careless as to the future, he would spend one morning the £20 he had won at cards the night before on a breakfast to his brother officers, and next day borrow money to buy tea and sugar for himself and barley for his horse. Brave as a lion, he would lead a forlorn hope, start on a three months' march across the desert, or go on parade with equal coolness and indifference, and with about the same amount of preparation. In fact, he had entered on the Khiva campaign with only three days' supply of provisions.

Andrei Alexandrovitch is a good linguist, but by no fault of his. When he was a child, he had English, French, and German governesses, and he thus learned these languages as he had learned his own, without study or application. He has now spent several years in Turkistan, yet he knows scarcely a word of the Tartar language. Whatever he knows of military affairs—and he knows a great deal—he has learned, not from books, but from actual experience. He has literary talent, too, of no mean order, and can coin French verses with a facility which is remarkable.

After the Khivan campaign he received two decorations the Saint Vladimir and the Saint Anne. He was offered promotion, likewise, but this he refused "You see," said he to me, "the difference between the pay of an ensign and that of a lieutenant is so small that it is not an object At my age, I would just as soon be one as the other. It is not everybody either that can be an ensign at thirty-eight."

"I think I would prefer the promotion to the decoration," I observed. "Ah, there you would be wrong. I have a respected maternal relative who, when she hears I have won the Vladimir—the highest order, you know, next to Saint George—will probably come down with twenty thousand rubles." "How long do you think that will last you when you get it ?" I ask. "Why a year or two, perhaps. No use in having money unless you spend it, and get something for it, you know."

Andrei Alexandrovitch is a slightly exaggerated type of the Russian officer in Turkistan—I might say of a large class of officers throughout the entire empire. They have not all been reduced to the ranks several times, and they are not all ensigns at forty, but the career of each of them is parallel to that of Andrei Alexandrovitch in every other particular. They have all been in the Guard; they have all squandered their fortunes in it; they have all followed faithfully in the beaten track of their predecessors. All are careless of the future, determined to make the most of the present; and all lead the same easy, indifferent, vagabond kind of life. They pass most of their time in playing cards; the mania of the Russians of all classes, indeed, for play is most excessive. I have seen them sit down and play for forty-eight hours, scarcely ever rising from the table during the whole time I had thought only savages could evince such a passion for gaming; and the truth is, this passion among the Russians is a relic of barbarism, which still clings to them.

They never study, and they no more bother their heads about the future operations of the army, or even the orders for the morrow, than does one of their own soldiers. In most armies on a campaign like the present, the officers would all know and discuss the plan of operations, the movements about to be made, and what would be required for their execution. They would all have maps and all the information to be obtained regarding the route over which they were marching.

This was not the case with the Russians. They neither knew nor cared what were the movements to be made, nor their chances of success. Of the orders for the morrow, the preparation that might be required for their execution, they knew nothing. None of them except, of course, two or three of the staff, had maps; and none of them even knew how far it was to the next well. They simply obey orders, no matter what they are; and the possibility of executing an order is a thing they never discuss.

Although all good linguists, there were not three officers in the whole of Kaufmann's detachment that knew the language of the country.

It is not to be supposed from this that the Russians are poor officers. They are as brave as lions; and there is not one among them that would hesitate to lead a forlorn hope, or that would not walk up to certain death with as much coolness as to dinner. They obey orders with a kind of blind, unreasoning heroism, that is only equalled by that of their own soldiers. Generous, kindly, pleasant fellows withal, ever ready to offer you their hospitality or do you a favour, they are sure to win your affection and esteem.

The Russian officers have very strong likes and dislikes. For the Americans and the French they have feelings of the utmost friendliness. They speak, by preference, the French language; love French literature and French music; and they endeavour to imitate French ways of living. And their sympathies in the last war were altogether with France. The Germans they detest as cordially as they like the French; and, indeed, a Frenchman hates the German with a hatred scarcely more bitter than that of the Russian, civilian or soldier. The origin

of this hatred must be sought in the time of Peter the
Great. When that monarch determined to introduce
Western civilisation into his empire, he had, of course,
to cast about among foreigners for the men to carry out
this purpose. He naturally selected Germany, as the
country nearest to him, and Germans were chosen to fill
the highest offices in the state, civil and military. The
jealousy thus created still lasts; for many of the descendants of the Germans—although they are now, of course,
thorough Russians—still occupy foremost places in the
country. And thus it is that Russia is filled with hatred
for Germany, that has been so often her most steadfast
friend; and with love for France, that has been in past
times her greatest enemy. The feelings of the Russian
officers towards the English are very different. They
look upon the English, if not with liking, at least with a
good deal of respect: but none the less anticipate a time
when the collision of Russian and English interests may
bring Russian and English armies into conflict. But into
such a contest they would bring no feeling of national
and ineradicable hate. And just as Russian and English
officers, during the days of truce at the Crimea, smoked
cigarettes, and exchanged friendly and courteous conversation with each other, so Russian officers would fight
with Englishmen without any great personal grudge,
but, on the contrary, with a chivalric feeling of respect
and esteem.

CHAPTER XX.

IVAN IVANOFF.

IVAN IVANOFF is a soldier in the regiment of Andrei
Alexandrovitch.

Ivan Ivanoff was born the serf of Andrei Alexandrovitch.
and he is a very different sort of person from that young
gentleman. In order to form a just estimate of the character of Ivan Ivanoff, it will be necessary to know something of his father, Ivan Michailoff. Ivan Michailoff is a
peasant; and his fathers have been, for generations, serfs
of the fathers of Andrei Alexandrovitch. He has never
known anything but the severest toil and the hardest fare.
Until emancipated, he had to work for his master four
days out of the seven, finding his own food, implements,
and horses; and had to support himself and family by his
labour during the other three days.

When it is remembered that half the year in Russia one
cannot work at all, owing to the deep snow, it will be
easily imagined that Ivan does not make a very good living.
Often, after performing a hard day's labour for his master,
he would work half the night for himself; and he never
tasted anything but soup and black bread. He lives in a
hut consisting of one room, in which the children—girls
and boys, old and young—all herd together. His grown

sons, with their wives and their children, live with
him in the same house, and the same room. Under these
circumstances, it can hardly be expected that Ivan
Michailoff should be distinguished for education, enlightenment, or refinement. He is, on the contrary, rather
remarkable for the absence of these qualities. He is
ignorant and superstitious to the last degree, but Ivan
Michailoff has, nevertheless, some good points. He is
neither brutal nor cruel by nature, nor is he the slave of
any degrading vices. He has some independence of
thought, too; and although religious and pious in the
extreme, has more or less contempt for his priest, who is
scarcely less ignorant than himself. Ivan Michailoff's
weak point is that of Napoleon I. It is his fatalism.
It affects him in a different way, however; instead of
making him hope all, and risk all, it makes him despair.
He emphatically does *not* believe in his star. He does
not even know he has a star; or, if he does, he considers
it a baleful star—a star to be mistrusted, doubted, and
detested.

If his house gets on fire, it is the will of God;
and he lets it burn. It would be flying in the face of
Providence to attempt putting it out. If he gets sick, he
refuses to take medicine for the same reason. If he has
the misfortune to make a mistake, and appropriate goods,
chattels, or moneys belonging to another, he maintains it
was *Chort*, the devil, who drove him to do it, and declines
to take any responsibility in the matter.

The truth is, Ivan Michailoff feels that he is not a free
agent. Centuries of oppression, ages of tyranny through
which his ancestors have passed—the iron hand of des-
potism that he himself has always felt upon his throat,
hard, unrelenting, and inexorable, has rendered him thus

fatalistic. Why resist the inevitable? Why struggle against the inexorable? Ivan's whole turn of thought and sentiment is, therefore, pervaded by a sombre tinge of sadness and depression.

His·stories all have tragic endings. Instead of Jack killing the giant by superior cunning and skill, it is the giant who kills and eats poor Jack. Ivan is persecuted and beset by vampires, and ghouls, and demons, from whose demoniac intelligence and pitiless voracity there is no escape. His songs are of hopeless love; and his music all in the minor tones, weird and melancholy as a funeral dirge.

Ivan Ivanoff, his son, is all this, and something more. Torn in early youth from village home and friends, to give fifteen or twenty of the best years of his life to the Tsar, he leaves all the hopes and desires of ordinary men far behind him. For twenty years he has nothing to look forward to but the routine of camp life. There are no pictures of wife and children, and pleasant fireside for him. Most of the friends of his youth he will never see again. He knows that long ere he returns to his village father and mother will be dead, sweetheart married, brothers and sisters grown old, and himself forgotten. His whole life has been changed; he has become another kind of being. Perhaps the change at first was bitter; he may have wept at it His poor home was not very attractive and comfortable; but it was home, nevertheless, and he will never see it again. But the great machine of State soon crushed him to uniformity, and moulded him to his place. Thenceforth he has only been an animated automaton, moved by a will far above and beyond his comprehension; he has submitted blindly and unresistingly to his fate The iron yoke is so solidly fixed that he never thinks of trying to throw it off. It is not in his character to struggle against the inexorable. God has willed it. It would be sinful as well as useless to repine, and he determines to make the best of a hard lot.

But amid the bustle and excitement of a soldier's life he loses the pensive sadness of his father, isolated in his remote far away village. He has little to hope, it is true; but then he has nothing to lose, and that is a source of unhappiness removed, and he becomes the merriest fellow in the world.

Ivan's chief source of amusement is singing. He sings from morning until night. On the march he keeps it up for hours. He has songs five hundred verses in length, which he sings through from beginning to end, with much apparent consolation and satisfaction. In the midst of the desert—at Irkibai, at Khala-ata, at Alty-Kuduk, when the heat was terrible, and he had an allowance of a pint of water a day, you might have seen him, at almost any hour, with fifteen or twenty comrades standing around in a circle, singing at the top of his lungs. It must be remarked, too, that he regards this act of singing as a matter of importance: a task not to be performed negligently. Therefore, when he sings, he stands up; and his comrades gather around him, serious and attentive, and join in the chorus, which occurs at the end of almost every line. There is something exaggerated in his good-humour. The indecency of some of his songs is so grotesque as to lose all character of indecency, and to be only laughably absurd and ridiculous.

Ivan Ivanoff has a confidence in the integrity and ability of his officers, which is highly commendable and edifying He believes them to be infallible; he is sure they always do the best thing that is to be done, and in the very best way. Therefore he never mutinies. Another soldier may grumble if he have not milk for his coffee, or meat at least once a day. Ivan is far above complaining of such trifles. If no meat is given him, it is evidently because there is none. Or if the meat furnished is rotten, it is because of the hot weather, and there is no help for it. If his shoes are worthless, and his feet get frozen, it is by reason of the cold. If his biscuits are worm-eaten, it is the fault of the worms. He never thinks of blaming anybody If by any bungling mistake he is brought under fire, where his comrades fall around him by the hundred, and his regiment undergoes sure annihilation, it is the will of God, and must be submitted to. Nor does it ever occur to him to correct the judgment of his officers by running away. In short, Ivan Ivanoff thinks, with Pope, that whatever is is right, and therefore is willing to take things as they are. He will live happily on black bread and tea, and never think of complaining.

Ivan Ivanoff has nobody to love but his comrades and his officers, and them he loves passionately, although in a stolid, unconscious sort of way. It is no uncommon thing for eight or ten soldiers to be killed in attempting to carry off a wounded comrade. There is nothing melo-dramatic about Ivan, either He will make the most heroic exertions without even being aware that he is doing any-thing out of the way, or that merits commendation. There is a kind of unconscious heroism about Ivan that is sublime. This is what made Napoleon say of him, " It is not enough to kill a Russian soldier; you must knock him down."

Ivan has peculiar notions about foreigners. For him they are all rebels against the Tsar English, French, German, or Asiatics, they are all insurgents alike, and he looks forward with pleasure to the early subjection of all the races of mankind to their rightful sovereign. Ivan never seems to have any personal ill-will against his foes; he never calls them names. Apart from the fact of their being rebels, he is ready to acknowledge that they are a very good sort of people. He will even admit that they are very brave. You never, therefore, hear him express contempt for his enemies, which is so common a thing among other soldiers. This is one reason, perhaps, why he never becomes panic-stricken. He is never astonished by any sudden attack on the part of the foe, for it was only what was to be expected.

In short, Ivan Ivanoff is the officer's ideal of the soldier; and, everything considered, is the best soldier in the world.

The whole story of his life is well told in one of his own songs, translated by Mr. Robert Michell.

> For God and for the Tsar,
> I've served in peace and war
> These five-and-twenty years.
> I left, when young, my house and kin,
> My wife and child; and theirs the sin,
> Who sold me for a bribe and parted us in tears
> I'm not so old, though wrinkled, scarr'd, and worn.
> I've bearded the Turk,
> I've snatched the threat'ning dirk,
> And stuck the mountaineer;
> I've toiled, and marched, and bled.
> Nor rested under shed,
> Nor broken bread for days; and borne these woes
> To spread the faith and lay the Emperor's foes.
>   For God and for the Tsar, &c.
>
> My term at last expired,—
> Bleeding, infirm, and tired,—
>   I drained a parting cup;
> Embraced my comrades well;
> Brushed off the tears that fell,
>   Then gave my bayonet up.

I took my pass and pay,—
Due at three groats a day;
A pipe, and hardened crust
Within my bosom thrust,
The money safely placed
Within my boots, I faced
The road, and went—
To Holy Kief bent.
An ashen staff my rest,
And all my pride—my medals on my breast.
       For God and for the Tsar,
        I've served in peace and war
       These five-and-twenty years.

25

PART III.

—

THE TURCOMAN CAMPAIGN.

.

CHAPTER I.

THE TURCOMANS.

THE Turcomans are the bravest and most warlike race of Central Asia.

They are a nomadic people, scattered over nearly all the country between the Oxus and the Caspian, as far east as Afghanistan, and as far south as the frontier of Persia. Their means of existence are various; those on the shores of the Caspian live in great part on fish; those farther east and north on their flocks and herds. But one of their principal resources hitherto has been catching Persians, and selling them as slaves in Khiva and Bokhara.

Parts of six tribes have settled in Khiva, viz., the Imrali, numbering 2500 kibitkas, the Chandors, 3500; the Karadashli, 2000, the Kara Jigeldi, 1500; the Alieli-Igoklens, 1500; the Yomuds, 11,000.—in all, 22,000 kibitkas, which, at an average of five persons to the kibitka, would make a population of 110,000 souls.

A wild and turbulent people, they have never been subjected to any regular form of government, and flout all authority, whether of Khan, Emir, or Tsar.

Each tribe is divided into many smaller subdivisions, which probably are formed by family ties and connections, and which are presided over by head men, or chiefs.

But the state does not exist among the Turcomans. There is no body politic, no recognised authority, no supreme power, no higher tribunal than public opinion. Their head men, it is true, have a kind of nominal authority to settle disputes; but they have no power to enforce decisions. These the litigants can accept, or fight out their quarrel, just as they please. And yet they have such well-defined notions of right and wrong as between themselves, and public opinion is so strong in enforcing these notions, that there are rarely dissensions or quarrels amongst them.

The Khan of Khiva has never been able to exert any control over the Turcomans inhabiting his dominions. In fact, the reverse is nearer the truth, for they always have exercised a very decided control over him. While allowing him a kind of nominal authority as ruler of their neighbours, the Uzbegs, they resist all attempts to extend that authority over themselves. Although intruders on Khivan territory, they decline to bear any portion of the general burden; and so far from paying any taxes, are rather disposed to exact tribute. They are always ready to fight for the Khan, however—when not fighting against him; and it is on them he principally relies for his soldiers. They have given over their nomadic mode of life to a great extent, but they have by no means abandoned their predatory habits. This has given rise to a continual feud between them and the Uzbegs; scarcely a year passing without a fight between them. Indeed it was the marauding propensities of the Turcomans that furnished the principal pretext for the Russian invasion of Khiva.

The Khan has several times tried to subdue them, but always without success. In spite of their want of artillery, they have been able to hold their own against very superior numbers, and to exert a very powerful influence on the affairs of the Khanate.

The Khan's usual plan of operation is as follows. He assembles an army, marches into their country, camps, and fortifies himself. The Turcomans instantly attack, or pretend to attack, galloping around the camp, shouting, yelling, firing their matchlocks, and cutting off small bodies of the Khan's troops who may rashly expose themselves outside of their earthworks. The Khan replies by throwing solid shot at them from his cannon; but as it requires the expenditure of several tons of iron in this way to kill a single man, the damage to the Turcomans is very small. As the Khan never marches out of his camp, their respective rules are reversed, and instead of his subduing the Turcomans, it becomes a question of their subduing him. This usually continues for some weeks. The Turcomans enjoy the thing immensely, and this time is for them a kind of holiday. When the Khan has expended all his munitions, and exhausted his provisions—the Turcomans easily succeed in cutting off his supplies—he makes a treaty with them, which changes their relations in nothing, then marches back in triumph to his capital, and then—the Turcomans resume their ordinary occupations.

Everything considered, however, the Khan had more reason to be satisfied with the Turcomans than otherwise. In spite of these little misunderstandings, they were always faithful to him. Although they refused to acknowledge his supremacy over themselves, they helped him willingly enough to maintain his authority over others. If they refused to pay taxes, or allow any interference in their affairs, they were ever ready to draw the sword in his defence, to protect him against domestic pretenders and foreign foes. It was they who made the only serious resistance offered the Russians, it was they who continued the struggle after he himself had abandoned it as hopeless, and when, terror-stricken by the bombardment of General Verévkin, he fled the city, and his own subjects turned on him, and elected his brother Khan in his stead, it was with the Turcomans he found a refuge. Forgetting all this, the services they had rendered him, the fidelity and bravery they had displayed in his cause, he denounced them to the Russians as robbers and outlaws. During the course of the negotiations with Kaufmann, relating to the payment of the war indemnity, he declared he could not take the responsibility of the payment of their portion; that they never had paid anything in the shape of taxes; that they would not now, and that it was beyond his power to compel them. More than this, in order to regain possession of his cannon, he even asserted that without artillery he could not keep them in check, nor even assure his own safety on the throne.

Kaufmann, having no use for the cannon, returned the Khan eighteen or nineteen of the twenty-one pieces captured at the fall of the city—a fact which shows that the Russians feel very sure of their own strength. As to the Khan's representations, they may not have influenced Kaufmann in the course he adopted towards the Turcomans; he had already determined to take the collection of the war indemnity into his own hands.

He accordingly issued a proclamation ordering the Yomuds to pay 300,000 rubles—about £41,000—about 16s to each man, woman, and child—within two weeks. To this they replied by sending several deputations, promising to pay, but asking for time, assuring him that so large a sum could not be collected on so short a notice. Kaufmann, nevertheless, determined to insist upon immediate payment. He therefore made preparations to invade their country, and attack them without giving them the time asked for.

He was severely criticised for adopting this course by some of his officers. He knew very well, they said, it was not possible for the Turcomans to pay in the specified time: he had allowed himself to be hoodwinked by the Khan; and was becoming a mere tool in his hands for the furtherance of his schemes of conquest over the Turcomans. The officers were likewise of opinion that the Turcomans were more exact in fulfilling their promises than the Khan himself; and that, in spite of their somewhat turbulent character, they were far better men than their neighbours the Uzbegs.

Some of these views I do not agree with. I do not think that Kaufmann was so easily hoodwinked, nor that he allowed himself to be unduly influenced by the Khan's assertions. What he did, he did with a full knowledge of the case, and upon his own judgment. Rightly or wrongly, he professed to place no reliance on the Turcomans' promises to pay; and not to believe in their professions of future good conduct They could not, he said, be relied upon to keep the peace until they should be completely crushed. Besides, he wished to conciliate the Uzbegs, who would only be too rejoiced to see their turbulent neighbours conquered, and reduced to submission. In addition to this, they were an independent people, who flouted all authority—the unpardonable sin in the eyes of the Russian government. It was necessary to make an example of them, and enforce obedience to royal authority, even though that authority were only personified in the person of the Khan of Khiva.

For my part, I think Kaufmann was wrong. I think that of the two peoples, the Uzbegs and the Turcomans, it would have been better to conciliate the latter. They are a better, braver, and nobler race. Almost free from Mohamedhan prejudices, and entirely exempt from the disgusting and degrading Mohamedhan vices, they would have made far more powerful and reliable allies than the degenerate, vice-stricken Uzbegs. Their bravery in the field, and their fidelity to the Khan, should rather have been recommendations in their favour. And it is a well-known fact, that of all the peoples of Central Asia the Turcomans are the only ones who can be relied upon to keep their promises. As to the Khan himself, cowardly, treacherous, and ungrateful, his wishes need not have been consulted at all.

It will be said that the Turcomans are all slave-dealers, and that they deserve punishment, if only for that alone. These Turcomans, however, did not own as many slaves as the Uzbegs, and were not implicated in slave-dealing at all. It is the Tekki Turcomans, on the shores of the Caspian, who carry on the slave-trade, the horrors of which were so graphically described by Vambéry. The Turcomans of Khiva were, therefore, less culpable than the Uzbegs.

Whatever were Kaufmann's views with regard to the Turcomans, one thing he did was hardly justifiable. Twelve Yomuds who came to negotiate with him were seized and detained as prisoners. They were released during the campaign, but their detention was simply a breach of faith.

CHAPTER II.

FIRE AND SWORD.

THE Yomuds, whom Kaufmann had decided to attack, are by far the most numerous and powerful tribe of Turcomans They number 11,000 kibitkas, as many as the five other tribes together.

On the 19th of July, five weeks after the fall of Khiva, a force, under Major-General Golovatchoff, composed of eight companies of infantry, eight sotnias of Cossacks, ten guns—including two mitrailleurs—and a battery of rockets, was advanced from Khiva to Hazavat, where the Yomud country commences.

The way led through gardens, beneath overhanging elms, whose dark green foliage was reflected in the clear little pools lying dark and cool around their roots. The apricot-trees were still aglow with their golden rosy fruit, miniature rice-fields, still green, were pleasantly varied by yellow stubbles of wheat and barley, now cut and gathered unsheaved in huge stacks like hay, waiting to be threshed by horses' feet.

As we marched forward, the Uzbegs came out in groups, and offered us bread, fruit, and milk, and watched with wondering eyes the dread array of artillery, glittering grimly in the sunshine, as it rolled noiselessly forward over the dusty road.

Five miles from Khiva our way began to skirt the desert, which here made a deep inroad upon the oasis. So often do the arms of the desert run in such fashion into the cultivated land like sea-inlets, that the oasis of Khiva may be said to be made up of a series of small islands, between which and the surrounding desert there is a continual struggle for the mastery. The warfare here between sand and soil is unremitting and unending. The former, driven by the furious winds of the desert, sweeps over the frontier, and buries the rich soil with its vegetation far beneath. But the water penetrates and permeates the sand, pouring in its rich deposits from the Oxus; the sand itself becomes fertile, vegetation again appears, and the soil is victorious—to be again overwhelmed and buried. This contest must have been going on for centuries, without much advantage on either side. Within the last few years, however, the sand—judging by traces of former irrigation that may be seen in many parts of the desert—seems to be gaining ground, but the line between soil and sand is as distinct and clearly defined as that between land and water.

At eleven o'clock the advance reached the canal of Hazavat, sixteen miles from Khiva, and camped on its banks; but the rear-guard did not arrive until five, to such a length had the column been drawn out by the narrow tortuous road. The canal on which we had camped served as an outlet for the superfluous water of the main arik of Hazavat, and emptied itself about a mile below us into the desert, where it formed a marsh. It was about thirty feet wide, and ten deep; the clear soft water poured

TURCOMAN FARM-YARD. *From a design by Verestchagin.*

through at the rate of five or six miles an hour. It may be stated that all of the principal canals of the oasis, receiving far more water than is necessary for the irrigation of the land, have outlets of the kind, by which an immense amount of water is poured into the desert, and wasted by evaporation. This proves that, with a little exertion, the oasis might be extended much farther to the south than it now is; and there is little doubt that, with the domination of the Russians, this will be eventually done.

Here the army remained encamped all next day; ostensibly for the purpose of seeing if the Turcomans would come forward and pay; really, I believe, because General Golovatchoff, who did not much relish the expedition, wished to give them an opportunity of escaping.

The detachment again moved forward early on the morning of the 21st. A march of two hours brought us within the territory of the Yomuds. The country was rich and fertile, cut up everywhere by deep canals, whose banks were bordered with long lines of poplars, and the little prairies were covered with a rich growth of grass, with here and there thickets of brushwood.

Agriculture among those people appears much less advanced than among the Uzbegs. There were fewer fruit-trees; less ground devoted to grain, and far more to pasturage. The population was thinner, the dwellings much ruder. Nowhere did you find the heavy battlemented walls and beautiful elms that characterise the dwellings of the Uzbegs. The houses were generally low mud inclosures, comprising stables and winter dwellings beneath one roof, with a kibitka or two placed outside, in which the people always live in summer. Everything, in short,

denoted a people in the transition state between a nomadic and a settled life; a people who have not yet
become sufficiently attached to their dwellings to make
any attempts at beautifying them.

The houses were all deserted. Not a single piece of
furniture was left in the rooms, and the farm-yards were
equally bare; not a chick nor a child was to be seen. In
some of the houses the fires were still smouldering—
clear proof that the flight of the inhabitants was very
recent.

At this point the General halted the vanguard, and
waited until the whole army got up. The Cossacks separated from the rest of the troops, and scattered themselves
all over the country, while the infantry continued its
march along the road. Soon, and unexpectedly, the
meaning of this movement was revealed to me.

I was still musing on the quietness and desolation of
the scene, when all at once I was startled by a sharp
crackling sound behind me. Looking round, I beheld a
long tongue of flame darting upward from the roof of the
house into which I had just been peering, and another
from the stack of nicely-gathered unthreshed wheat near
it. The dry straw-thatched roof flashed up like powder,
and the ripe wheat-straw burned almost as readily. Huge
volumes of dense black smoke rose out of the trees in
every direction, and rolled overhead in dark ominous-
looking clouds, coloured by the fiery glare from the flames
below. I spurred my horse to the top of a little
eminence, and gazed about me. It was a strange, wild
spectacle. In an incredibly short space of time flames
and smoke had spread on either side to the horizon, and,
advancing steadily forward in the direction of our course,

TURCOMAN FARM-YARD. *From a design by Verestchagin.*

slowly enveloped everything Through this scene moved the Cossacks like spectres. Torch in hand, they dashed swiftly across the country, leaping ditches and flying over walls like very demons, and leaving behind them a trail of flame and smoke. They rarely dismounted, but simply rode up to the houses, applied their blazing torches to the projecting eaves of thatch, and the stacks of un-threshed grain, and then galloped on. Five minutes after-wards, sheets of seething flame and darkling smoke showed how well they had done their work. The entire country was on fire.

In half an hour the sun was hidden, the sky grew dark; for, as though the sudden lighting of so many fires had produced some change in the atmosphere, a rain set in— a thing almost unknown in Khiva, and which added one dismal feature more to the already dismal scene It was a slow, drizzling rain, not sufficient to put out the fires, but only to beat off the ashes and make them burn brighter, to drive down the smoke, and make it hang over the trees in heavy, sullen masses, darkening the air, and forming a lowering background to the blood-coloured flames This was war such as I had never before seen, and such as is rarely seen in modern days.

It was a sad, sad sight—a terrible spectacle of war at its destructive work, strangely in keeping with this strange wild land!

We moved slowly along the narrow winding road, the flames and smoke accompanying us on either flank, until about noon, when the vanguard reported the flying inha-bitants in sight; a body of men on horseback had halted to parley with the advance-guard. When asked what they wanted, they replied, that they wished to know why the Russians were invading their country. They had never made war on the Russians; why were the Russians making war on them?

The guard invited them to go to General Golovatchoff, who would listen to their complaints; but, declining this offer, they launched forth into a torrent of threats. "We are," they said, "many thousands, and if the Russians overrun our country, severe shall be their punishment." And they were, they said, determined to fight. As this was all the Russians wanted, there was nothing more to be said, and they galloped off to rejoin their flying companions.

The Russian cavalry was only too eager to give chase. Several times the officer in command of the advance-guard sent back a messenger asking for permission to begin the attack. General Golovatchoff hesitated a long time, however, before issuing the order, with the motive, as it appeared to me, of giving the Turcomans a chance to escape. Among them were women and children in great numbers, and these he would, I think, have gladly spared.

At length they were reported turning off into the desert, where they might laugh at our pursuit; and if the attack was to be made, it must be done instantly. The order was at last given for the Cossacks to pursue the fugitives. As soon as I heard the order, I galloped forward to the head of the column. The troops were just on the edge of the desert, drawn up in double lines, each sotnia with its colours flying in the wind; horses and men alike were eager for the fray. About two miles away to the south, just disappearing over the summit of a long, high, sandy ridge, were the flying Turcomans, an undistinguishable mass of men, women, and children, horses, camels, sheep, goats, and cattle, all rushing forward in wild frightened confusion. There are two or three thousand, perhaps, in all—merely a detachment of laggards from the main body, which is a few miles farther on. In two or three minutes they had disappeared over the brow of the hill, and were lost to view.

CHAPTER III.

THE MASSACRE.

SIX sotnias of Cossacks were selected to pursue the enemy
Riding along in front of their line, I catch sight of Prince
Eugene, who welcomes me to the front with a hearty
shake of the hand, and kindly puts me in one of his
squadrons, as a good point of observation.

The order to advance is passed along the line, and in
another moment we are dashing over the desert at a
gallop. Ten minutes bring us to the summit of the hill,
over which we had seen the fugitives disappear; and we
perceive them a mile farther on, crossing another low
ridge. Already the body has ceased to be compact
Sheep and goats scatter themselves unheeded in every
direction; the ground is strewed with the effects that
have been abandoned in the hurried flight—bundles
thrown from the backs of camels, carts, from which the
horses have been cut loose, and crowds of stragglers
struggling wearily along, separated from friends, and
rapidly closed in upon by foes.

Down the little descent we plunge, our horses sinking
to their knees in the yielding sand, and across the plain
we sweep like a tornado.

Then there are shouts and cries, a scattering discharge

THE CHARGE.

of firearms, and our lines are broken by the abandoned
carts, and our progress impeded by the cattle and sheep
that are running wildly about over the plain. It is a scene
of the wildest confusion.' I halt a moment to look about
me.   Here is a Turcoman lying in the sand, with a bullet
through his head; a little farther on, a Cossack stretched
out on the ground, with a horrible sabre cut on the face;
then two women, with three or four children, sitting down
in the sand, crying and sobbing piteously, and begging for
their lives; to these I shout "*Aman, aman*," "Peace,
peace," as I gallop by, to allay their fears.   A little
farther on, more arbas or carts, carpets, and bed coverlets,
scattered about with sacks full of grain, and huge bags
and bundles, cooking utensils, and all kinds of household
goods.

Then more women toiling wearily forward, carrying
infants, and weeping bitterly; and one very fat old
woman, scarcely able to carry herself, with a child in her
arms, which I somehow take for her grandchild.   Then
camels, sheep, goats, cattle, donkeys, cows, calves, and
dogs, each, after its fashion, contributing to the wild
scene of terror.

I am at first shocked at the number of Turcomans I see
lying motionless.   I can't help thinking that if all these
be killed, there are no such deadly marksmen as the
Cossacks.   After a while, however, the mystery is explained; for I perceive one of the apparently dead Turcomans cautiously lift his head, and immediately after
resume his perfectly motionless position.   Many of them
are feigning death, and well it is for them the Cossacks
have not discovered the trick.

Delayed somewhat by the contemplation of these scenes,
I perceive that I am left behind, and again hurry forward.

Crossing a little ridge, I behold my sotnia galloping along the edge of a narrow marsh, and discharging their arms at the Turcomans, who are already on the other side, hurriedly ascending another gentle slope. I follow down to the marsh, passing two or three dead bodies on the way. In the marsh are twenty or thirty women and children, up to their necks in water, trying to hide among the weeds and grass, begging for their lives, and screaming in the most pitiful manner. The Cossacks have already passed, paying no attention to them. One villainous-looking brute, however, had dropped out of the ranks, and levelling his piece as he sat on his horse, deliberately took aim at the screaming group, and before I could stop him pulled the trigger. Fortunately the gun missed fire, and before he could renew the cap, I rode up, and cutting him across the face with my riding-whip, ordered him to his sotnia. He obeyed instantly, without a murmur; and shouting "*Aman*" to the poor demented creatures in the water, I followed him.

A few yards farther on there are four Cossacks around a Turcoman. He has already been beaten to his knees, and weapon he has none. To the four sabres that are hacking at him he can offer only the resistance of his arms; but he utters no word of entreaty. It is terrible. Blow after blow they shower down on his head without avail, as though their sabres were tin. Will they never have done? is there no pith in their arms? At last, after what seems an age to me, he falls prone in the water, with a terrible wound in the neck, and the Cossacks gallop on. A moment later I come upon a woman, sitting by the side of the water, silently weeping over the dead body of her husband. Suddenly, my horse gives a leap that almost unseats me, my ears are stunned with a sharp, shrieking, rushing noise, and, looking up, I behold a streak of fire darting across the sky, which explodes at last among the fugitives. It is only a rocket, but it is followed by another, and another; and, mingled with the shrieks of women and children, the hoarse shout of the Cossacks, bleating of sheep and goats, and howling of cattle running wildly over the plain, made up a very pandemonium of terror. This lasted a few minutes.

Then the Turcomans gradually disappeared over another ridge, some in this direction, and some in that, and bugle-call sounds the signal for the reassembling of the troops. As we withdrew, I looked in vain for the women and children I had seen in the water. They had all disappeared; and as I saw them nowhere in the vicinity, I am afraid that, frightened by the rockets, they threw themselves into the water, and were drowned. It was all the more pitiable, as, with the exception of the case I have mentioned, there was no violence offered to women and children. I even saw a young Cossack officer, Baron Krudner, punishing one of his own men with his sword for having tried to kill a woman

The roll having been called, search was made for the wounded, and the doctors immediately attended to the injuries of those who were found. A boy, thirteen or fourteen years of age, was picked up with a dangerous sabre cut in the head. He was accompanied by his mother, who was distracted with grief, and watched the doctor dressing the wound with wild, eager eyes. To her primitive ideas, it was scarcely credible that the same people should first try to kill, and then try to cure her son. When the wound had been carefully dressed, and the doctor had assured her that the child would not die, she seized his hand and kissed it with a burst of grateful tears.

For awhile we rested our horses ; then detaching a number of Cossacks to drive in the captured sheep and cattle, some 2000 in number, we started off for the camp. Many a look we cast behind, for there stood in the midst of the vast desert a sight that our eyes unwillingly lost sight of. It was this mother, who sat watching with her daughter over the wounded boy. Around her lay the wreck of all her worldly wealth; possibly not far away the dead body of her husband; and disappearing in the far distance were the routed ranks of her nation. So she stood a picture of ruin and despair.

CHAPTER IV.

A PICTURE OF WAR.

THE next morning we continued our march, burning and
ravaging everything as we proceeded. We left behind
us a strip of country, about three miles wide, in which
there was nothing left but heaps of smouldering ashes.
The value of the wheat destroyed must have been many
thousand rubles. Wishing to observe more closely the
incendiary operations, I rode out with Prince Eugene,
who had been ordered to burn everything on the right of
the road. He did not seem to enter upon the operation
with any great degree of zeal, but executed the order
faithfully and conscientiously. The task was, of course,
repulsive, but nevertheless had some very exciting and
interesting features, combining just enough of lawlessness
to make it gratifying to that spirit of destruction which
probably exists in a latent state in even the most peaceable
and civilised men.

We galloped hither and thither, leaping ditches and
walls, breaking through hedges and beating down gates;
marking our progress at every step by columns of smoke,
and angry flames.

The quietness of these households, which we thus

destroyed, formed a queer contrast with the tumult and violence of our proceedings. Absolute silence reigned in them all. In many we could still find the traces of the tranquil everyday life of their late inhabitants—the marks of children's tiny feet, the remnants of women's household work, the simple implements with which they plied their toil.

Here they lived in quiet peaceful contentment—for whatever they had to do with war was far away in the Persian and Russian frontiers—in their little oasis surrounded by the great desert, as isolated from the outside world as an undiscovered island in the South Pacific. But the torch was applied, and they learned all too dearly something of this great outside world.

We seldom found anything in the houses. A few cooking utensils, sometimes a few chickens, which the Cossacks instantly seized, an old horse, or a young calf, unable to follow in the hurried flight, and often a cat sitting placidly on a wall or a roof, making her toilet, and complacently watching the proceeding, until the scorching flames drove her off. Sometimes, but rarely, we found a dog that had been left behind, or that, perhaps, with a cat-like instinct, had refused to leave the house, who ran off at our approach, howling dismally Once I was shocked by the terrified shrieking of a number of young puppies that had suddenly discovered themselves in the midst of impassable flames.

We breakfasted about ten o'clock on roast chicken, in an orchard adjoining a house we had set on fire. As we had left the infantry far behind, and were consequently in no hurry, we stretched ourselves on the grass under the trees, some to sleep, some to watch the flames, whose hot breath scorched and withered the trees, and sometimes reached us in hot, angry puffs. The heavy black smoke hung in thick columns, and settled down over the trees, half hiding the Cossacks gleefully making their tea and the horses picketed in a line, and feeding luxuriously on the rich wheat of the Turcomans. Above all rose the banner of Russia, seen indistinctly through the smoke, flapping lazily, like some great vulture gloating over the sinister scene.

We marched into camp by two o'clock in the afternoon, having made twelve miles from our last starting place, and halted for the rest of the day at a point forty miles from Khiva.

The next day's march was like the preceding: we continued our incendiary operations, applying the torch to everything that would burn, and leaving the country behind us a blackened waste. At noon we arrived on the plain of Kyzil-Takyr. This plain is barren, open, and sandy, with only one or two farmhouses within a circuit of several miles. In every direction, however, it was cut up by canals, in some of which there was still water, showing that the place had once been in a high state of cultivation. Some such war as this we were raging had probably turned the gardens into this bleak and barren desert. This was the place where Markosoff should have first struck the oasis after traversing the Turcoman desert. We camped on the plain about noon, near a house and garden that had apparently been abandoned a long time.

The heat by this time had become excessive, so that it was necessary to halt a day, in order to rest the troops. I soon learned that a Turcoman boy had been captured in the course of the morning. Unconscious of all the storm around him, the poor lad had been found asleep in the shade of a tree near a house; he was about twelve years old, but strangely hard-featured for a child, with very large head, prominent high cheek-bones and eyebrows, a short turned-up nose, yellow skin, and large black eyes, fierce and bright He said he had neither father nor mother. His uncle, who used to take care of him, had gone off and left him while asleep. This desertion of the child, we afterwards discovered, was not intentional, for the uncle, when the campaign was concluded, hearing that the child was with the Russians, came and claimed him, and manifested the greatest joy at seeing him again. The boy followed us during the campaign, and was made a kind of pet by the soldiers, who gave him a new suit of clothes from the plundered effects of his countrymen, a donkey to ride, and taught him Russian.

I profited by the time we lay here to visit the ruined fortress of Imukchir, near which we were camped. In extent it is about four acres, and the walls, which were in some places thirty feet high, were in a tolerable state of preservation ; moreover, they were built, not of sun-dried bricks, but of excellent fire-brick, a pale red in colour, six inches square, and an inch and a half thick ; all which showed that they were not of Khiva manu-facture. The fortress probably dates from either the Chinese or the Persian domination. While here, the Yomuds, who had been imprisoned at Khiva by order of Kaufmann, passed us on their way to rejoin their flying brethren. They had been liberated—after two of their number had been killed in an attempt to es-cape—with instructions to try and induce their country-men to accede to the Russian demands, and pay the war indemnity. Judging from what followed, their efforts in that direction, if they ever made any, were of little avail.

On the morning of the 24th we were again on the march. This day, however, there was no burning, as we were in one of those streaks of sand that cross the oasis where there was nothing to burn. In fact, we had by this time completely traversed the country of the Yomuds, and had ravaged nearly 100 square miles of territory; and now we approached a part inhabited by the Uzbegs, who were friendly to us. On the way we found a Persian, who had been left for dead in the sands by the Yomuds. He had received no less than fifteen or twenty horrible sabre cuts. His wounds were dressed by the doctor, and he was put in an ambulance, but his life was despaired of for the moment, although I believe he eventually recovered.

By ten o'clock we were again in sight of gardens and green trees, and by eleven we encamped among them, just on the edge of the desert, and about two miles from the town of Iliali. As we were pitching our tent, the welcome cry of "A bazaar!" was heard. Every one dropped whatever work he had in hand and rushed to the indicated spot. Our anxiety was intelligible, for we had been without either fresh bread, fruit, or milk for many days; and a bazaar, as we knew, meant a supply of these longed-for dainties.

The term "bazaar," I should explain, is applied to any place, great or small, rich or poor, in which anything is sold. Though the whole stock-in-trade consists of but a cartful of melons or a bagful of bread, the lofty-sounding word is used. In our bazaar we found five or six carts full of melons, hot wheaten-cakes, and jugs of milk. Need I say that we laid in a plentiful supply of these delicacies? The place was kept by some twenty Uzbegs, who—as I have had already often occasion to remark—had throughout

27

the expedition food for the hunger and drink for the thirst of the Russian invader.

We pitched our tents in the shade of apple and poplar trees, spread our carpets on the grass, and soon our tea-urns were playing their welcome tune. After the heat, pleasant is the shade of these trees; pleasant after fasting this delicious meal; pleasant after a long march this stretch in the grass! We give ourselves up to the impulse of the moment, talk but in languid monosyllables, and after a while let " tired eyelids fall on tired eyes."

All at once the bugles sound an alarm : the Turcomans are reported approaching over the desert. Immediately we jump from the ground, tighten up our clothes, buckle on our revolvers, and climb upon carts, or other elevated vantage ground, to see the enemy's approach.

CHAPTER V.

THE SKIRMISH.

THEY were leisurely approaching in irregular masses over the desert, all on horseback, but apparently bent on a reconnaissance rather than an attack.

In order to understand what follows, it must be remembered that we were encamped, as it were, between the desert and the gardens on the side of the road by which we had arrived. This road here entered the gardens, and continued along just inside their edges as far as the town of Iliali, two miles distant, and was completely hidden by the trees and walls. To the south and west was the desert, stretching away in a broad, slightly uneven plain covered with a little, low, weedy grass.

It was on the desert side the Turcomans were advancing. Two companies of infantry had already been sent out to meet and skirmish with them, and orders were sent to the cavalry to prepare for action. General Golovatchoff and his staff had advanced just outside of the camp on a little eminence, from which they were watching the progress of events.

I mounted and rode out to the skirmish line, now advanced about half a mile from the camp. I found it deployed along the embankment formed by a dried-up canal, the right under command of Colonel Dreschern, the left under Colonel Navamlinsky. The Turcomans were about half a mile distant in considerable numbers, galloping backwards and forwards over the plain, but not showing any disposition to advance nearer. The sharpshooters were firing occasional scattering shots, and there was from time to time the rattling crash of a mitrailleur, which did not seem, however, to produce any effect.

This had gone on about a minute when, looking towards the camp, I saw rising over the trees, and moving rapidly along the road from Ihali, a dense cloud of dust evidently caused by a body of horsemen advancing at a gallop.

It was an attack on the camp from the other side, and one which threatened to prove successful, as everybody—soldiers and officers—had gathered on the side next the plain, to watch the operations on our skirmish line; and then the attacking party was covered by trees and walls.

Nobody in camp as yet seemed to be aware of their approach, and it looked for a moment as though the Russians were to be completely taken by surprise by one of the most simple and artless of *ruses*. The object of the enemy's appearance on the plain, and their apparently senseless galloping back and forth, was now evident.

I wheeled my horse to give the alarm, when I perceived that Colonel Navamlinsky had seen the movement almost at the same moment, and was just wheeling his men preparatory to repelling it. In another second his troops were rushing forward at a run in the direction of the Ihali Road.

By this time the Turcomans had emerged from the trees, and we could see their dark forms indistinctly in the dust, half-hid by the foliage of the bushes, not more than 200 yards from the camp.

Had the enemy boldly rode on then, sabre in hand, they would undoubtedly have gained at least a momentary victory over the Russians, who, gathered on the other side of the camp, watching the proceeding on the plain, were entirely unconscious of the danger which threatened them. Instead of this, however, they stopped and commenced driving off the camels and horses that were wandering about near the camp. This gave time for the alarm to be sounded. The Russians rushed to their arms, the soldiers forming in order of battle, without even the aid of their officers.

In the meantime Navamlinsky had arrived within 200 yards of the road, taking the Turcomans in the flank. He ordered a half-turn, with the rapidly succeeding commands, "Load," "aim," "fire." A sharp crash broke the air, as a volley of rifle-bullets went shrieking over the little meadow that separated us from the Turcomans. This was followed by three more volleys in rapid succession from the American breech-loaders. A fire so heavy and well-directed was too much for the Turcomans, and wheeling their horses, they retreated as rapidly as they came. I saw several of them fall, and likewise saw their comrades halt and pick them up, in spite of the murderous volleys we were pouring in upon them.

Had they dashed through the camp—which would have been a very easy matter—they would have entirely escaped this raking flank-fire and met a party of their comrades, who, as we soon learned, were making a diversion on the south.

On the south, a picket of five men had been placed only about 200 yards distant from the camp. While the events I have just related were going on, a short but desperate fight occurred between this picket and a body of Turcomans. How it happened was never known. A young officer, Lieutenant Kamenetsky, who was going the rounds, had arrived at this picket when the fight on the other side had commenced, and it is probable that they were watching so intently the proceeding on the other side of the camp that they allowed themselves to be surprised. After the fight on our side was over, the bodies of the six were found, stripped naked and headless. That it should have occurred within 200 yards of the camp without being seen by anybody, speaks well of the skill and audacity of the Turcomans.

In the meantime, four or five sotnias of Cossacks had advanced out on the plain where the enemy had first appeared, to see if they were disposed to give battle. Wishing to see as much as possible of this strange kind of warfare, I followed them, and was soon again with the combatants.

The scene was somewhat amusing as well as picturesque.

The Turcomans are hovering around in considerable numbers, but although they keep up a shouting and yelling, and gallop about, they show no disposition to come to blows, and their splendid horses make it impossible for us to get any nearer than they find convenient. We fire occasional shots at them, and offer special inducements for attack, by getting in disorder, and shouting to them to come on; but they decline.

In fact, the whole thing is a kind of lark which we enjoy immensely. The horsemanship displayed by the Turcomans is really admirable, and we can see that there is no lack of individual bravery among them With discipline, they would be most formidable cavalry.

They have old-fashioned ideas of chivalry, too, and dare us out to single combat. They advance, one, two, and three at a time, within fifty yards of us, and salute us with their curved sabres, proffering at the same time divers remarks and observations in an unknown tongue—probably of a very personal nature.

Some of our Circassians are anxious to go out and fight them, and, but for the prudence of the Colonel, we might have a series of splendid tournaments, ending possibly in a general hand-to-hand fight. Judging by what I saw afterwards, I am now inclined to think it was well for us it did not end in that way.

One fellow, on a splendid black horse, rides up within fifty yards of us, and halting, salutes us with a graceful movement of his sword. The Cossacks commence firing at him. Nothing daunted, he spurs his horse into a gentle canter, and passes along our whole line, while each Cossack in turn empties his piece at him. We can see where the bullets knock up the sand, sometimes under his horse's feet; but he escapes unharmed, and returns to his own side, with evidently as great contempt for our marksmanship as for our bravery.

"Would you like to take part in a charge?"

"Certainly."

"I am going to take a sotnia, and charge that mass you see away there to the right. Tighten your saddle-girth, and get ready."

It is Prince Eugene who has spoken to me. He wears a white uniform and white Cossack cap, with white handkerchief pinned to it to protect his neck, which makes his dust-begrimed, sun-burned face look as swarthy as a Moor's.

We are drawn up in line—100 of us, with drawn sabres. The Turcomans are distant some 300 yards, grouped in an irregular mass, numbering perhaps 300 or

400. "Gotovo!" "Charge!" shouts the Prince, and we are down on them like an avalanche. A cloud of dust, the panting of horses, the rattle of harness, a flash of sabres, and we are there.

But the Turcomans are not.

Three hundred yards further on we see them; they are going in a gentle canter, not seeming to be in the slightest hurry, and evidently not in the least apprehensive of our overtaking them. We continue the chase a short distance, with no result. It is exasperating. We might as well charge a flock of wild geese, and we give the thing up.

After a little more skirmishing, without any loss to either party, we turn and start back to camp. The Yomuds instantly wheel about, and follow us with derisive shouts, giving us to understand that they regard us as the most cowardly of cowards.

We returned to the camp, paying little attention to them, however, with the exception of an occasional shot, when they got too close. They followed us to within half a mile of the camp, and then retired. On the way back we found the bodies of two of them that had been killed by the sharpshooters, one of whom had been shot through the head, and the other through the breast. These were, I believe, the only dead left on the field, though, from what I saw during the attack on the camp, they must have lost several by the fire of Navamlinsky's sharpshooters.

The Russian loss was six in all, so that they rather had the advantage of us.

The heat during the day had been excessive, and we were glad when we, returned to camp to throw off our accoutrements and stretch ourselves under the shade of the trees on our carpets for a rest. We were soon gaily engaged in discussing the events of the day, together with a good dinner of roast mutton, milk, melons, and fresh wheaten cakes, hot from the ashes, which had been furnished us by the Uzbegs

CHAPTER VI.

AN INTERVAL.

THIS attack by the enemy showed that they really meant to fight, and if they had carried it on as well as they had commenced, it might have gained a very serious advantage. We discovered that we had been estimating their courage far too lightly, and that they were by no means an enemy to be despised. We remained encamped here next day, inactive. The Uzbegs again brought us in provisions; and I thought how curious it was that they should have such unlimited confidence in us as to trust their property and lives within our grasp, when we were using their neighbours so harshly. For my own part, I could see but little difference between them and the Turcomans either in dress or complexion; and it was only when they took off their heavy sheepskin caps, and showed the shape of their heads, that one could detect the difference. Even then it was in most cases difficult, as the two races, living so close together, have naturally intermingled, and the types peculiar to each have become more or less modified. In truth, for all we knew to the contrary, half of these Uzbegs may have been Turcomans who came in to reconnoitre. However, as there was no sure way of distinguishing between them, and the Uzbegs not liking the

Russians well enough to denounce their brother Mahom-
medhans, and as they would really understand nothing of
Russian military ways when they saw them, no measures
were taken to guard against spies.

Another delegation of Turcomans came in during the
day, apparently for the purpose of treating; but I could
find out nothing regarding the nature of their propositions
further than that they were rejected.

That they were willing to make peace, and that they
had no particular ill-will against the Russians, was
shown by the way in which they treated the troops of the
Orenburg detachment that had passed through this same
country only three weeks previously.

All along the road they had come out in great numbers
with melons, fruit, milk, and bread, which they offered in
the most hospitable manner, without asking pay. And
Count Shuvaloff afterwards told me the troops of this
detachment, which was then some forty miles farther
down the river near Kuna-Urgench, were living on the
most friendly terms with the Turcomans, while we were
burning and ravaging their country in every direction.
He said some of the Yomuds even came to them, and
tried to make an offensive and defensive alliance against
our detachment. They said naïvely, "We have sworn
friendship with you, and consider ourselves your allies.
Now the other tribe of Russians from Turkistan are
making war upon us, and we think you ought to help us
against them just as we would help you against your
enemies."

CHAPTER VII.

THE BATTLE.

WE lay here all day inactive. General Golovatchoff, as it appeared, towards evening, was collecting information as to where the mass of the Turcomans had taken refuge, preparatory to making an attack upon them. After dark it began to be whispered about the camp-fires that we were to march out before daylight next morning, and attack and surprise the enemy in their camp, only six or seven miles distant. About ten o'clock the rumour was confirmed by an official order, which was passed round. The baggage was to be left behind under a guard, and we were to march at one in the morning.

The Turcomans, it was said, were on the other side of Iliali, some five or six miles distant, and were going to make a stand.

About eleven o'clock, when everybody was going to sleep, an alarm was sounded, some shots were fired, and we rushed to arms, in the momentary expectation of an attack. All became quiet, however, and the picket reported he had seen a black form creeping up in the darkness, and had fired. Nothing further appearing, we all lay down again to snatch a hasty nap. Again we were aroused a little before one o'clock by a shot and a wild terrified cry, that brought us to our feet like an electric shock. There is another rush to arms, a moment's confusion, every man gains his place, and then all is silence—we are awaiting the attack. This time it is not a false alarm, as the picket had fired upon something very near him in the darkness, and then picked up a sabre— very good proof that some of the enemy were prowling around.

This decided General Golovatchoff not to march at one, as was originally intended, but to wait until three, just before break of day.

Accordingly, about three we are aroused by the reveille; our baggage is packed, and all placed within a hollow square formed by the arbas, of which there are 200, and left under a guard of 300 men. This having been accomplished, with no little confusion in the darkness, the General, with his staff, mounted and took up his station just outside the camp, to wait for the infantry to file out under his eyes.

It should be remembered that we were in the same place in which the little affair of two days before occurred; and we were about to march out on the open plain to the west, in the direction of Iliali, as preferable to following in the darkness the more direct road through the gardens. The faintest streak of day could be seen in the east, but towards the west, in the direction we are marching, the darkness is black and impenetrable. There is something curious in the air, a kind of strange agitation almost electric, which makes one somehow feel that there is going to be a storm. A white horse, broken loose, rushed madly about here and there through the lines in a wild, absurd, crazy way—an incident I remembered afterwards with a curious interest.

The cavalry has already passed out on the plain, and is probably half a mile distant; the infantry are just forming in marching order under the eyes of the General; two or three of us are discussing the probability of taking the Turcomans by surprise, when all at once a wild fierce yell, a horrid confused sound of frightened shouts, scattering shots, and a trampling rush of horses, breaks upon our startled ears. Everywhere—before, behind, around—the air is filled with the wild revengeful yell, the plain alive with the Turcomans. Our expectations of a surprise are fulfilled in a somewhat unexpected manner.

Then there is an irregular discharge of firearms, that flashes up like lightning, then a long hissing streak of fire, that rends the darkness with a fearful, crashing, nerve-shaking sound, and explodes with a murderous report; then bouquets of blue, green, and red flame, that leap up and disappear; then more streaks of fire, the whizzing of bullets, the trampling of frightened horses, and the occasional gleam of sabres.

For a moment we sit spell-bound in our saddles, too much amazed to do anything but gaze in dumb astonishment.

General Golovatchoff gives a hurried order for the infantry and artillery to advance; and the next moment we are dashing through the darkness after him, without knowing whither we are going. In an instant we are in the midst of the combatants. By this time the rockets have ceased, partly because, being damaged, they often exploded in the hands of the gunners; partly because the Turcomans are so close, that at the lowest angle at which they could be fired, they passed over the enemy's heads, and failed to either injure or frighten them. The rifle firing was brisker than ever, and a kind of irregular discharge was kept up from both sides, by whose light strange, fearful glimpses were caught now and then of a dark, savage face and glittering sabre, instantly lost again in the darkness, while the shouts and yells continue ten times more demoniac than before. The Cossacks seem to have been thrown into some confusion, and are slowly retiring. Here and there the Turcomans have penetrated the lines, and it becomes a hand-to-hand fight. In the confusion I am separated from General Golovatchoff. When I find myself again by his side, he is calmly issuing orders, but is covered with blood. He has received a sabre cut; Colonel Friede, his chief of staff, is near him, likewise bleeding profusely from a bullet-wound in the head. The Turcomans have already penetrated or flanked the lines in many places, and one of them had wounded General Golovatchoff.

Now there is a confused rush of Cossacks backwards, that carries me along. It is, perhaps, not a flight, but something that very much resembles one, or the beginning of one; and besides, there is something fearful in the air, something the like of which I have never experienced before nor since, and which I can only compare to the ominous threatening atmosphere said to always precede an earthquake; above the uproar, the cries and shouts and confusion, a low, ominous, frightened murmur, like the commencement of a cry of despair; we are on the verge of a panic. The Cossacks have lost their Colonel, and looking at them closely, I can see their scared, anxious faces, and know well what that means! A rout —a massacre; not one of us will escape the Yomuds, with their fleet-footed horses. Looking towards the camp we had left, I see a long line of dark figures gallop in between, their tall, black forms easily seen against the brightening eastern sky; we are completely surrounded. Away to the right is heard the crash of the mitrailleuse, which proves that the fight is widely extended.

Prince Eugene dashes past, with smoking pistol, apparently in search of General Golovatchoff. He had, as I afterwards learned, been surrounded and almost cut off; had shot down two of the foe with his own hand, while the officer in attendance on him was almost cut to pieces. Not knowing whither the Cossacks may carry me in their backward movement, I determine to get out from among them. I do so, and then find myself on the extreme front, with nothing between me and the enemy. They are advancing from the west, where all is in the most profound darkness; but I can distinguish, at a distance of probably fifty yards, a dark irregular mass of horsemen coming forward at a gallop. They are all screeching like fiends, and by the flashes of fire, I can catch glimpses of their fierce, dark faces, and the gleam of drawn sabres. It did not take me long to perceive that I could not stay here, and quickly wheeling my horse, I dash off, first emptying my revolver at the mass. Almost at the same instant a company of infantry arrives on my left.

They come up in marching order at a run, and with a movement something resembling that of a lasso, the officer has thrown them into line of battle. I quickly spur my horse behind them, feeling for the moment extremely happy. They stand in line, the left foot foremost, their rifles ready; in another second the order rings out "Fire!" and the air is rent with the crash of a volley and the shriek of flying bullets.

The discharge was followed by another, and another, in quick succession. It was time; the Yomuds were so close,

PRINCE EUGENE.

that many of them fell dead at the very feet of the troops. And now away to the right begins to be heard the loud, fierce roar of the cannon, which have arrived on the scene, and are belching forth grape and canister.

The coming of daylight has probably been retarded for a few moments by the dust and smoke that were hanging over us, for now smoke and dust are cleared away by a small puff of wind, and, as if by magic, the darkness rises and discloses the Turcomans flying over the plain on their swift-footed horses, in full retreat.

I look around me. About a hundred yards away I see General Golovatchoff's banner, a number of Cossacks, and several officers grouped around; the rest of the Cossacks collected here and there in irregular groups; the infantry stretched around in a broken circle, about 300 yards in diameter, still in line of battle; the artillery-men, beside their smoking pieces, watching the retreating enemy, and hesitating about giving them a parting shot. The battle is over.

CHAPTER VIII.

AFTER THE BATTLE.

NEAR me were two or three Russian soldiers lying dead, and three or four wounded. A little farther away, Colonel Esipoff, whom I shook hands with half an hour before as he marched out, lay stark and cold, with a bullet through his breast, his Cross of St. George bespattered with blood. He had died the death of the brave.

I rode up to where the General's standard was waving, anxious to learn whether he was badly wounded. His arm was bandaged and his white coat covered with blood, but he still kept his saddle. The wound was only a sabre cut in the arm, and had been given by a man on foot.

We rode over the field, to count the wounded and the dead. The bodies of Turcomans were strewn about in great numbers. Here was one lying on his side, both hands still clutching a long stick, to which was tied a short crooked scythe. He was barefoot, bareheaded, and was clad only in light linen shirt and trousers; the dark scowl of hate still clung to his hard, rough features, and there was still the stamp of the fierce savage spirit that had led him with such unequal weapons to face the breech-loaders of the Russians.

Here, three or four lying side by side, as though shot down at the same instant, and three, four, or five tumbled together about the body of a beautiful horse, as if successively killed, along with the noble beast, in trying to help each other. Then more horses, more men lying about, half hidden among the low weeds in the little hollows of sand. In one spot the ground was literally covered with them. But there were no wounded; no groans, no cries for help. I was astonished at this at first, as although the Turcomans always try to carry off their wounded, they, of course, could not have carried all the Russians must have wounded in the recent engagement.

I soon had an explanation of the phenomenon, as horrible as it was unexpected. I saw a soldier cautiously approach one of the dead Turcomans. His movements were so strange, they excited my curiosity, and I drew up my horse at the distance of twenty or thirty feet to watch him. He was so intent on what he was doing that he did not observe me; and I could see a wild scared light in his eye, that reminded me partly of a crazy man, partly of a frightened child. Suddenly, before I had in the least comprehended what he was going to do, he plunged his bayonet deep into the Turcoman's side. I uttered an involuntary cry of horror; he looked up, saw me, and slunk away without a word. The Turcoman had only been feigning death, but even now he did not utter a groan, nor open his eyes, while the blood gushed from his side and mouth in a crimson stream; and I might even now have thought him dead, but for the convulsive clutching of his fingers and spasmodic quivering of his limbs. I turned away sick at heart, for I knew the poor fellow was past all human aid.

I am glad to be able to say, however, for the honour of the Russian troops, that, to the best of my knowledge, this was the only case of such cold-blooded barbarity that occurred. Although I scanned the field closely, I saw no more incidents of this kind. This soldier was evidently one of the cowards who had been terribly frightened, and was only having his revenge.

But the absence of wounded was explained. They were all feigning death, for fear of being killed. We counted in all about 300 bodies lying scattered about, or piled up in heaps, with a good many horses, but the enemy afterwards acknowledged a loss of 500. The Russians' loss was only forty in killed and wounded, which may be accounted for by the fact that the Yomuds were only armed with sabres and scythes. It was a bold and brilliant attack, and, but for the steadiness displayed by the Russian infantry, might have proved very disastrous to us. If a panic had once ensued, not one of us would have escaped. And yet this was the first affair in which these troops had ever been engaged. The coolness displayed by General Golovatchoff during the action was admirable, and probably had very much to do in preventing a panic.

The General took a hasty survey of the field, gave orders for the care of the wounded and burial of the dead, and then resumed the march. By this time the sun had risen, and threw long shadows over the desert; an oppressive silence reigned around, instead of the din and uproar of the conflict, and we marched silently forward, talking to each other in low voices.

The truth is, the attack had been so sudden, so unexpected, so fierce and desperate, that we were for the moment awed at the danger we had so narrowly escaped.

As there was now no particular reason for keeping to

I ... ... me to say, however, to the honour of the ... troops, that to the best of my knowledge this was the only case of such cold-blooded butchery that occurred. Although I examined the field closely, I saw no more acts of this kind. This soldier was evidently one of the cowards who had been terribly frightened, and was only taking his revenge.

But the absence of wounded was explained. They were all feigning death, for fear of being killed. We counted in all about 500 bodies lying scattered about, or piled up in a ... with a good many horses, but the enemy afterwards acknowledged a loss of 600. The Russians' loss was only forty in killed and wounded, which may be accounted for by the ... that the Yomuds were only armed with sabres and scythes. It was a bold and brilliant attack and but for the steadiness displayed by the Russian infantry, might have proved very disastrous to us. If a panic had ensued, not one of us would have escaped. And yet this was the first affair in which these troops had ever been engaged. The coolness displayed by General Golovatchoff during the action was admirable, and probably had very much to do in preventing a panic.

The General took a hasty **survey** of the field, gave orders for the care of the wounded and burial of the dead, and then resumed the march. By this time the sun had risen and threw long shadows over the desert; an oppressive silence reigned around instead of the din and uproar of the **conflict**, and we marched silently forward, talking to each other in low voices.

The **truth** is, the attack had been so sudden, so unexpected, so fierce and desperate, that we were for the moment awed at the danger we had so narrowly escaped.

As there was now no particular reason for keeping to

GENERAL GOLOVATCHOFF.

the open ground, we turned to the right, and were soon
in the road leading through the gardens to Iliah. In
half an hour we espied through the trees its mud battlemented walls, grey and frowning in the shadows of
morning. The road led around the town. The inhabitants had gathered in a large crowd at the gate to
receive us, with presents of freshly-baked cakes, melons,
grapes, and peaches.

CHAPTER IX.

THE PURSUIT.

THE people of Ihali were Uzbegs, with whom we had no quarrel.

Although they knew we were not making war upon them, they were, nevertheless, frightened at the noise of the combat; and they watched us with scared looks as we rode by, dust-covered and grimy, and gazed with awe upon General Golovatchoff, whose white coat was all bespattered with blood, and whose arm was in a sling.

We did not enter the town, but followed the road leading around the walls, and continued our march to the north-west.   In an hour we were again in the desert. Our road lay along its edge, which was irregular and crooked, so that we were continually crossing alternately streaks of sand and points of cultivated land.   We were in search of the Turcoman camp, which we had intended to surprise when marching out in the morning, and which was supposed to be some five or six miles from Ihali.

The Turcomans had entirely disappeared immediately after the fight, and for two or three hours we saw no more of them.   About nine, however, we began to see them scudding along the horizon on our left.   In half an hour the plain was covered with them; the battle was on once more, if battle it could be called. They showed themselves in considerable masses to the right and left, as well as before us, so that we were obliged to be prepared for an attack at any point. We had thrown out skirmishers and sharpshooters, under cover of the banks of the canals, which in many places afforded excellent protection. The enemy showed considerable daring, in spite of their defeat of the morning, often coming within easy range of our rifles, and sweeping by at a dashing gallop.

We were aproaching their camp, and their object was to retard our march as much as possible, in order to give the non-combatants time to escape.

Our progress under these circumstances was very slow. Advancing in marching order, with a line of sharpshooters thrown out on our left, while our right was protected by the cavalry, we were obliged to halt every few minutes to rearrange our broken ranks or change our front. Although having a wholesome dread of the infantry, the Yomuds were by no means so afraid of the cavalry, whose inability to cope with them they had discovered in the morning. Several times they dashed down upon the Cossacks in the most determined manner, and were only brought to a halt by a volley from the infantry, or a shell shrieking through their ranks.

This kind of running fight continued for two or three hours, the Yomuds careering around us in all directions, shouting, yelling, and firing their matchlocks. They did not appear to have any definite plan of action or attack, further than riding down upon us in irregular masses, without order or system.

Once half a dozen of them had gathered behind a ruined house, about 300 yards from the road, and as we passed they dashed out one at a time, and galloped off unharmed, under a rattling fire from the skirmish line.

General Golovatchoff seeing some masses of them away in the desert to the left, about a mile and a half, sent them a dozen shells, as a signal to the Orenburg detach- • ment. This detachment was supposed to be approaching from the other side, at the distance of eight or ten miles, for the purpose of completely hemming the fugitives in. These shells, fired without any particularly wicked intent, did the Yomuds a good deal of harm, as we afterwards learned. They 'had fallen into the camp we were in search of, which, hidden in a little hollow, had escaped our observation, and so caused the enemy to fly in such haste as to abandon everything.

This we learned from the Orenburg troops, who came upon the deserted camp the next day, and found several hundred arbas or carts of the country, which had been abandoned, together with some dead bodies, and a great quantity of baggage. The poor people had been so frightened by the bursting of the shells, that they had mounted their horses, and left everything, not even taking time to carry off their dead.

Among the curious things found was a quantity of papers of Lieut. Shakespeare, who went to Khiva on a mission from the English, during Perovsky's unfortunate expedition in 1840. Lieut. Shakespeare, it will be remembered, went to Khiva to bring about a peaceable settlement of the difficulties between the Khivans and the Russians.

One of these papers was a copy of a letter from Lord Palmerston, in which the British ambassador was instructed to inform the Russian Government that the annexation of Khiva might be regarded by England as a *casus belli*.

Our detachment did not discover the camp in which these papers were found at all. The guides had all disappeared in the affair of the morning. Nobody knew exactly where the camp was situated, and we marched by without seeing it, leaving it about two miles to our left.

At noon we reached the canal of Ana Murat, which poured a strong current of water into the desert; and crossing it, halted. Here we found ourselves on the site of an old fortified camp, made by the Khan during wars with these same Turcomans. It was about ten acres in extent, and the mud walls were in many places ten feet high, and nearly intact. The Khan gave Kaufmann a history of this war, which was curious.

Exasperated beyond endurance by the refusal of the Turcomans to pay taxes or recognise his authority, he determined to make war, and subjugate them. He assembled an army of Uzbegs, between whom and the Turcomans there exists, as I have before remarked, the most bitter animosity. The Khan marched his army into the country of the Turcomans; and arriving at this place, which offered a strong position in the deep canals that protected it on two sides, fortified himself.

Here he remained several weeks, during which time the Turcomans made real or feigned attacks upon his camp every day; which—judging by what we saw of them—they must have enjoyed immensely.

As the Khan never marched out to fight them, they had it all their own way. He threw solid shot at them with his cannon, but as it takes several tons of iron to kill a single man in that way, he did not do them much harm, while they careered around the camp on their horses, shouting, yelling, firing their matchlocks, flourishing their sabres, and enjoying the fun immensely. This continued for several weeks, at the end of which time the Khan, having exhausted his munitions and men, marched back to his capital in triumph. The Turcomans returned to their homes, and resumed their ordinary occupations.

This was the camp in which we now found ourselves; and the position being a good one, General Golovatchoff decided to remain here the rest of the day.

The Yomuds for their part made good use of the time thus allowed them, and continued their flight. As we had already passed them, they doubled on their track like hunted hares, and returned over nearly the same road we had come, taking their way to the south-east. All day and night they continued their hasty and terrified retreat, and thus gained several miles start of us.

The next morning at daylight we were on their trail. We had not gone far when we found the body of a Russian soldier, stripped naked, and decapitated; a picket whom they had probably surprised during the night. All that day we followed the trail of the fugitives, only stopping once to allow the troops time to breakfast. As we were encumbered with little baggage, our march was very rapid. We again passed near Iliali, leaving it to our left, and after crossing a small oasis, found ourselves on a wide open plain, which, judging by the numerous canals by which it was cut up, must have been at no far distant period in a state of cultivation. We saw no signs of the fugitives until nearly sunset, when a cloud of dust on the horizon showed we were fast overtaking them.

We camped soon afterwards on the banks of a canal, which afforded a plentiful supply of water; in a few minutes the Cossacks had scattered over the plain in search of forage for their horses. They found some hay, which had just been cut and saved by the Yomuds, a mile distant from the camp. But this confused dispersing of the Cossacks over the plain resulted in a deplorable accident. One of the native guides, who had ridden off some distance in advance of the others, was mistaken for a Yomud, fired upon by one of the Cossacks, and so dangerously wounded that he died in a couple of hours, in spite of the efforts of the army surgeon.

CHAPTER X.

THE FLIGHT.

EARLY next morning we were again on the trail, and soon began to perceive signs of the fugitives. Here an arba loaded with baggage, which had been hurriedly abandoned; there a cow or a calf that had not been able to follow; now an old woman hid in a hut, and almost paralysed with fear, supposing she would be immediately led out to execution; then an old man, ragged, and dust-covered, and miserable, who, leaning on a staff, watched us march past with haggard eyes. Later we began to come upon little flocks of lambs and kids, then flocks of sheep and cattle, and more arbas.

Golovatchoff now ordered the cavalry ahead to overtake and attack the fugitives, and if possible, force them to give battle. Judging, from what I had seen the first day, that this attack must necessarily be on the laggards and stragglers, I determined to stay behind with the staff.

The cavalry soon disappeared in a cloud of dust; the infantry continued to move steadily forward. In half an hour we came to a deep narrow canal, full of water, which traversed the plain at right angles with our line of march, and here a strange and fearful scene met our gaze

THE FLIGHT. *From a design by Verestchagin, 'Illustrated London News.'*

Scattered over the plain in every direction were hundreds of arbas, or carts, loaded with the household goods of the Yomuds. Unable to cross the canal on the one narrow bridge, they had cut their horses loose and fled, abandoning everything. Some, however, had failed to make their escape; either because they had no horses, or possibly because they trusted too much to the clemency of the Russians. These had been overtaken and cut down by the Cossacks.

Everywhere, lying among the thickly standing arbas, were the bodies, with sabre-cuts on head and face, bloody and ghastly. But worse still to see were the women cowering under the carts, like poor dumb animals, watching us with fear-stricken faces and beseeching eyes, but never uttering a word, with the dead bodies of their husbands, lovers, and brothers lying around them. They expected to be treated as they knew their own husbands, brothers, and lovers would have treated the vanquished under like circumstances.

I observed one, however, who gave no attention to what was passing around her. She was holding in her lap the head of a man who was dying from a terrible sabre-cut in the head. She sat gazing on his face as motionless as a statue, not even raising her eyes at our approach; and we might have taken her attitude for one of stolid indifference, but for the tears that stole silently down from her long dark lashes, and dropped on the face of the dying man. There, at least, was no dread of the Russians. Grief had banished fear.

But worst of all to see was a number of little mites of children, whose parents had probably been killed. Some were crawling about among the wheels, crying; others, still sitting in the carts among the baggage, watched us with curious, childish eyes; one little girl crowed and laughed at the sight of General Golovatchoff's banner.

I took one of the crying infants to a woman with wild eyes, who was sitting under a cart; but she paid no heed to it, for, in passing afterwards, I saw the little thing lying on the ground near her, screaming its lungs away.

The General and staff stopping here a few minutes, I rode slowly forward alone. Everywhere were the abandoned arbas, piled full of carpets, cushions, cooking utensils, threshed wheat, spun silk, and clothing; and now and again the body of a sabred Yomud. Here an old woman, eighty I should say, was sitting prone in the middle of the road, with an infant in her arms, over which she was bending in an attitude of resignation and despair. With closed eyes she waited, as though resolved not to look on the sabre she expected would cut off both their lives together. She would not abandon her little grandchild, though perhaps the mother had. Farther on was a young and pretty woman under an arba, with bleeding face, and torn robe, and a woe-stricken countenance that told its own story. Acting upon an unreasoning impulse, I offered her money; but she flung it back, and bowed her head in her hands with a sob.

I must say, however, that cases of violence towards women were very rare; and although the Russians here were fighting barbarians who commit all sorts of atrocities upon their prisoners, which fact might have excused a good deal of cruelty on the part of the soldiers, their conduct was infinitely better than that of European troops in European campaigns.

A little farther on was an old woman lying near the road, wounded with a bad sabre-cut in the neck; but she might easily have been taken for a man, as she wore no turban. The orders were to give the men no quarter, whether they resisted or not. This was the only woman I saw wounded, though I was told there were three or four other cases.

I had now advanced some two miles on the plain, which was still covered with the abandoned carts. They were scattered about in groups of five or six; some in the road, some a quarter or a half a mile to the right and left, as though their owners had hoped to escape into the desert, when the approach of the Cossacks forced them to abandon the attempt.

Fifteen or twenty Yomuds on horseback now showed themselves a short distance away in the desert, and as the infantry was some two miles behind, and the cavalry probably three or four in advance, I thought it prudent to halt. While waiting here, a Yomud, who had probably been hiding somewhere in the vicinity, suddenly appeared coming towards me. He was only armed with a stick, but his manner was so defiant, that I seized my revolver. Even then he did not show the slightest sign of fear, but crossed the road before me, at a distance of not more than ten feet, scowling at me with his fierce black eyes, as though half tempted to attack me with his club, in spite of my two revolvers and my breech-loading rifle.

My first impulse was to make him throw down his stick and tender his submission to me, as one of his conquerors, but the fellow had such an audacious, independent bearing, that he excited my admiration; I thought, besides, it would not be a brave thing to do, with such odds in my favour. He walked off without so much as bidding me good-day, and disappeared among the low hillocks of sand.

The infantry soon came up, and the march was continued some four or five miles farther. More sheep, more cattle, more camels, young and old, but no horses. It is not a little remarkable, that although many thousand head of sheep and cattle were captured during the course of the campaign, not a single horse was caught; and it shows how wise the Yomuds were in prizing so highly their splendid beasts. Probably only those who had no horses were caught and killed in this day's chase.

Seeing two or three Cossacks pillaging a group of carts a short distance from our line of march, I rode out to inspect the operation. The bodies of two Yomuds were lying on the ground; and a little girl, three years old, standing beside the dead bodies, watched the pillaging operation in a bewildered way, peculiar to children, and wept quietly, but bitterly.

As the little thing, if left here, would have died of thirst, I took her upon my horse, with the intention of leaving her with the next woman I should find. Soon after perceiving another, I handed the first over to the care of my comrade, Chertkoff, and went after the second. The poor child had a great gash cut in her foot, as though she had stepped on a sabre; and the wound, full of sand and exposed to the hot sun, must have been painful. She was not shedding a tear, but stood watching the Cossacks pillaging an arba, probably her own father's, with bright, curious, but defiant eyes. When I offered to take her on my horse, she ran away, and I was obliged to dismount in order to capture her.

Then she struggled and scratched, and bit like a little wild cat; and not till I had exhausted all my vocabulary of Tartar on her did she at last consent to go with me. But when I succeeded in persuading her of my peaceful intentions, she put her arms around my neck and went to sleep. The poor little thing was completely covered with dust and dirt, and looked as though she had been dragged through a mud puddle. She had probably not been washed since the flight had commenced more than a week ago, and the fugitives had been travelling in clouds of dust during the whole time.

I cut a rather ridiculous figure riding along the lines with the little barbarian's arms tightly clasped around my neck, and her little queer-shaped head, covered an inch thick with dust, lying on my breast. I soon found I was in good company, though, for I met an officer of the staff with a like acquisition—also a little girl. The Yomuds seemed to have abandoned their girls with less reluctance than their boys.

About eleven o'clock we overtook the cavalry, which had halted to rest their horses, and we camped for the morning.

The fugitives had scattered in every direction, but the great mass of them, mounted on their fleet horses, was some miles further on, and it would be useless to attempt overtaking them. General Golovatchoff therefore decided that as the greater part of their baggage, as well as live stock, had been captured, they had been sufficiently punished, and determined to march back to Ilali.

Even here, so far from the oasis, there were two or three large canals, one of which was full of water, showing that the plain, barren though it be at present, was formerly under cultivation, and might be easily reclaimed. From what I have observed, the limits of the oasis of Khiva must have formerly been much greater, for everywhere over these plains, from a point near the city itself, which is almost on the frontier between sand and desert, are signs of former irrigation.

Before arriving in camp I saw five or six women, to whom I offered my little protégée, but they refused to accept it, pointing to their own children. They did not certainly appear to be in a condition to take charge of another child, as they each had four or five already; so I carried mine into camp, not knowing exactly what to do with her. The most practical plan seemed to be to throw her away and have done, but I might as well have left her in the desert at once, to feed the jackals. While debating the matter, I made a bed for her under a cart, with a pile of cotton, of which masses were lying about along with rugs, carpets, and cooking utensils, the remains of the pillaged carts. Then, with the aid of the doctor, I washed and dressed her wounded foot.

She was a brave little thing, and won our admiration by the way in which she stood the dressing of the wound. Although it was terribly swelled and inflamed, and full of sand, and must have hurt her dreadfully when we were cleaning it, she never shed a tear. After a good deal of scrubbing, I got her face clean enough to see what she looked like, and found her rather pretty. She drank water greedily, probably being the first she had tasted that day. Seeing a soldier milking a captured cow, I bought as much fresh milk as she could drink, after which she went to sleep on her bed of cotton. In short, I got so interested in the little outcast, and she was such a brave little thing, that it was with reluctance I gave her up to the mother, whom I afterwards found. The mother, although overjoyed to find her child, did not seem particularly grateful to me, and never looked at me once afterwards. This was rather hard, I thought, considering I had returned the child with a well-appointed wardrobe I had pillaged for the occasion, besides a piece of gold, which will probably go to make up her marriage portion, ten years hence. Perhaps she thanked the Kafir in her heart of hearts, though, all the same.

After a halt of three hours, during which time we pillaged and set fire to all the carts that were captured here, we took up our march back to Iliali.

Some fifty or sixty women were captured here, but they were allowed to remain behind, and were probably soon rejoined by their friends.

The soldiers were ordered to take everything of value and burn the rest; and the Cossacks executed the order with a right good will. Carpets, silk stuffs, and articles of clothing, with occasional silver ornaments, were the principal objects of value; and the road was soon strewn with unspun cotton, raw silk, old carpets, which the soldiers had not thought worth taking, together with grain, flour, cooking utensils, skins of milk, and all sorts of household goods.

It was sad to see the poor, simple articles of household use, wrecks of so many simple happy homes, trampled in the dust. For with these simple people every article of the household is an old and well-known friend, to which they have become attached by long use, and with which are associated many remembrances and souvenirs; over which has been told many a mystic charm. It is sad to think of the women coming back over this road, trying to save something from the general ruin, and weeping, perhaps, over some familiar prized article, that would remind them of a happy home now in ashes.

But there were other things sadder still to excite one's sympathy and compassion.

In one place were the bodies of three Yomuds, lying in their blood, and near them six children, of the ages of four to eight, all alone with their dead. The eldest, a sturdy little fellow, was taking care of the others, as well as he could. He was engaged in making up a bed for them, under a cart, with bits of cotton, silk, worn-out rugs, and old carpets—all that was left of their once well-furnished kibitka. He did not pay the slightest attention to me when I rode up, but continued his task, without even looking up; and, I have no doubt, his little baby heart swelled with rage and indignation at the sight of me. Twenty years hence, some of the " Kafirs " will probably feel how well the child had learned to hate them.

I took care that the soldiers should not burn the cart under which the children had taken refuge, found them a skin of milk, and rode off after the rear-guard, leaving them alone with their dead in the wide, wide, desert. Well has Victor Hugo said: " Ceux qui n'ont vu que la misère des hommes n'ont rien vu; il faut voir la misère des femmes. Ceux qui n'ont vu que la misère des femmes n'ont rien vu; il faut voir la misère des enfants."

I only saw one child that had been killed. It was a very young infant, and looked as though it had received a simple blow from a horse's hoof or some other object, as there was no sign of blood on it.

Our march all the way back was marked by fire and flame. Arrived at the canal before spoken of, where were the first mass of arbas, I found they had been completely pillaged, and that nearly all the women and children had disappeared. A few still remained, however; and it was curious to see a Cossack stop from his work of plunder to give a child a piece of bread, or a drink of water from his flask, in the gentlest manner possible, and then resume his occupation.

I found the little girl that had crowed so gleefully in the morning at the sight of General Golovatchoff's banner still sitting in the same cart. It was now near night-fall, and the poor little thing had been there all day in the hot sun, with nothing to drink, waiting patiently till she should be taken away. I found a skin of milk among the thousand other things that lay scattered about, and gave her to drink, not without difficulty, as I could not find a single drinking cup.

There were some five or six hundred arbas here, so closely packed together, that one or two having been fired, the flames spread rapidly, and were now approaching the one in which sat the little girl. I took her away far enough to be out of danger, and put her down on a piece of carpet, wondering what I should do with her. Although there were three or four women still here, the fact of their having left her all day alone was sufficient evidence that they could not be depended upon to take charge of her. It was now near dark, and the Yomuds could hardly be expected back before the next day; in the meantime the jackals were plentiful, and could already be heard howling in the distance.

I had about decided to take her into camp, when I observed a woman approach, whom I had not yet seen, leading two children. I showed her the child and asked, "Yours?" "Yok," "no," she replied; and pointing to a Yomud stretched out on the ground, added, "his." "Any mother?" I ask. "Yok," "no." Then I told her by signs I would take it with me to camp. She did not seem to relish the idea, so I asked her if she would take charge of it herself. This she did readily. I gave her a piece of gold, and told her to not stay here. She took the little girl in her arms, and walked off along the canal, across the wide open plain, with the two others trudging wearily after her, wandering, God knows whither.

The rear-guard did not reach camp until long after dark, owing to the great numbers of sheep, cattle, and camels we had captured, and which made our progress necessarily slow. Their bawling and bleating, filling the whole plain, was mournful enough in the darkness; while low down on the southern sky could be seen the glare of the burning arbas, telling a sad tale of blight and ruin.

CHAPTER XI.

THE WAR INDEMNITY.

GENERAL KAUFMANN, with a considerable force, met our detachment at Iliali. Communication with General Golovatchoff had been cut off for several days, and this, coupled with a flying rumour of a great battle which had reached Khiva, had alarmed the Commander-in-chief. Hastily assembling, with the Khan's assistance, as many arbas for transport as he could in half a day, he immediately set off to our relief. On the way he received General Golovatchoff's despatch containing the account of the affair of the 27th of July, which of course relieved his fears.

The power of the Yomud Turcomans was broken; their ruin complete. The greater part of their live stock had been captured. All of their wheat, grain, and forage, upon which they depended for subsistence during the winter, had been burned, and their dwellings laid in ashes.

It would seem that their proud spirits were still unbroken, for they refused to submit and return to their ravaged homes, as they were invited to do by Kaufmann They wandered about the desert, hanging on the frontier of the oasis, living as best they could for some weeks, until Kaufmann had crossed the Oxus and was on his way back to Tashkent. Then, from what I have learned since my arrival in Europe, they fell upon their Uzbeg neighbours and pillaged them, until they had partly made up for the losses inflicted by the Russians.

Now, however, their position must have been deplorable. Kaufmann told me he had learned they had sent an embassy to the Tekke-Turcomans on the Caspian and Attrek, asking permission to emigrate to their territory, to which request the latter replied, in a very brotherly manner, that they might come, but that they would have to give up all their property which had escaped the Russians. However true this may be, few of them, I believe, went to the country of the Tekkes.

Kaufmann camped at Ilıalı, and issued a proclamation to the other Turcomans, informing them he had assessed a war indemnity upon them, which he expected them to pay within a week, and threatening them with the same punishment he had inflicted upon the Yomuds, in case they failed to comply within the specified time.

' To this proclamation they responded by a delegation of their head men, who promised to pay, but asked for time. It would be, they said, impossible to collect the money on so short a notice. Kaufmann therefore granted them fourteen days.

The assessment of this war indemnity was at the rate of fifteen tillas, about £4 1s. of English money, to the kibitka, for all the tribes except the Kara-djigeldis, who were assessed at the rate of twenty tillahs, or £5 7s. The whole amount thus levied was about £42,500. Considering the comparative wealth of the two peoples, this was a considerably higher war indemnity than that levied on France by the Germans. In a day or two, the Turcomans, true to their word, sent in a small instalment

of a few thousand rubles, consisting of the small silver
coin of the country, and some pounds of silver in the
shape of bracelets, and other female ornaments.

The camp for the next few days presented a curious
spectacle. There was probably not enough coin in the
country to pay this—to the Turcomans—enormous sum,
so they brought in horses, and carpets, and camels to eke
out the amount. These they sold, at good round prices,
to the officers. Many of the Russians were anxious to
possess a genuine Turcoman horse, whose superiority
had been so well demonstrated by the fact that, during
the whole campaign, not a single one was captured.

From what I saw of them, however, I should say
that these Turcomans either did not bring in their best
animals, or that their horses are greatly inferior to
those of the Yomuds. Few of them, as far as I could
judge, possessed any of the points indicating either speed
or bottom. Narrow chests, with the fore-legs planted
against each other like those of a rabbit, large head and
ears, almost entire absence of mane, and a very thin
tail, together with a great height, being their principal
characteristics. Lieutenant Stumm, judging by the specimens that had been captured during the march upon
Khiva, was disposed to infer that the race of Turcoman
horses had deteriorated, and were now no better than any
other, and perhaps inferior to those of the Kirghiz. I am
inclined to think, however, that he had not seen any real
Turcoman horses; the truth being that their owners
prize them more highly than they do their daughters,
and part with them less readily.

Although during the campaign against the Yomuds,
our cavalry had charged them several times, they had
never been able to approach nearer than a hundred yards,

and so conscious did the Yomuds seem of the superiority
of their beasts, that they did not even appear to hurry,
but galloped off in an easy canter, as though disdaining
to urge their horses for us; and this while we were
applying the whip and spur, and straining every nerve
to overtake them. And yet the Cossacks have excellent
beasts.

The Turcoman horses, however, whatever their merits,
brought very good prices, the Russian officers paying
from £20 to £50 for one.

The Turcoman carpets, too, were very much in demand,
and sold readily, in spite of the high prices demanded for
them and of the fact that hundreds had been "looted" in
the campaign against the Yomuds. A carpet, four yards
long by two wide, brought £4 to £5. A curious feature of
the sale was, that although the Turcomans must have been
hard pressed for money to pay the indemnity, they could
not be induced to lower their prices a single kopeck.
They simply named their price, and you might take the
article or leave it, as you pleased. The carpets are made
by the women, and will compare favourably with the best
carpets made anywhere. Each family has a different
pattern, which is handed down from generation to generation as an heirloom, without undergoing the slightest
change. The colours are principally red and white, in-
terspersed with small patches of green and brown, and
are really very pretty, as well as durable.

The principal part of the war indemnity was paid,
strange as it may seem, by the women. Every Turcoman woman possesses a great number of ornaments, such
as bracelets, necklaces, buttons, and head-dresses, in solid
silver. In fact, the principal wealth of the Turcomans,
apart from horses, seems to consist in these silver orna-

TURCOMAN WOMAN.

ments. They brought in hundreds of them, which Kaufmann accepted at the rate of twenty-five rubles to the pound of silver. The ornaments were all of the purest silver, of very rude workmanship, and usually very massive; a pair of bracelets often weighing more than a pound. These bracelets were always very wide and thick; in shape like a letter C, sometimes traced with gold, and always set with cornelians.

It was sad to think with what pain these simple objects must have been surrendered by the women to satisfy the insatiable maw of the "Urus." These ornaments had often been in the family many generations. Their mothers, and grandmothers, and great-grandmothers, had worn them on their bridal days, and they looked forward to seeing their daughters and their granddaughters wear them in their turn; and now the hated Kafir had come and demanded them all. One can imagine them shedding bitter tears over the poor simple articles, with which they were wont to deck themselves so bravely on great days, as they spread them out on the floor of their tents, and counted them over, and admired them for the last time.

A commission of officers was appointed to weigh and estimate the silver, and for ten days they were busily engaged in this occupation from morning till night. Nevertheless, at the expiration of the time fixed by Kaufmann for the payment of the indemnity, they had only received some £20,000—less than half the sum demanded. As the Turcomans had given sufficient evidence of their intention to pay, however, and as the impossibility of collecting so large a sum in so short a time was only too apparent, Kaufmann decided to give them another year to pay the remaining £22,500 It was very evident that the Turcomans, with the greatest good-will, would not be able to collect the whole sum under several weeks; and it was necessary that the army should cross the Oxus, and be ready to start back to Tashkent by the 1st of September, in order to get across the desert before the intense cold should have set in.

The difficulties the Turcomans had to surmount in collecting a large sum of money were really very great. Besides the scarcity of the money itself, was the difficulty of apportioning the amount to be paid by each kibitka. As before remarked, the State does not exist among the Turcomans. There is no supreme authority to fix rates or apportion taxes, nor any recognised power to enforce their payment. They have no assessment or estimate of taxable property, nor anybody who knows how to make such an estimate, because they have never had any taxes to pay. The difficulty, therefore, of organising an internal revenue department, as it were, must have been very great. Kaufmann tried to give their head men all the instruction possible under the circumstances, in order to assist them. He told them how to distribute the amount assessed on each kibitka, according to the number of cattle, sheep, horses, and camels possessed by each man, but it was hard to get them to understand. They said that those who often had the most live stock were those who had the least ready money, and were, therefore, the least able to pay; while those who had money, hid it, and refused to pay it out for the general good. Kaufmann tried to explain to them that those who had money should lend to those who had none; and endeavoured to show them how the head men should borrow money from those who had it, in the name of the people at large, who might next year pay it back to them in sheep and cattle. In short, he did his best to give them some idea of how they should organise themselves into a State, as well as raise a national

debt. But it was too complicated for them ; and Kaufmann
had to leave them to their own devices.

All this time we encamped in a large garden, surrounded by a high wall, adjoining the town of Iliali. It
is a small place of perhaps 2000 inhabitants; completely
enclosed by a heavy mud wall, which forms a rectangle
about 300 yards long by 200 wide. It has a bazaar, but
no mosque ; and is half in ruins, the result of some internecine conflict ; and, although the country around is
fertile and rich, presents but a wretched and desolate
appearance.

To those of us who were not occupied in counting and
weighing Turcoman silver the twelve days we spent here
were passed wearily enough. The dull tedium of the
camp was unbearable after the excitement of the short but
interesting campaign. Eating, drinking, and giving each
other dinners and entertainments was all we had to do ;
and we threw a spirit and ardour into these occupations
which even astonished ourselves.

We actually came to look upon Khiva as the great
metropolis for business, news, and pleasure, and to regard
it as one does London, Paris, or St. Petersburg after a
long sojourn in some little rustic village far away from
any railroad. As to seeing London, Paris, or St. Petersburg themselves, a visit to them was so dimly distant in
the unknown future, that we thought of it as something
that might take place years hence. Khiva was the object
of all our interest, and we longed for a sight of its bazaar,
as some of us often had yearned before for the boulevards
of Paris.

It was, therefore, with light hearts that we sprang
into our saddles again, and turned our horses' heads
towards Khiva. An easy march of five days brought us
to the capital.

CHAPTER XII.

THE TREATY.

Soon after the fall of Khiva, Kaufmann drew up the draft of a treaty to be made with the Khan. This draft he sent to St. Petersburg, with a courier, for the Emperor's sanction. It was duly approved by the Emperor, and returned in time to be signed before the army left Khiva. A copy of it in the Uzbeg dialect was given the Khan two or three days in advance, so that he might have time to get a knowledge of its contents before signing.

On the 23rd of August, the treaty was signed by Kaufmann and the Khan, in the presence of all the officers of the staff. I give it in full:

1. Said Muhamed Rahim Bogadur Khan, declares himself the humble servant of the Emperor of All the Russias. He surrenders the right of keeping up direct relations with neighbouring Khans and rulers, of concluding commercial or other treaties with them, or of declaring war without the permission of the supreme Russian executive authority in Central Asia.

2. The frontier between the Russian and Khivan territiories shall commence at Kukerth, and follow the western channel of the Amu-Darya to the Aral Sea.

From there the frontier will follow the shores of the sea to Cape Urga, thence it will follow the foot of the Chink on the south of the Ust-Urt, and what is usually called the old bed of the Amu-Darya, to the Caspian Sea.

3. The right bank of the Amu, with all the neighbouring territories which formerly belonged to Khiva, pass from the possession of the Khan to Russia, with all the peoples who inhabit them, including the nomads. Lands within the ceded territory, which the Khan has given to dignitaries of the Khanate, shall nevertheless belong to Russia, and no claims on the part of ancient proprietors will be admitted. The Khan may indemnify them by giving them other lands on the left bank of the river.

4. In case the Emperor should wish to transfer a part of the right bank to the Emir of Bokhara, the Khan will recognise the Emir as the legal sovereign of this part of his ancient domains, and renounces all intention of re-establishing his authority over them.

5. The navigation of the Amu is accorded exclusively to Russian vessels Khivan and Bokhariot vessels cannot navigate the river without the special permission of the supreme Russian authority in Central Asia.

6. The Russians have the right to establish ports on the left bank of the Amu, at all points which may appear to them necessary. The government of Khiva is responsible for the safety of these ports. The choice of places for the establishment of ports lies with the Russian supreme authority in Central Asia.

7. Besides these ports, the Russians have the right to build warehouses on the left bank of the Amu, for the purpose of storing their merchandise. The government of Khiva agrees to give unoccupied lands, which may be necessary for the purpose of constructing their warehouses

and magazines, the dwellings of the employés, and accompanying farms at the points which may be indicated by the Russian supreme power in Central Asia. These warehouses, with the merchandise they contain, and all the people who inhabit them, shall be under the protection of the government of Khiva, which is responsible for their safety.

8. All the towns and villages of Khiva are open from this time forward to Russian commerce. Russian merchants, with their caravans, may pass through the country in all directions. The functionaries of the Khan' government are obliged to protect them, and the government of Khiva is responsible for their safety.

9. Russian merchants are freed from paying the *ziaket*, as well as all other taxes, and are placed on the same footing as Khivan merchants in Russia, who neither at Kazala, Orenburg, nor any of the ports on the Caspian, pay taxes of any kind.

10. Russian merchants have the right to transport their goods to countries adjoining Khiva, without paying any duties in traversing the Khanate.

11. Russian merchants have the right, if they should wish it, to have at Khiva, and in all the other towns of the Khanate, their own agents (*karavan bashis*), to keep up relations with the functionaries of the Khanate, and to manage their commercial affairs.

12. Russian subjects have the right to acquire landed property in Khiva, and the taxes assessed on such property shall be subject to the approval of the Russian supreme power in Central Asia.

13. Contracts made between Russians and Khivans shall be faithfully executed by both parties.

14. Complaints of Russians against Khivans shall

be immediately examined and adjusted by the Khan's government. Where debts are due to Khivans and Russians, the Russian claims shall have the priority.

15. Complaints of Khivans against Russians, even when the latter inhabit Khiva, shall be forwarded to the nearest Russian commandant, who alone has the right to pronounce judgment.

16. The government of the Khan shall not receive any emigrant from Russia who arrives without a passport giving permission of the Russian authority to come to Khiva. If a criminal Russian subject come to Khiva to escape the pursuit of justice, the government of the Khan is obliged to seize him, and send him to the nearest Russian commandant.

17. The emancipation of the slaves, as well as the prohibition against slavery in all future time, remains in full force; and the Khan's government binds itself to the strict accomplishment of this edict.

18. A war indemnity of 2,200,000 rubles is levied upon Khiva, to pay the expenses of the campaign, which was solely caused by the government and people of Khiva. As it would be impossible for the government of Khiva to pay this sum at once, permission is accorded to pay the sum in instalments with interest at five per cent. The two first years the Russian government shall receive 100,000 rubles each year; the two following years, 125,000 each year, in 1877 and 1878, 150,000 rubles each year, the two following years, 175,000 rubles each year; and in 1881, that is at the end of eight years, 200,000 rubles; and each year after, until the end of the payment of the indemnity, the sum of 200,000 rubles. The payments may be made in Russian paper-money or in Khivan coin. The time for the first pay-

ment is fixed for December 1, 1873. The Khivan government is allowed to collect taxes on the right bank of the river, to contribute to the first payment, at the same rate as previous years. The collection of these taxes must be accomplished by the 1st of December, 1873. The payments shall be made on the 1st of November of each year. After paying 200,000 rubles for the year 1893, there will only remain, after nineteen years on the 1st of November, 1893, the last sum of 73,557 rubles. The Khivan government has the right to pay more than the sum specified each term, but not less.

CHAPTER XIII.

RUSSIA AND ENGLAND IN ASIA.

I HAVE hitherto refrained from saying anything of the causes of the Russian campaign against Khiva. These causes may be summed up in a very few words. First among them was the detention at Khiva of twenty-one Russians, held there as slaves; who were, however, liberated before the campaign was commenced. Next were the occasional attacks of Khivans upon caravans of Russian merchants, which the Khan of Khiva would not, or could not, hinder, and which had been going on for many years.

It will be seen by the treaty of peace, that they had other and more important objects in undertaking the campaign. They wished to reduce to subjection the only remaining Khanate in Central Asia which still refused to acknowledge their supremacy, as well as to advance their frontier to the Oxus, and gain complete possession of that river as far up as the boundary of Bokhara.

Summing up the Treaty, the result is. The Russian frontier has been advanced 300 miles farther south, 80,000 square miles of territory have been annexed, and complete possession of the lower Oxus has been obtained.

The river, when Kaufmann left Khiva, had already been explored; and it appeared that after the artificial obstructions put in the channel by the Khivans should have disappeared, it would be easily navigable for the Russian steamboats as high as Khiva, and perhaps higher The communication thus between Kazala and Khiva will be easy and rapid.

It is not known to a certainty how many people have been added to the population of Russia; but as the right bank of the river is thinly inhabited, a guess of 50,000 souls would probably be not far astray.

I do not know what were the exact terms of the agreement entered into by Count Shuvaloff and Earl Granville. It is, I believe, generally understood that the Russians simply agreed not to annex any territory south of the Oxus.

It will be seen by the treaty, that the Russians have not broken their agreement, while, at the same time, they have reduced the Khan to the most complete state of vassalage, besides depriving him of a large share of his dominions He cannot stir hand nor foot without the consent of the Russians, while he has at the same time all the responsibility of government. The arrangement, indeed, leaves every advantage on the side of the Russians. As will be remarked, they receive about two-thirds of the whole revenue of the Khanate, without any expense or trouble, or the odium attached to the collection of it. The people are as completely in their power as though they really occupied the place; and Russian traders may come and go freely, as in their own country.

The arrangement is far more advantageous to the Russians than the actual occupation of the country; and I doubt very much whether they would have annexed it immediately, even without the promise made to Earl Granville.

Under existing arrangements, the Khivans are becoming accustomed to the presence of the Russians, their prejudices are gradually wearing off, and the way is thus paved for Russian rule by the Khan himself. Indeed, I have little doubt that long before the war indemnity is paid, the death of the Khan, or some other event, will enable the Russians to quietly take possession, perhaps at the demand of the people themselves.

It may be expected that I should say something of the political situation of the Russians in Central Asia. On this subject, however, I have but little to say. I do not deem that the mere fact of my having been in Central Asia during a short campaign, enables me to say anything new on the question, and there are men who have never been there at all far more competent to speak on it than myself.

Such men as Sir Henry Rawlinson, Mr. Michell, and others, who have studied the question for years, must be looked to for information, and to the works of these gentlemen I would refer the reader who wishes to obtain a correct and comprehensive knowledge of Central Asian affairs. Mr. Schuyler, too, and Mr. Ashton Dilke, are about publishing works on Central Asia, which will contain much valuable and new information on Russian politics and Russian administration in Turkistan.

It would be idle in me to say anything of the general views or the general interests of Russia and England in Central Asia. So far as these are questions of fact, abundant information has already been supplied by other writers, and so far as they are questions of opinion, those acquainted with the subject have already made up their minds.

I would simply remark that, in my opinion, the

conquest of Khiva, and its occupation, should that follow, have no great significance, so far as Russian advances on India are concerned. Of course, the fall of Khiva must exercise a strong moral influence upon all the Mohamedhan populations of Central Asia. Khiva was considered impregnable and inaccessible; it was the last great stronghold of Islamism in Central Asia, after Bokhara had fallen; and its conquest will tend to confirm the belief, already wide-spread in these countries, that the Russians are invincible.   •

But apart from the prestige thus gained, the conquest of Khiva has little importance. In the present situation of the Russians in Central Asia, there are two lines of advance to India. The one from the southern shores of the Caspian, along the northern frontier of Persia to Herat, and thence on to the western frontier of Hindostan,—in all a distance of 1000 miles. Whatever the possibilities of an invasion being accomplished by this route, a glance at the map will show that Khiva would not be of the slightest use to an army from a military point of view. The other, and more probable line of march upon India, would be from Samarcand across the Khanate of Bokhara to Kerki, and thence up the Oxus to Kunduz. Khiva is 375 miles north-west from Kerki, and, therefore, that distance behind what the direct line of march would be. The greater part of this distance, too, is a desert; for even the banks of the Oxus for most of the way are uninhabited. Khiva would, therefore, be of as little use to an army marching by this route as by the other.

It may be said that the Russians could employ their steamboats for transporting troops down the Syr, across the Aral Sea, and up to the Oxus. But, apart from the fact of the Russians having but a few small boats on the

Aral, utterly insufficient for the transport of a large army, there is little probability the Oxus is navigable as high up as Kerki; and a scheme of this kind would, therefore, be impracticable.

I am not of those who believe in a traditional policy of aggression on the part of the Russians in Central Asia. The Russian advances have been made rather through the ambition of military chiefs, who were only too glad to take advantage of the blunders and perversity of Central Asian despots to distinguish themselves, or win a decoration. Nor do I believe that the Russians have any immediate designs on India. But they see that there is a certain amount of territory lying between the English and Russian possessions which must sooner or later fall into the hands of either power. I think they are disposed to seize as much of this territory as they conveniently can, and this comprises their whole policy at present.

Whether, however, they follow a traditional policy of aggression or not, the result is, it must be admitted, very much the same. They are steadily advancing towards India, and they will sooner or later acquire a position in Central Asia which will enable them to threaten it. Should England be engaged in a European war, and not show herself sufficiently accommodating on the Bosphorus, then, indeed, Russia would probably strike a blow at England's Eastern empire. At present, however, the Russian forces in Asia are not sufficient to make any such attempt. They have occupation enough in keeping the Central Asia populations in subjection.

But when a railroad is laid from Samara to Samarcand, the question will assume a very different aspect. Suppose stores to have been collected at Samarcand in advance, an army of 100,000 might, by means of a railroad, be concentrated in Kerki in thirty days. From Kerki to Kunduz, along the valley of the Oxus, is only 250 miles, and from Kunduz to the summit of the Hindu-Kush, only 100 miles; and an army might make this distance easily in twenty days The annexation of Bokhara, and the occupation of Kerki, would, therefore, be the next steps in the advance of the Russians on India.

Bokhara is at present completely under Russian tutelage; and, I believe, no existing agreements between them and the English Government prevent them from occupying that country.

And Bokhara occupied, the Russian frontier would be within 150 miles of Cabul.

CHAPTER XIV.

HOMEWARD.

I WOULD here record an act of daring performed by
Colonel Skobeloff, of the Caucasus, whose name I have so
often already mentioned.   It was a matter of great interest
and importance to determine whether Colonel Markosoff,
who led the expedition starting from the base of Attrek,
would have been able to reach the oasis, had he continued
the march instead of retreating.   In order to form an
opinion on this point, it was necessary for some one to
cross the desert to the point where Markosoff had turned
back.   But it would be an expedition of great hardship
for a large force, and very hazardous for a small one, for
the desperate Yomuds were prowling about in that direction.   Besides, the matter was not of sufficient importance
to justify a great loss of men.   One or two men should go
over the road alone, make a hurried map of it, examine
the wells, and determine about how much water they
could be relied upon to furnish, and should trust to their
own skill and the fleetness of their horses for safety.
This duty was undertaken by Colonel Skobeloff, and
carried out in the most gallant manner.   Disguising
himself in a Turcoman costume, he took three Turcomans,
who had been long in his service on the shores of the

31

Caspian, and, the day we marched for Khiva, plunged into the desert in the opposite direction.

We did not see him again for ten days, and had given up all hopes of his return, when he suddenly appeared among us, tired and exhausted with his long ride, but with the object of his undertaking accomplished. It appeared from his report that any attempt on the part of Markosoff to proceed farther with enfeebled camels, horses, and men could only have resulted disastrously, owing to the scarcity of water in that part of the route which still remained to be traversed.

On the 24th of August, the Russians started from Khiva, and took up their march for the Oxus. On the morning of that day, the Khan rode out to the camp, took leave of Kaufmann and the officers of the staff, shaking hands with them all round. I happened to be in the city of Khiva while this leave-taking was going on; but on my way back to the camp, I met the Khan, accompanied by fifteen or twenty followers. My interpreter was absent, so that we could not open a conversation; but he shook me by the hand, smiled good-naturedly, and greeted me with the words usually employed in saying farewell. There was about his manner a little of that ostentatious good-nature which people, well pleased with their circumstances. are accustomed to lavish on all comers; joy at the departure of the Russians had probably the effect of securing for.me an unusual display of friendly feeling.

Colonel Skobeloff, who had just returned from the dangerous expedition through the desert of which I have just spoken, had not yet drawn up a report for General Kaufmann, and this report he had made up his mind to finish before leaving Khiva. He asked me to stay behind with him in the summer palace of the Khan, where the Russian troops had been encamped, to keep him company. The troops started about two o'clock; by three, they had all disappeared, and then the Colonel, his two servants, and myself were left alone—an insignificant remnant of the victorious Russians, in the midst of the multitudinous enemy.

The Colonel at once applied himself to the preparation of his report and of an accompanying map, while I endeavoured to pass the day in alternately reading back numbers of the 'Revue des deux Mondes' and in wandering about the deserted camp of the Russians. Curious, indeed, was the spectacle presented by the ground which the troops had lately occupied. Silence, in place of movement and bustle; the ground strewn with pieces of old carts, old carpets, and old tents; and a Persian slave or two wandering about in a *chiffonnier*-like search for deserted valuables.

At night we went to sleep in the interior of the small court of the palace. All night through the Colonel slept the sound sleep of one utterly worn out by hard work; but his servants and I were less fortunate. Three times in succession we were awakened by loud reports, like those of a cannon. Anxiously we climbed to one of the upper porches, and looked towards the town. We could see nothing, however, but the glare which usually hangs over gas-lit cities. But Khiva is unlit by gas-lamps, or lamps of any other kind, so we concluded that the reports and the glare came from bonfires lit by the Khivans in celebration of the departure of the enemy.

Early next day we set out for the army. It was a beautiful, sunny morning; and not without regret did we take a last look at the domes, minarets, and walls of

Khiva. Bathed in the sunlight of early morning, their
squalidness had changed to beauty ; and a residence of
two months and a half had given us a familiarity with the
place that threw a tinge of not unpleasant melancholy
over our departure. For three or four hours we rode
through the pleasant fields and gardens of the oasis,
occasionally meeting some Uzbegs, who saluted respect-
fully, but with a certain amount of gaiety, that betrayed
their delight at seeing the last of the Russians. Not one,
however, showed the slightest inclination to molest us ;
and our small party of four rode on with as little appre-
hension as if we were a column a thousand strong.

We overtook the rear-guard at Khanki, and in a quarter
of an hour more were on the banks of the Oxus. That
night the army encamped by the river, and next morning
the passage was commenced. The transport of the troops
was not accomplished without considerable difficulty. In
the first place, the number of *kayuks*, or ferry-boats, was
quite insufficient. Secondly, there were two islands in
the river at the point where the army crossed. The
result was that, when the boats reached the first island,
the troops had to get out, then march across the island,
and once more enter the boats. The same process had to
be gone through on arriving at the second island, although
it was separated from the mainland but by a narrow
channel. The result of all these obstacles was that the
passage of the river occupied nearly two weeks.

Meantime, General Kaufmann and his staff surveyed the
right bank of the river, for the purpose of selecting a proper
site for a fort, finally, they chose a spot just below Shura-
khana, and the works were immediately commenced. The
place chosen was a large garden, planted with trees and
surrounded by a thick, heavy, mud wall--a place which, in

point of fact, was already a fortress in itself, and required scarcely any addition to make it sufficiently strong for the purposes of the Russians. The fort was constructed on the same scale as those erected all over Central Asia. The walls, already standing, were strengthened by earthworks; and places were constructed for the reception of cannon. Situated on the bank of a river, in a fertile country, where the heat of summer is not too oppressive for this part of the world, and the cold of winter is not over severe, this fortress is by no means the worst station in Central Asia. It is about twenty-five miles from the capital. The garrison consists of two battalions of infantry, 1000 men; 200 Cossacks; and six pieces of artillery, together with two heavy guns, captured from the Khan. This, it will be seen, is not an enormous garrison; but it is quite sufficient to strike awe into the Khivans, and keep them in submission.

Colonel Ivanoff and Colonel Dreschern were left in charge; the latter in command of the fort, the former as military governor of the district. No better selection could have been made. Colonel Ivanoff and Colonel Dreschern are thoroughly capable officers, devoted to their profession, fond of study, and take a lively interest in the populations with whom they have to deal. In addition, they are extremely popular with the soldiers, as well as with their brother officers. These two gentlemen, together with Baron Kaulbars, are among the very best officers in Turkistan.

It was determined that the different detachments should go home by the routes by which they had come Verevkin's detachment accordingly started for Orenburg, and Lamakin's for Kinderly Bay, both departing a week before Kaufmann, on his way to Tashkent. The greater part of the Kazala column remained at the fort on the banks of the Oxus.

It was decided to send the sick and wounded in the kayuks down to the mouth of the Oxus, where the flotilla, under Lieutenant Sitnikoff, was stationed. They were to proceed thence up the Aral Sea to the mouth of the River Syr, and up that river to Fort No. I. Having a wish to see the lower Oxus, I decided to accompany this detachment. As all the boats were required for the passage of the army across the Oxus, we had to wait until the greater part of the troops were on the other side before starting. At last twenty large kayuks were provided for us. There was an escort of about fifty men, about thirty or forty wounded or sick soldiers, together with a number of officers who had received leave to go by this route to Tashkent, St. Petersburg, and other places. Among the officers was General Kolokoltsoff, one of the bravest and most experienced officers in the Russian army; and there were besides, Baron Korf, whom I had first met at Alty-Kuduk, and General Pistolkors, who has probably more wounds than any man in the Russian army. About ten or fifteen men were placed in each boat; awnings were constructed out of the reed mattings, and most of the officers had beds made for them. In one end of the boats there was a place where our food could be cooked; and altogether the voyage was undertaken with every convenience that could be expected under the circumstances.

On the morning of the 1st of September, we pushed away from the Khivan shore, proceeding through a narrow canal, which, in about a quarter of an hour, brought us into the Oxus. We went down the river at a moderate speed, half gliding, and half rowing with the

THE KAYUK. *From a design by Verestchagin.*

stream. At this point the current was about four miles an hour, but as we descended the river it grew much slower, and when we reached the Aral Sea it was not more than half a mile an hour.

The voyage was indeed a very pleasant one. We had furnished ourselves with a sufficient supply of provisions. Twice during each day we landed in order to keep the boats together, and to rest the men who had been rowing. Then we cooked our food, ate our meals leisurely, and lay down on the grass, in the shade of the trees, before pushing off again. Every night, for the first few days, we encamped on shore, finding it impossible to steer through the darkness. The days were passed in a pleasant, do-nothing kind of way. Sometimes we played cards, sometimes we fished, generally once a day we took a swim; and often we lay for hours, tired and languid, on our beds, listening to the singing of the soldiers, which, with the plash of the oars, made very pleasant music.

The shores presented but little signs of life; we scarcely ever caught sight of a human being. We saw plenty of houses, however, embosomed and almost hidden from view by gardens and fruit-trees. We also caught frequent glimpses of the graveyard mosques, which form as prominent a feature of Khivan scenery as the country church of the English landscape. These mosques have a tall, slender façade, about twenty feet wide, forty or fifty feet high, and square at the top. Behind this is a dome, which is very often covered with green tiles. Dome and façade, seen above the tops of the trees, present a very imposing appearance. The Khivan tombs are everywhere like those I have described within the walls of the capital—small semi-spherical mounds of mud or clay, which are often ornamented here and there with a burnt tile or two, and with an inscription from the Koran in blue.

We caught some very fine fish, and we were able to have fresh caviare the whole way. It may be worth mentioning that a fish—the *Scaphyrhyncus*—has been found in the Oxus which up to this time has only been caught in the Mississippi. The naturalist who accompanied the expedition gave to this new species the name of *Oxianus*.

The Oxus varied in breadth from three-quarters to two miles and a half. In some places it was spread over an immense amount of country. The first halt we made was on the Khivan shore. Afterwards we always encamped on the right bank, which, according to the treaty of peace, is now Russian territory. The Khivan bank was covered with gardens, trees, and houses; while on the right bank there was, half the time, scarcely anything but reeds and tall grass; and there were signs that the river occasionally overflowed on that side.

We sometimes met other boats coming slowly up the river, loaded either with wood or with fish. As the stream was too swift to row against it, these boats were generally dragged along by two men on shore, while two others steered. Once or twice we passed a boat-load of Kirghiz who were going in the same direction as ourselves. They were probably an aul on its annual migration.

We camped opposite Kiptchak; there is a slight torrent, but not sufficient to impede the navigation of the river. Down to the point where the Ulkun-Darya branches off from the Oxus, and in the Ulkun-Darya itself, there are no falls or rocks; and the river, in fact, is perfectly

navigable up as high as Khiva. A short distance below
the Kiptchak, we saw a low range of mountains, or rather
hills, on the right bank. These were bare, and of the
same rotten sandstone formation which I had seen in
the mountains of the Kyzil-Kum. Here the river grew
narrower, the stream deeper, and the current carried
us backwards and forwards from shore to shore. Next
day — we were about a 100 miles from Khiva — the
mountains disappeared on the right bank, and the fields
and gardens on the left; and then there was nothing
to be seen on either side of the river but wild reedy
marshes. About thirty miles below Khodjeili, we entered
a branch of the Oxus, called the Ulkun-Darya, which
is much narrower and deeper than the main stream, and
therefore more suitable for navigation. It is, however,
very crooked, and sometimes the turnings were so short,
that it was with difficulty our heavy boats could be got
around them. Sometimes, too, we were almost caught in
the thick reeds, which grew to a great height on all
sides.

Before passing Khodjeili, the Governor of Kungrad had
come to meet us in a small boat, with one or two atten-
dants. His demeanour to the Russians was very different
now from what it would have been at the time he sent the
request to General Verèvkin, to give him three days to
collect his cannon. He undertook the duty of guiding us
through the Ulkun-Darya; and from this point forward
he could be seen, always gliding before us in his little
narrow kayuk, leading the way. We now found it impossible to land, as the reeds grew so thick in the water
on each side that the boats could not penetrate through
them. In fact, for three days we never even saw terra-

firma; at night, we had to tie our boats to the reeds. During these three nights, those who had not nets suffered greatly from the mosquitoes. So bad had they become before this, that the officers one night went on shore, lit a flaming fire of dried reeds, and so kept them off them till morning; but during these three nights no such resource was possible.

On the evening of the seventh day, the narrow channe' of the Ulkun-Darya spread out into a wide lake; and here the water was almost at a stand-still. The lake was some eight or ten miles in extent, and full of little floating islands of reeds and bushes. Rowing across it, we at length, in the afternoon, beheld in the distance the slender masts of ships rising out of the vast reedy plain.

Towards nightfall we emerged from the reedy marshes in which we had been involved for more than three days; and here again the channel Ulkun-Darya had become narrow—scarcely more than 100 or 200 feet wide. About sunset we reached the flotilla, and were soon on board, exchanging greetings with our friends and acquaintances.

Lieutenant Sitnikoff was somewhat surprised to see me, as he had imagined when I left Kazala that I simply intended to go on to Tashkent. He had received some vague account of my adventures, and we had a hearty laugh together over the trick I had played upon my friend Captain Verestchagin at Kazala.

Among others I found young Count Schuvaloff. This brave young officer, it will be remembered, received a contusion in the storming of Khiva. He had been sent home with the Orenburg detachment; but he became so much worse on the road that he had to be sent in a *tarantass* to the flotilla. I am glad to have heard that his health is now completely restored.

The flotilla consisted of two steamers—the 'Samarcand' and the 'Perovsky'—and three barges. The sick were all put on board; the 'Perovsky' took one barge in tow, and the 'Samarcand' two; and next day we abandoned our kayuks, and started down the Ulkun-Darya in full steam for the Aral Sea. We reached the mouth of the river, which was about forty miles from the station of the flotilla, the same night, and cast anchor, as it was impossible to cross the bar in the darkness. Early next morning we were again under steam. In half an hour we had crossed the bar and were rushing through the blue waters of the Aral Sea. Two days and one night on the Aral brought us to the mouth of the Syr-Darya, and in thirty-six hours more I was once again in Kazala, for which I had started so many months before. From this point some officers went to Tashkent, and others to Orenburg, on their way to St. Petersburg.

Here for the first time I met Mr. Ker, who had been sent by the 'Daily Telegraph' on the same mission as myself. I was sorry to find that, less favoured by fortune than I, he had been unable to accomplish his undertaking. He has since published his experiences; and, having read his book, I can testify that the pictures of the country through which we both passed are as accurate as they are graphic.

I had to make a stay of three days, waiting my turn for post-horses. I bought another tarantass, and on the 15th of September was once more on the post-road to Orenburg.

The distance from Kazala to Saratof, which in the previous march had taken six weeks to accomplish, I now—when the horses were fresh from the summer pastures—made in fourteen days. The journey calls for no further comment. So here I end the account of my travels, and bid the reader—farewell.

INTERESTING WORKS

OF

TRAVEL AND ADVENTURE

PUBLISHED BY

HARPER & BROTHERS, NEW YORK.

☞ HARPER & BROTHERS *will send either of the following works by mail, postage prepaid, to any part of the United States, on receipt of the price.*

☞ HARPER's NEW AND ENLARGED CATALOGUE, *with a* COMPLETE ANALYTIC INDEX, *sent by mail on receipt of Ten Cents.*

SCHWEINFURTH'S HEART OF AFRICA The Heart of Africa or, Three Years' Travels and Adventures in the Unexplored Regions of the Centre of Africa From 1868 to 1871. By Dr. GEORG SCHWEINFURTH Translated by ELLEN E. FREWER With an Introduction by WINWOOD READE Illustrated by about 130 Woodcuts from Drawings made by the Author, and with Two Maps. 2 vols., 8vo, Cloth, $8 00.

STANLEY'S COOMASSIE AND MAGDALA. Coomassie and Magdala · a Story of Two British Campaigns in Africa. By HENRY M. STANLEY With Maps and Illustrations. 8vo, Cloth, $3 50

VINCENT'S LAND OF THE WHITE ELEPHANT The Land of the White Elephant: Sights and Scenes in Southeastern Asia A Personal Narrative of Travel and Adventure in Farther India, embracing the Countries of Burma, Siam, Cambodia, and Cochin-China (1871-2) By FRANK VINCENT, Jr. Magnificently illustrated with Map, Plans, and numerous Woodcuts Crown 8vo, Cloth, $3 50.

TYSON'S ARCTIC ADVENTURES Arctic Experiences containing Captain George E Tyson's Wonderful Drift on the Ice-Floe, a History of the Polaris Expedition, the Cruise of the Tigress, and Rescue of the Polaris Survivors. To which is added a General Arctic Chronology. Edited by E VALE BLAKE With Map and numerous Illustrations 8vo, Cloth, $4 00

DAVIS'S NIMROD OF THE SEA. Nimrod of the Sea, or, the American Whaleman By WILLIAM M DAVIS. With many Illustrations. 12mo, Cloth, $2 00.

MACGAHAN'S CAMPAIGNING ON THE OXUS. Campaigning on the Oxus and the Fall of Khiva. By J. A. MACGAHAN. With Map and Illustrations Crown 8vo, Cloth, $4 00.

GILLMORE'S PRAIRIE AND FOREST Prairie and Forest a Description of the Game of North America, with Personal Adventures in their Pursuit. By PARKER GILLMORE ("Ubique"). Illustrated 12mo, Cloth, $2 00.

HOPPIN'S LIFE OF ADMIRAL FOOTE. Life of Andrew Hull Foote, Rear-Admiral United States Navy By JAMES MASON HOPPIN, Professor in Yale College With a Portrait and Illustrations Crown 8vo, Cloth, $3 50

HARPER'S HAND-BOOK FOR TRAVELERS IN EUROPE AND THE EAST. Being a Guide through Great Britain and Ireland, France, Belgium, Holland, Germany, Italy, Egypt, Syria, Turkey, Greece, Switzerland, Tyrol, Denmark, Norway, Sweden, Russia, and Spain. With over One Hundred Maps and Plans of Cities   By W PEMBROKE FETRIDGE, Author of "Harper's Phrase-Book" and "Rise and Fall of the Paris Commune " In Three Volumes, 12mo, Full Leather, Pocket-Book Form, $3 00 per vol (*the vols sold separately*); or the Three Volumes in one, similar Binding, $7 00.

PIKE'S SUB-TROPICAL RAMBLES. Sub-Tropical Rambles in the Land of the Aphanapteryx By NICOLAS PIKE, U S Consul, Port Louis, Mauritius Profusely Illustrated from the Author's own Sketches, containing also Maps and Valuable Meteorological Charts Crown 8vo, Cloth, $3 50.

TRISTRAM'S THE LAND OF MOAB The Result of Travels and Discoveries on the East Side of the Dead Sea and the Jordan. By H B TRISTRAM, M.A , LL.D., F R S., Master of the Greatham Hospital, and Hon. Canon of Durham With a Chapter on the Persian Palace of Mashita, by JAS. FERGUSON, F.R.S. With New Map and Illustrations. Crown 8vo, Cloth, $2 50.

THE DESERT OF THE EXODUS. Journeys on Foot in the Wilderness of the Forty Years' Wanderings; undertaken in connection with the Ordnance Survey of Sinai and the Palestine Exploration Fund By E H PALMER, M A , Lord Almoner's Professor of Arabic, and Fellow of St. John's College, Cambridge. With Maps and numerous Illustrations from Photographs and Drawings taken on the spot by the Sinai Survey Expedition and C F Tyrwhitt Drake Crown 8vo, Cloth, $3 00.

NORDHOFF'S CALIFORNIA California For Health, Pleasure, and Residence A Book for Travelers and Settlers. Illustrated. 8vo, Paper, $2 00 , Cloth, $2 50.

NORDHOFF'S NORTHERN CALIFORNIA, OREGON, AND THE SANDWICH ISLANDS Northern California, Oregon, and the Sandwich Islands. By CHARLES NORDHOFF, Author of "California for Health, Pleasure, and Residence," &c., &c. Profusely Illustrated 8vo, Cloth, $2 50.

SANTO DOMINGO, Past and Present, with a Glance at Hayti By SAMUEL HAZARD. Maps and Illustrations. Crown 8vo, Cloth, $3 50.

AROUND THE WORLD. By EDWARD D. G. PRIME, D D With numerous Illustrations Crown 8vo, Cloth, $3 00.

ALCOCK'S JAPAN. The Capital of the Tycoon: a Narrative of a Three Years' Residence in Japan. By Sir RUTHERFORD ALCOCK, K C.B., Her Majesty's Envoy Extraordinary and Minister Plenipotentiary in Japan. With Maps and Engravings. 2 vols., 12mo, Cloth, $3 50.

ANDERSSON'S OKAVANGO RIVER. The Okavango River. a Narrative of Travel, Exploration, and Adventure By CHARLES JOHN ANDERSSON With Steel Portrait of the Author, numerous Woodcuts, and a Map showing the Regions explored by Andersson, Cumming, Livingstone, and Du Chaillu 8vo, Cloth, $3 25.

ANDERSSON'S LAKE NGAMI. Lake Ngami; or, Explorations and Discoveries during Four Years' Wanderings in the Wilds of Southwestern Africa By CHARLES JOHN ANDERSSON. With numerous Illustrations, representing Sporting Adventures, Subjects of Natural History, Devices for Destroying Wild Animals, &c 12mo, Cloth, $1 75

ATKINSON'S AMOOR REGIONS Travels in the Regions of the Upper and Lower Amoor, and the Russian Acquisitions on the Confines of India and China. With Adventures among the Mountain Kirghis. and the Manjours, Manyargs, Toungous, Touzempts, Goldi, and Gelyaks the Hunting and Pastoral Tribes By THOMAS WITLAM ATKINSON, F.G S., F R G S With a Map and numerous Illustrations 8vo, Cloth, $3 50.

Lightning Source UK Ltd.
Milton Keynes UK
UKHW030632170322
400211UK00006B/474